PAUL McGEOUGH was the only [ ]
cover the entire war in Baghdad. He is a former editor
of *The Sydney Morning Herald*, and is now its New
York-based writer-at-large. He has been a reporter for
almost 30 years, covering international conflict since
the 1990–91 Gulf War. McGeough's work has earned
Australia's highest journalistic honours, including the
Perkin and the Walkley awards. His reporting on
Afghanistan won a prestigious SAIS Novartis
international award in 2001.

Australian reporter to

IN BAGHDAD

A reporter's war

Paul McGeough

ALLEN&UNWIN

First published in 2003

Copyright © Paul McGeough 2003

Allen & Unwin
83 Alexander Street
Crows Nest NSW 2065
Australia
Phone: (61 2) 8425 0100
Fax: (61 2) 9906 2218
Email: info@allenandunwin.com
Web: www.allenandunwin.com

National Library of Australia
Cataloguing-in-Publication entry:

McGeough, Paul, 1954- .
In Baghdad: a reporter's war.

    ISBN 1 74114 219 9.

    1. McGeough, Paul, 1954-. 2. Iraq War, 2003—Personal
    narratives, Australian. I. Title.

956.70443

Typeset by Bookhouse, Sydney
Printed by Griffin Press, South Australia

10 9 8 7 6 5 4 3 2

CONTENTS

Iraq and its neighbours

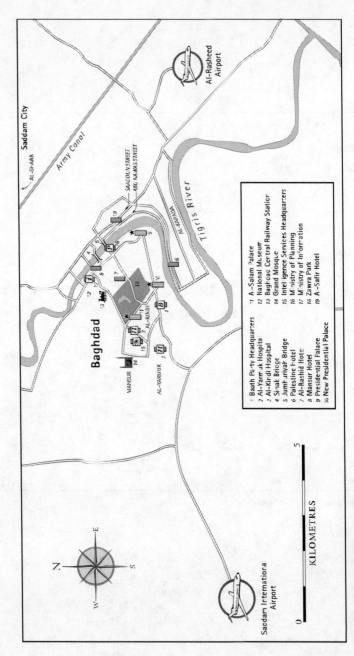

Central Baghdad and surrounds

IN BAGHDAD

DAY ONE

First Attack

Filed Thursday, 20 March at 1.25pm local time   **Palestine Hotel**

The first US strike against Saddam Hussein was a pinprick, not the much-promised 'Shock and Awe'. But when the Iraqi president addressed the nation three hours later he seemed weary, rattled even.

A single, powerful detonation created a power-surge that moved beds in our city hotel. It was followed in quick succession by a series of muffled explosions to the south-east of the capital at about 5.20am, all of which was a dramatic switch to a US battle plan that was expected to open with 48 hours of missile mania, which Washington hoped would fracture the morale of the Iraqi military and the top layers of the regime.

But, acting on information from the CIA, President George W. Bush apparently decided at the last minute to short-circuit what could become a bloody war by going after the man, not his machines. Iraqi officials claimed that the missiles—about 40

1

of them, zeroing in from the south—fell left and right of their target, a bunker at the sprawling al-Rashid military complex in which Saddam and five of his senior officials were said to be hunkered.

And, according to street talk in the capital, the US also targeted an elaborate presidential palace adjacent to Saddam International Airport, just south of Baghdad.

Reports from Washington say that the CIA was convinced that it had a surveillance fix on Saddam in a bunker within the al-Rashid complex. Both sites are close to one of Saddam's more impressive personal security facilities—the palace is cheek-by-jowl with the airport, from which a French construction contractor built Saddam two escape routes in the mid-80s, a tunnel and a separate access road.

As this morning's air-raid sirens sounded across the city and ranting speeches blasted from mosque minarets, exhorting their listeners to fight, Baghdad's anti-aircraft batteries opened fire. The lead role in this coordinated, if futile, barrage was taken by two stations atop the Information Ministry in central Baghdad. Coloured tracer fire—by which the gunners gauge the trajectory of their fire—arced in a silver dawn.

Iraqi forces fired three missiles into Kuwait, one of which was taken out by a US-operated Patriot missile battery before it neared Kuwait City. The other two reportedly landed harmlessly in the deserts of north Kuwait. Iraqi officials said that one person had died and several had been injured in US-led attacks on a customs post on the Jordanian border and on a TV station at Ramadi, a Saddam stronghold just west of Baghdad.

Baghdad—the regime and the city—emerged in the early hours of today dazed from the first US strikes and fearful of what might be in store for them in the coming night. The regime was belligerently angry, but many ordinary Iraqis continued with a remarkable behaviour change which has emerged in recent days—voluntarily displaying their pleasure in seeing Saddam get whacked. One old-timer was so conflicted that in the space of five minutes he cried with worry over his grandchildren having to endure a war and then laughed and made up ditties about the demise of Saddam.

The streets were deserted of all except military traffic—save for a few of Baghdad's orange-cornered taxis and its red double-decker buses, which continued to ply their routes. Two men who claimed that their vehicle had been attacked from the air west of Baghdad managed to drive into the city before fleeing into the suburbs. Soldiers wandered aimlessly in the vicinity of their bunkers as a group of staff at the al-Rashid Hotel took to the lawns to view the fighting.

Security and armed forces traffic shot about the city at speed. As we crossed the Jumhuriyah Bridge on the Tigris River—moving to pre-arranged back-up hotel accommodation after receiving a late warning that the al-Rashid Hotel was a 'high value target'—we were overtaken by a Nissan pick-up travelling at breakneck speed, with a soldier at the ready at a machine-gun mounted on its tray.

After a time, light traffic returned to Baghdad's streets, but only during daylight hours. The telephone system was either shut down or on the brink of collapse. International calls were impossible; local calls were a lottery. Virtually all shops remained closed. Foxholes and revetments were still being built around the city, and what I presumed to be a pile of waste cardboard on a busy intersection proved to be a secret foxhole when several soldiers were seen emerging from beneath it.

Nationalist music on Iraqi radio and television was interrupted first by a plea from Saddam's older son, Uday, for all Iraqis to fight. But an hour later Saddam himself appeared on TV, apparently determined to disprove speculation that he had been killed in the attack.

Saddam repeatedly referred to his notes in an unusually brief speech that lacked his usual calm and rhetorical flourishes. He seemed to be shocked and a telltale sign of the haste with which his appearance had been organised was the appearance of glasses on his nose—his deep-seated vanity normally means that he never publicly displays the weakness of being shortsighted. But there was speculation too that the speaker might have been one of the doubles that Saddam purportedly uses to confuse his enemies on his whereabouts.

Saddam shed no light on the US attack. He urged all Iraqis to 'sacrifice yourselves, even the children'. He claimed that Mr Bush was guilty of a crime against Iraq and he urged the people to take up their weapons. He said: 'Victory is ours already. We will win, we will defeat this enemy. Take up your swords and find glory. Victory is ours, Iraq will win. In all this darkness there is a spark, a fire that will burn the losers. But no one wins without sacrifice, so pray to God to heal your wounds.'

Addressing those around the world who had rallied against this war, he declared: 'We will stop these invaders till they lose patience; they will be defeated, along with their Zionist supporters. Long live Iraq! Long live Palestine! Long live jihad!' Shortly after Saddam's speech the air-raid sirens sounded again, but the all-clear came within an hour.

A hectoring Information Minister, Mohammed Saeed al-Sahhaf, accused Mr Bush of deliberately attempting to assassinate Saddam Hussein. He said: 'Bush has committed a despicable crime against humanity. The only way to describe the rulers of the US and Britain is that they are mercenaries and war criminals.' Like most of his colleagues, Mr Sahhaf arrived at the press conference in the drab military ensemble of the Baath Party.

Most senior officials have switched to the same garb—even the Director-General of Information, Uday al-Tai. Yesterday he arrived at work in the early hours in a smart suit and tie, but by mid-morning he too was in fatigues.

In Baghdad yesterday, six foreign reporters were released after being detained by the regime for alleged currency violations as they attempted to leave Iraq in the last few days. But there was concern about the whereabouts of one of the six, a female Mexican reporter, who during their detention had been subjected to what a member of the group described as 'tasteless banter' from their guards.

One of the detainees told the *Herald* that, when the journalists were about to be released, their guards had insisted that the five males—from APTN and NBC—return to Baghdad to be fined as much as $50 000 and have all their cash confiscated, but that the guards would escort the woman, Nera Moncao of Mexico Radio 13, directly to the border. The group was held at Ramadi, a security centre for Saddam just west of Baghdad. The reporter who was released yesterday said: 'We insisted that she come with us to Baghdad. She was very upset. She might be perfectly safe by now, but we don't know.'

▲

Email from: Robert Whitehead, Editor, *Sydney Morning Herald*
To: Paul McGeough, Baghdad

Hi Paul, Have tried you numerous times but unable to get through. Any further information about reasons for the NYT ordering Burns to get out? Any other intelligence? Alan Revell and I believe now it would be better if you were out. Please call at any hour. Regards, Robert.

Eventually, when he did get a line through to me, I conceded, telling him: 'Robert, I'll get out. We'll organise a convoy and get out as quickly as we can.'

I was admitting that the edginess in Baghdad had finally got to me; I was agreeing that I would head for the border and attempt to cross into Jordan before the opening strike of the war.

This exchange took place on Tuesday, March 18. Two days later, when the war actually began, I still couldn't believe that I had actually uttered those words after investing so many months in preparing myself to report this war—as a humanitarian crisis and as the opening of a fault line that was likely to run through world affairs for decades to come.

During the previous months I had criss-crossed Iraq, spending more time here than at home in New York. Late last year I had reported on Iraq's suspected production of weapons of mass destruction, but had seen little evidence to support the strident claims of the US and Britain; later I had gone to the north, to document Saddam's appalling treatment of the Kurdish communities. Since arriving back in Baghdad a month ago, I had visited the oppressed Shia cities of the south—Basra, Karbala and Najaf—and in the south-east I had been to some of the last remaining communities of the Marsh Arabs.

But during the last weeks the focus had been on Baghdad, where the passing of each day hyped nervous agitation in the 500-strong press pack. In recent days the angst had become obsessive—about staying alive; about the heavy-handed bureaucrats and intelligence agents who could cancel our visas in a trice; and about avoiding intelligence raids for sat-phones we might have hidden in our hotel rooms.

But the greatest anxiety had been about visas. For a month now they had been renewed for ten days at a time, with an unlucky 50 or so reporters being forced to leave the country in each cycle so that some of the 700 others clawing at the grille on the visa window at the Iraqi Embassy in Amman could get in. Rumour thrived in the press pack, with everyone focused on the key objective—staying in Iraq so as to reserve the right to be here to cover the war. The slightest hint that your visa was at risk was a crisis that could wreck your day during this period.

I had been locked in a struggle with the icy Mr Kadhim, a senior member of the sinister Mukhabarat secret service, whom the regime had planted in the Information Ministry's Press Centre to observe and manipulate our movements and those who normally managed us.

When I had first attempted to bribe Kadhim—with an envelope of cash inserted among the copies of my reports he had demanded as part of my visa renewal (a frequent demand by the regime)—he had extracted the envelope and waved it in the air for all in his crowded office to see, before yelling sharply: 'You are forbidden to pass personally addressed letters to us.'

This had seemed like an attempt to protect himself because few, if any, press visas had been issued in Iraq without a bribe. In fact, bribery had become such an accepted part of the process that, when an Amman-based fixer was told that a new Iraqi diplomat would be difficult to bribe, she had exploded: 'But that's unethical!'

I got a ten-day visa extension on this occasion, but I was warned I was unlikely to get another extension, so I made enquiries about other avenues. A local fixer, whom I had retained over the years, informed me that his uncle was a member of the high-ranking Information Ministry committee that approved visa extensions, and could be persuaded to back any application I filed in exchange for $US1000. Done!

With that deal I entered a visa twilight zone. Kadhim knew that I had bought protection—and that it was good protection. But he was so angered that he refused to process my paperwork and, when I went around him to lodge the paperwork at a higher level in the administration, he and his colleagues would sit on the approval when it was returned to their office for them to issue my new papers. This nerve-wracking process was a nightmare for all media, keeping us continuously on edge. No sooner did you have your paperwork than you had to start the whole process again.

The relationship between the Information Ministry and the press was both vexed and tense. They were desperate to control us wherever and whenever they could, and minders regularly monitored radio and TV reports as they were transmitted from the country. Filing by email to a newspaper made it difficult for them to censor what I wrote, but the ministry had its own suite of pressures for print journalists.

It controlled where I could go. Special written requests to undertake specific assignments were required and all travel beyond Baghdad's city limits was outlawed during the week when the war finally began. The ministry controlled whom I spoke to, and a minder assigned to me by the ministry sat in on all my interviews with Iraqis. And it decided for how long I could stay in the country.

Within this straitjacket, the foreign press was welcomed. Clearly there was a tug-of-war within the regime about our usefulness, but it had seemed that Saddam did know the value of the media. And, instead of hostility, ordinary Iraqis were embarrassingly generous in their offers of hospitality, even to reporters who hailed from countries like the US, Britain and Australia, members of Bush's so-called coalition of the willing.

Apart from visa extensions, the biggest challenge in Baghdad up to now had been to report on the lead-up to war without being distracted by the incessant planning and workshopping essential to cover a very different story—the war itself. This is a serious business—there's no cockiness. Younger reporters seek out the old hands, quizzing them on the imperfect art of survival—there are ways to stay safe and at the same time be able to cover a story that needs to be reported.

But the Pentagon and the British Ministry of Defence had for weeks been pressuring editors to evacuate their staff from Baghdad. British editors were told that, if only half of what the military expected to go wrong went wrong, we'd all still be in diabolical trouble. This advice was well meant, but the consensus until now among many of the big media organisations was that it should be treated with caution and that any decision to quit Baghdad should be left to the reporters on the ground.

Governments and the military do not like reporters in a war zone, unless the army can limit their access to communications and can control what they see and hear. In this case we were going a step further than that—as far as Washington, London and Canberra were concerned, we were behind enemy lines.

As the 48-hour ultimatum George W. Bush had delivered to Saddam on Tuesday, March 18 ticked away, rumour was rife in the city about the imminent bombing. The tension covered us like a blanket. The last evacuation flights and diplomatic road convoys had long gone and, with only hours left before the war might start, many correspondents were ordered to leave by their editors. But as the first of them arrived at the Jordanian border, reports filtered back to nervous colleagues in Baghdad of arrests at the border on trumped-up currency and sat-phone violations and of media convoys that had been turned around and ordered to drive back to Baghdad.

This was the atmosphere in which five of us—myself, John F. Burns of *The New York Times,* Jon Lee Anderson of *The New Yorker*, Melinda Liu of *Newsweek*, and Burns' photographer colleague Tyler Hicks—sat down to work through our options. The critical management view was always going to be that of the *NYT*—once it ordered Burns and Hicks out, it would be difficult for the rest of us to argue to the contrary. Burns had now been told to go and the rest of us caved in. If we left quickly, we might all just get out in time.

Baghdad was emptying of all who could afford to leave and soldiers were taking up their positions behind sand bags on every street corner. We had a convoy on standby for the five-hour desert drive to the border. But we had failed to take into account the nicotine-stained Mr Jamal, the man without fingernails who was the collector of the exorbitant Information Ministry fees we were obliged to pay. And we would not be allowed to cross the border without a receipt issued by Jamal.

Our window of opportunity was slamming shut.

Jamal could not process the paperwork in time for us to attempt the drive in daylight. First, he could not be found; and when he was found, he was busy with other matters—bundling small mountains of US dollars into bags. Just as we were meeting again in Melinda's cubby-hole office to discuss what to do, CNN flashed the news of Saddam's rejection of the Bush ultimatum—which meant that now the war could start at any time. For us to head for Amman meant risking arrest at the Iraqi border on trumped-up infractions; or being made to return to Baghdad in government custody, as other reporters had been forced to do; or possibly even detention in an Iraqi prison, conceivably as the first bombs were falling. They were chilling options.

The decision made itself—it was safer to stay. Our editors agreed, though not happily.

In the days before this, like most of my colleagues, I had been hotel-hopping around Baghdad looking for a room from which to observe the war but which would not also become a target. Some reporters, with their hapless drivers in tow, had already hauled their gear through three or four hotels, but still they were uncertain about where best to stay.

I had been staying for the last few weeks at the al-Rashid Hotel, as had others. As a back-up, I had booked a suite at the family-run al-Hamra Hotel, in the city's north-west, where many of our colleagues had concluded they would be safe. I had arranged to share this suite with Jon Lee Anderson, a writer for *The New Yorker* magazine, whom I had met in Baghdad the previous year. But when an anxious Iraqi friend suggested we make a more detailed inspection of the immediate area there, we found the palace known as 'Uday's place', home to Saddam's older son, plus a huge Republican Guards barracks, rambling residential compounds for senior members of Saddam's secret service and homes belonging to members of Saddam's extended family.

As a result, we opted to share a room that Anderson had booked at the al-Safir Hotel on leafy Abu Nuwas Street, on the banks of the Tigris River. And, as an absolute emergency, we also had the use of a safe house in the diplomatic quarter, in suburban Mansur, that had been offered to Anderson. We thought we were fixed on the accommodation front.

We then went out on what we believed would be our last big shopping expedition. I had brought a limited supply of military-style meals ready-to-eat (MREs), but we figured that war would quickly halt food supplies to Baghdad, so we stockpiled the basics—tinned fruit and vegetables, pasta and the like. But, after we had split and stored the food and other supplies between the room at the al-Safir and the safe house in Mansur, the manager of the al-Safir informed us that he was under orders to direct all journalists to the al-Rashid or to a tawdry high-rise, the Palestine Hotel, a few blocks south along the river. As if to make his point, a team of labourers then arrived to start bricking up the al-Safir's ground-floor doors and windows, to prevent looting.

For most journalists, this search for the perfect room in a few, fast-filling hotels was affirmation of their wish to stay in Baghdad for the looming war. But it went in tandem with an intense and, for some, acrimonious debate with senior editors over the wisdom of even staying in Baghdad. Last year I had met Mitch Potter of the *Toronto Star*, when we both enrolled in a hostile environment survival course in the US. On Tuesday he had lost the stay-or-go debate with his editors, so he agreed to turn over Room 905 at the Palestine Hotel to Anderson and myself.

The two of us spent a cramped, unpleasant night in Room 905 before deciding to head back to the comparative creature comforts of the fast-emptying al-Rashid. In undertaking this move we found ourselves persuaded by the sage-like wisdom of *The New York Times'* John F. Burns. His argument was that to be anywhere in Baghdad was to be in the US bull's-eye, and therefore debating the relative safety of one hotel over the next was a marginal pursuit. Burns claimed it made more sense to choose one's address in Baghdad on the basis of how comfortable one would be as much as how safe one might feel.

Quickly convinced of this, Anderson and I moved back to the al-Rashid just before lunchtime on the Wednesday and miraculously found ourselves at the head of the queue for the allocation of suites. The hotel had been re-shuffling its rooms as the world's media were abandoning the al-Rashid in the belief that it might be a US target.

Anderson and I both frequent the hellholes of the world, where divvy hotels are the norm. We had often slept in the open, in barns, under tables and in cars, but neither of us had ever had a full-on hotel suite. But, entirely by an accident of fate, by Wednesday we were the proud occupants of four linked rooms on the eighth floor of the al-Rashid—one room for each of us to sleep in, one in which to work and live, and a room at the end of a corridor for our local drivers, Sabah and Mohammed. The westerly aspect was perfect to sneak a phone signal from the satellite over the eastern Atlantic, in defiance of the Iraqi Information Ministry's ban on the use of sat-phones from any location apart from the official Press Centre. But, conscious of the need for back-ups, we decided not to relinquish Room 905 at the Palestine.

I managed to get a few hours sleep on Wednesday night, but Anderson wrote through the night to meet his weekly deadline and his head had hardly hit the pillow when the first bombs in the first US strike against Iraq shook the hotel shortly after 5am on Thursday morning. The sirens wailed as I made coffee. Our plan was to pull a couple of armchairs up to the windows to watch the opening assault on Saddam Hussein's regime.

Then the phone rang. It was the *Herald*'s foreign desk in Sydney with a message that was as well sourced as it was frightening: 'You have to get out of the al-Rashid immediately— the Department of Foreign Affairs has called to say it's a "high-value" target.' Peter Kerr, my foreign editor, had attempted to extract more information from the source of the warning by arguing that surely the streets of Baghdad were unsafe while the bombing raid continued. But the response, perhaps a touch too melodramatic, was that right now the streets were safer than the al-Rashid.

Anderson was furious—he hadn't even slept in his bed and already we were being forced out of the suite. But even then we hung on to the keys, just in case the Palestine soured, in which case we'd need the al-Rashid as a fallback—if it was still standing. As we left the al-Rashid we kicked at the door of the room next to us, that of the *Los Angeles Times*. And we banged away at Room 610—John Burns of the *NYT*—but we got no answer. It looked as though we were destined to slum it at the Palestine . . . again.

The warning that the US was targeting the al-Rashid rekindled our speculation about Saddam's special communications bunker beneath the hotel, and we decided that we could not leave without passing a warning on to the hotel staff. When I explained it all to Salman at the cashier's desk, he became troubled as he pondered what it meant.

'We can go to the bunker in the basement?' he asked. No, I explained, the US was likely to use a very powerful bunker-buster bomb that would pass through the shelter used by staff and guests to get to Saddam's hideout, which was even deeper under the hotel. 'Oh,' he said. 'We will have to go into the garden.'

As percussion rocked the city, we loaded our essentials into Sabah's white Mercedes Benz and he rushed us across town, through desolate streets and back to the dumpy Palestine Hotel. Piled high around us in Room 905 was enough food and equipment for the siege of Baghdad: six big tanks for washing water; hundreds of bottles of drinking water and slabs of cool drinks; a long flex that would drop from our ninth-floor balcony to our portable generator in the hotel garden—which Sabah and Mohammed would later retrieve from a store room at the al-Rashid; our armoury of chemical warfare suits, bullet-proof vests and hard hats; first-aid kits, including self-administered syringes of atropine, the antidote for nerve-gas attacks; a short-wave radio; and walkie-talkies.

I emailed the *Herald*'s foreign desk in Sydney and my wife in New York: 'It's started—5.30am. Mostly distant for now, but heavy anti-aircraft fire ex Baghdad. Sat is jammed but Jon Lee has managed to hold this line. Will file as and when can. Cheers . . . '

Events in Baghdad were moving rapidly and, once the piercing wail of the air-raid sirens shattered Thursday's dawn, nothing else seemed to matter. An email bobbed onto my screen from John Burns: 'Bombs away, my friend. JB.'

DAY TWO

Lunge at the Heart of the Regime

Filed Friday, March 21 at 11.42am   **Palestine Hotel**

At least five cruise missiles slammed into the heart of Baghdad last night as the US piled psychological pressure on Iraqi forces, suggesting that Saddam Hussein might have been injured or killed and that key Iraqi military officers were talking surrender.

The attack, which hammered downtown Baghdad and set two government buildings ablaze, stabbed at the nerve centre of the regime—Saddam's palace compound on the banks of the Tigris River. It fell short of 'Shock and Awe', but its precision nature, hard on the heels of Thursday's dawn assault on a bunker in which the US believes Saddam was hunkered, points to a dramatic re-ordering of the Bush battle plan. Truth and propaganda become blurred in war, but US officials are seriously speculating that they might have injured or killed Saddam and that significant elements of his officer corps might be ready to turn after decades of his ruthless dictatorship.

The homes of members of Saddam's family also were targeted last night, with a spectacular wave of missiles that whipped in from the south, triggering huge fireballs and clouds of acrid smoke that hung above the capital until early today. To counter speculation that he had been incapacitated, Saddam appeared on state TV hours after the first strike, quoting the day's date to prove that the recording was made after the strike. And state radio reported that there had been no deaths in the second strike.

This is all a dramatic reverse in the American attack strategy. It has launched its ground offensive, with more than 60 000 troops pushing into southern Iraq 24 hours earlier than planned; and it is mounting a series of precision strikes instead of the promised opening shot of 3000 missiles in 48 hours. In the first 24 hours only 60 missiles have been fired.

Almost as though there had been no change of plans, Defence Secretary Donald Rumsfeld said in Washington: 'We continue to feel no need for a broader conflict if the Iraqi leaders act to save themselves. But if they don't, what follows will not be a repeat of any other conflict. It will be of a force, scope and scale beyond what has been seen.'

One of his senior officials added: 'We are trying to punish the regime and give his forces time to capitulate. If this last chance to oust Saddam doesn't work, we have plans to annihilate the military.' After months of the US attempting to cow the Iraqi military into turning on Saddam or simply refusing to fight, it is not clear whether the battle plan switcheroo was based on a serious belief in Washington that its first salvo in the early hours of Thursday had killed key officials or if it was just more psychological pressure. But Mr Rumsfeld said: 'We are communicating with some important people who are officials in the military at various levels and who are increasingly aware of what is going to happen.'

US intelligence sources insist that Saddam, and possibly his second son Qusay, were at the al-Rashid military complex, 15km south of Baghdad, when about 40 cruise missiles hammered in. One US official told the *Washington Post*: 'The preponderance of the evidence is that he was there ... and there's evidence that he was injured because of the medical assistance sought on his behalf.' Much of the international media coverage of the war is available to Iraqis—the elite, including vulnerable senior members of the military, have access to satellite TV and many more have access to short-wave radios. So, true or false, the Washington spin will play on their nerves.

Last night's strikes were accomplished in a matter of minutes. The air-raid sirens wailed at 8.48pm and twenty minutes later a building near the headquarters of Saddam's Oil Ministry was engulfed in a massive fireball. The missile whipped in from the south, exploding with a low-percussion thud that reduced the building to ghostly flames and a great plume of smoke.

The next target was metres away and it went up in a spectacular hit only minutes later. This building, which earlier in the day had two anti-aircraft batteries on its roof, and the office block adjacent to the Oil Ministry are next to Saddam's planning headquarters, where the Jumhuriyah Bridge meets the west bank of the river. A short time later, two missiles appeared to slam into the presidential compound.

The chances of the security-paranoid Saddam or members of his family being on the premises at a time like this are zero, but there were reports that a house in which the president's wife and daughters live was hit. The missiles produced none of the spectacular aftermath of the earlier strikes. But in the dark it was difficult to be precise about which buildings had been hit.

▲

I took a couple of hours to prepare Room 905 at the Palestine Hotel for war. It was a dark tangerine-painted box, with a single narrow glass door leading out to a small balcony—not the best for observing the battle across Baghdad's urban sprawl, but useful for our physical protection in the event of the windows being blown in.

When I dispatched Sabah, the driver, to get ten rolls of masking tape, he returned with the only colour available in all of Baghdad—a wild, garish pink. So as I X-ed and latticed and herring-boned my way around the room, each glass surface becoming a pink riot—the mirrors, the shower screens, the TV screen, the windows and even the pictures on the walls. Then I placed the mattresses from the two single beds head-to-head along the most sheltered wall and used the two bed bases, up on their sides, to create an L-shaped shield that would protect the mattresses from any flying glass. All of this was held together with half a dozen baggage straps. Anderson slept at one end; I slept at the other.

Mainly though, there was little sleep to be had in Baghdad. Stuck where it is on the globe, it is six hours behind Sydney, which meant that most of my writing was done late at night or early in the morning hours. I was pretty much going to bed at 1am and rising at 3am or 4am. And if the piece was big enough, I'd write all through the night. New York was eight hours behind us so, for us all to keep up with US developments, editors and, in my case, my spouse, day was always night and vice versa. It would become a murderous schedule.

Before the bombing I'd squandered hours waiting for Information Ministry approval to embark on the simplest task, like visiting a hospital. But now the war had started, we spent hours waiting for the bombing and watching it and, when it was over, haggling with the Information Ministry about getting out to witness the aftermath.

After the air attacks on Thursday night, Baghdad was deserted. But the ministry decided to further curtail our movement—by insisting that it bus us to locations around the city, rather than allow us to drive ourselves. This meant that we only got fleeting glances at buildings targeted by the US—such as a group of them in the north-east corner of the presidential compound that took a hammering that night. Shopkeepers had carted off the last contents of their shops and stores for safekeeping and I watched as the weight of some files, piled high on a trolley being pushed out of the Information Ministry, was so great that it collapsed on the pavement.

I returned to the al-Rashid to collect some gear and found the lobbies there were deserted—save for staff hanging kilim carpets to black out the floor-to-ceiling windows. The tension was palpable. City and hotel staff had stopped coming to work; people were queuing for petrol in the hope of fleeing to the countryside; the sand-bagging of government and military buildings had been stepped up even more; and ministerial staff were removing valuable equipment, like computers, to what they hoped would be safe storage. Those with money had rushed shops for the last tinned food and medical supplies.

Amidst the misery there were surreal moments —such as the sight of our Information Ministry minders glued to a documentary on al-Jazeera TV about the last days of the Russian Tsar. It must have made them wonder about the longevity of the regime they served. And the ministerial press conferences—where the anti-Western invective and rhetoric were in inverse proportion to any signs of serious preparations for the defence of Baghdad—were from the theatre of the absurd.

How do you attempt to reconcile the hyperbole of Foreign Minister Naji Sabri's defence of Saddam with the fact that Saddam executed a brother and a cousin of Sabri's in one of his regular purges of the regime? More to the point, how did Sabri reconcile it? The answer had to be fear. Or what about Deputy

Prime Minister Tariq Aziz, who looked at us straight-faced and insisted that Iraq was victorious in the 1991 Gulf War?

John Burns—known to readers of *The New York Times* as John F. Burns and to half of Baghdad as Mr John Fisher—cut an imposing figure on the streets of Baghdad, with his towering physical presence and a wild grey thatch that gave him the look of an old English sheep dog. He and I first met in Baghdad back in 1990–91, during the first Gulf War. Since then we'd been bumping into each other in one place or another around the world. In Baghdad he was de facto dean of the press pack—his masthead and the hard-nosed manner in which he wrote his stories made him a beacon for the irritable bureaucrats at the Information Ministry.

His reports were followed closely and frequently Uday al-Tai, the scar-faced Director-General of the ministry, would exclaim when Burns came into his line of sight: 'Ah! The most dangerous man in Baghdad!' It was as much a compliment as it was a warning and, at one stage, it led me to think aloud to Anderson about the extent to which we two might be deemed to be guilty by association with Burns because of the amount of time we spent in his company.

Burns' particular crime had been to deduce late in 2002 that the people of Iraq wanted an end to what the hagiographers called the Era of Saddam Hussein, and this informed his writing in a way that few other foreign correspondents dared from within Iraq. He was for a time blacklisted, but he acquired his visa to cover the war through a back-door channel in Amman. After being made to wait three days when he finally arrived in Baghdad, his suspicion that his newly appointed minder was a security agent was confirmed when the man snapped at him one day: 'You know who we are . . . '

Anderson also was early to sense the hunger by Iraqis to be freed from the yoke of Saddam. But, like me, he was sceptical about the ultimate intentions of the US in Iraq. As we drove past the al-Rashid Hotel on this Friday, he adopted an Elvis-has-left-the-building tone to declare: 'You are now passing the future US Embassy of the Democratic Republic of Iraq.' As we headed across town, he amused himself picking out likely locations for the first McDonald's and Taco Bell franchises.

We did not seem to have the problem that Burns had, with the Information Ministry poring over his every report in the *NYT*. I got confirmation of this when the loathsome Kadhim had asked for copies of my reports as part of the visa renewal process—I downloaded a dozen of my stories from a database and, before printing them out, I spent a bizarre couple of hours as a 'seeker of truth', during which I rendered much of what I had written for the *Herald* into mush that would be acceptable to the regime. So 'the dictator Saddam' now read as 'President Saddam' and lines like 'After Saddam's brutal suppression of the Shia in Karbala . . .' became 'After Saddam restored law and order in Karbala . . .'

The laconic Anderson had worked much the same part of Afghanistan as I did during the war that followed the September 11 attacks on New York and Washington, but it was not till late last year that we met—in Baghdad. Since then, we had been emailing each other about the difficulty we faced in getting a new visa to cover the coming war in Iraq and we had debated the merits of abandoning plans to cover it from Baghdad versus entering Kurdish northern Iraq via neighbouring Iran. Finally, in February, we each managed to acquire a visa for Baghdad.

As always, it was a last-minute thing and, when I packed to leave New York for Iraq in mid-February, *The New Yorker* sent me a huge swag of gear that Anderson could not purchase in Britain where he lived. It included a combat helmet, body armour and a chemical warfare suit, which I added to my own protective gear and another lot I was hauling for colleagues at *The*

Washington Post, as well as an extra chemical warfare suit for Jason South, who was an inspiring photographer from the two newspapers for which I was reporting, *The Sydney Morning Herald* and *The Age*, and would be with me for the first month in Iraq.

Anderson had already done me a favour. I had been working the phones and the only place in the world—literally—that would sell me atropine, the self-administered antidote for nerve gas attacks, was the Fleet Street Clinic in London. I emailed Anderson to ask if he would collect my jabs and take them to Amman, the foreign press gateway to Iraq. We could do the swap when we got there.

An unintended consequence of all this was my wife putting her foot down when she saw Anderson's helmet delivered to our midtown apartment and insisting that I was not going to Iraq without a helmet of my own. I had never used one in the past because I was always wary of looking too much like a soldier— a sure-fire way to be shot at. But she made her point pretty clear—this time they could be shooting from all directions, she said witheringly.

My plane was leaving JFK in eight hours. I raced downtown to the armaments shop that had supplied Anderson's helmet— 'Too late,' I was told, 'yesterday we sold the last one we had to *The New Yorker*.' The store manager also informed me that all his competitors had sold out of such gear and he urged me to try some of the army surplus stores. Working my mobile phone from the kerbside, I finally found such a store, across the Hudson River in New Jersey. It had the Kevlar helmet I needed, but the owner would not accept a credit card number over the phone and he refused to put a helmet in a taxi.

In desperation I called him back a couple of hours later at the urging of my wife, who had by no means given up, even as she and I had a farewell afternoon tea in the Palm Terrace at the Plaza Hotel. The surplus store manager seemed to have mellowed. He still insisted on a cash transaction, but he was prepared to have someone meet me on the road to the airport to exchange his helmet for my cash. I ordered one for Jason South as well—it would just have to fit his head.

At about 8pm, with two hours to take-off, the courier with the helmets and my taxi driver organised by mobile telephone that we might pull alongside each other on the approach to the Manhattan end of the Midtown Tunnel, where we made the exchange. It was February 14—Valentine's Day. As I went through customs at Amman's Queen Alia Airport, I had to talk very fast and produce letters of authority from *The New Yorker* and *The Washington Post* to explain to the authorities why I was carrying enough body armour for a small army.

In Baghdad, Sammi Majid was my official minder. A gentle, sickly man, who was always smartly turned out in a jacket and tie, he nonetheless was quietly courageous in ensuring that I got to where I wanted to be. In defiance of the ministry, he took me to Najaf, one of the twin shrine cities for Iraq's oppressed Shia majority, and he had a way of niggling the ministry till the right travel permit or interview approval was produced.

Not surprisingly he was obsessed about the safety of his family. They lived in the shadow of the al-Dura oil refinery, south of Baghdad, which in 1991 had been a prime US target and which he feared would be hit again. He wanted to get his wife and children away to the country. But, as we sipped glasses of hot, sweet tea from a kiosk in the ministry parking lot, he told me that greedy landlords were demanding a year's rent for run-down houses that they knew would be needed by the likes of Sammi for little more than a few weeks. I gave him some extra cash to help, but no amount of pushing by me could get him to actually pack his family off to the country.

The tension in Baghdad hastened the bonding process, although my ready supply of greenbacks was undoubtedly the glue between us. Sammi, the minder, and Mohammed Izzedine, my driver, earned more from me in a week than they could from Iraqi employers in six months. So we were also a vital part of their family economy—which is why I'll never forget the look of utter horror on Mohammed's face when I told him on the Wednesday before the war started that we might leave Baghdad.

The tension and the anxiety spread well beyond Iraq. In Perth, in Western Australia, my mother was working what a friend calls her 'heavy duty' rosary beads. She informed me by email that she was having a Mass said for the safety of myself, Burns and Anderson and that she and an Iraqi Muslim friend had agreed to 'swap' prayers for the safety of those whom they each knew and cared for in Iraq.

I thought we might have been able to drop our guard at the Palestine Hotel. All the rooms at the al-Rashid were bugged and we often had to resort to sign language or code as we discussed the day's developments or our own plans. But I was warned that the listening devices at the government-run Palestine were more plentiful and more sophisticated than at the al-Rashid. And at both hotels we had to keep much of our belongings under lock and key—last year my friend and colleague Sam Kiley, who was making a documentary for Channel 4 in Britain, caught Iraqi security agents red-handed as they went through his possessions at the al-Rashid, unaware that he had left a motion-sensitive camera running in his room.

But with the start of the war, my problems with Mr Kadhim finally no longer mattered. The visas for all foreign reporters had now expired, although the ministry still needed to rake in the extortionate fees it demanded from journalists—$US225 a day for those who used a satellite phone. We were issued with a pink press pass, but only after we produced receipts to show that all our fees had been paid.

DAY THREE

Long-Promised Shock and Awe

Filed Saturday, March 22 at 6.21am   **Palestine Hotel**

An awesome barrage of missiles hammered Baghdad last night, tearing apart its palaces, compounds and bunkers as blinding bursts of light and clouds of smoke lit the city like the wildest dreaming of Hollywood. At precisely 9pm local time, the US unleashed its long-promised 'Shock and Awe' air war against Saddam Hussein, with the first of more than 100 Tomahawk cruise missiles incinerating six or more key buildings in the main presidential compound.

In rapid succession, thunder-clap explosions and ghostly bursts of flame and debris erupted even as the next missiles could be clearly seen, zeroing in with devastating precision and a daunting, metallic whoosh. As a display of modern, high-tech war, it was more stunning than anything witnessed by correspondents here—from the last Gulf War to Bosnia and Afghanistan.

Iraqi anti-aircraft batteries retaliated helplessly, shooting through a blanket of thick smoke. Their red and white tracer fire arced incessantly through the night as silver-white surface-to-air missiles ripped into the darkness. Watched from the balcony of a city hotel that shook with the force of the explosions, the skyline became a fearsome necklace of light and dark, with other, more distant targets filling the background with lightning-like blasts and whooping explosions that rolled ominously across Baghdad's urban sprawl.

The roar when one of the missiles passed right by the hotel was so ferocious that the six of us bolted indoors, dropping to the floor. But we were back on the balcony in time to see its spectacular direct hit on one of the buildings in the compound.

At times three or four of the regime's iconic symbols of power would implode simultaneously. It was hard to keep a tally of what was happening around us, but such was the total destruction of the edifices of Saddam's brutal dictatorship that it didn't seem to matter.

The targets included Saddam's monumental green-domed Republican Palace, with its 300 acres of manicured grounds and hidden bunkers; what is referred to as Uday's Palace, home to Saddam's thuggish older son; the neo-imperial Council of Ministers, with its indulgent 25m ceilings; the Baath Party headquarters, which has been bombed three times in ten years by the US; the Sajida Palace, with its four huge busts of Saddam portrayed as the legendary Arab warrior Saladin; and the headquarters of Saddam's much-feared secret police, the Mukhabarat.

The exact regime role of many of these secret buildings is not known. Journalists usually make little headway when they ask officials about such details. If you ask three people in the street, you get three different answers. But the focus of the attacks was the presidential compound, a foreboding network of residential and office complexes set in luxuriant palm-fringed gardens on a 3km stretch of the west bank of the Tigris River.

There the building that was hammered again and again was an unidentified monolithic office block, buttressed with huge sloped pillars of concrete that give it the appearance of an Aztec temple. By night's end it was still standing—but it was ablaze and seemed to have been disembowelled after taking as many as six direct hits. As a *New York Times* photographer exclaimed: 'This is the most kick-ass thing I have ever seen.'

Time will reveal the accuracy of the strikes. But the target selection appeared to keep faith with previous US undertakings to spare Baghdad's civilian population and infrastructure. Only one ambulance siren was heard in the course of the night and there was no loss of electric power.

And as power shifts, so too does fear. Iraqis knew that a devastating attack was on the cards—short-wave news bulletins had reported the departure from the US air base at Fairford, in Britain, of a fleet of heavily armed B-52 bombers. But such was their confidence in the promised accuracy of the strikes that small groups of Iraqis gathered in the streets and on rooftops to watch on a cool, perfectly still spring night as the buildings that spoke the oppressive power of the state became sitting ducks on the expansive floodplains of the Tigris.

The regime has spent weeks emptying these buildings of staff, files and valuable equipment. So the chances are that the only casualties on the night will have been the hapless junior soldiers who are obliged to guard them. On Abu Nuwas Street, just across the Tigris from the presidential compound, a hotel worker went right on with his work, sweeping the pavement as a man rode past on a bicycle and the bombs went off.

An eerie silence settled on Baghdad in the aftermath of the attacks. But in recent days Iraqis have been speculating on the fate of the regime that has reduced what was once one of the richest and best-educated countries in the region to abject poverty, to an absence of human rights and to the constant threat of prison, torture and death for those who dare to question the regime.

Saddam has not been seen since he made his unusually brief—and shaken—appearance on TV in the aftermath of the opening missile attack and the White House continues to suggest that the rattled character who appeared on Iraqi TV may have been one of Saddam's doubles. The absence from public view of Saddam and his key associates has many Iraqis wondering if the great survivor has been injured, or maybe is even dead, along with key members of his inner circle.

Since Thursday Iraqi TV has run only old footage of Saddam with his son, Qusay, and two of his key henchmen—Vice-President Taha Yassin Ramadan and Saddam's cousin Ali Hassan al-Majid, the man he appointed as Governor of Kuwait in 1990 and who is best known for overseeing gas attacks on the Kurds in 1988. But ministers of the regime have appeared to harangue the foreign press. During a press conference yesterday Interior Minister Mahmoud Diab al-Ahmad brandished a silver-plated Kalashnikov, at one stage pointing it at reporters with his finger inside the trigger guard.

Like other members of the regime, the minister appeared delusional. Even as Iraqis in the south of the country were photographed and filmed by TV crews kissing the feet of invading GIs, he insisted that all Iraqis would sacrifice themselves for Saddam. Unaware of the destruction that would befall the symbols of his regime in Baghdad within the next hours, he defiantly declared: 'They might take Umm Qasr and Basra, but how will they enter Baghdad—it will be a big oven for them.'

But by the end of last night's onslaught it was hard not to conclude that, along with the bricks and mortar, the entire edifice of power in Iraq may well be crumbling. For years the likes of the Interior Minister have listened only to their own voices but, in the explosive assault on Baghdad we have just witnessed, those voices were drowned out.

▲

This morning the locals were sneaking a look at the damage to the presidential compound and other buildings. I watched people edging out onto the bridges that span the Tigris River, where they would stand against the guard rails for minutes at a time, heads apparently bowed as though looking into the water, but all the time taking furtive glances into the smouldering compound on the west bank of the river.

For the foreign press the Information Ministry organised bus tours of the city—to show how last night's awesome display of military might had, in the view of the bureaucrats, inflicted little or no damage. Baghdad is running normally, was the message. But to get to their version of 'Baghdad normal', the press buses skirted several of the wrecked palaces and other symbols of the regime—including the building I thought of as Aztec-inspired. It turned out that this was the executive office of the presidency and that the building was said to be a copy of the world's oldest standing building, which is at Ur, in the south of Iraq. It all proclaimed loudly the defencelessness of Saddam's capital.

The Iraqi response to the US-led attack was limited to igniting dozens of trenches filled with oil and to sounding the air-raid alarms to demonstrate that their air defence systems were still functioning. But the absence of any practical response to this airborne onslaught started me wondering if all Saddam's talk about a last stand in the capital was anything more than the swagger of a man who knew the game was up.

A bunch of us watched as best we could from the balcony of Room 905 at the Palestine Hotel. Apart from Jon Lee Anderson and myself, there were Burns and Hicks from the

NYT and reporter Matt McAllester and photographer Moises Saman from the Long Island-based *Newsday*. Amazingly, this was a war zone in which telephones, water and power still functioned so, as I juggled a stream of radio and television interviews from Australia, the others crowded onto the balcony—the photographers competing for the best angles and all the time threatening to knock Anderson's sat-phone dish over the edge.

The first bombs were electrifying and, truthfully, quite terrifying. My nerves steadied after a while but, when Friday's barrage started to smash Baghdad's palaces, compounds and bunkers the crowd on our quivering balcony had difficulty comprehending what we saw. I lost count—the Pentagon said 1300 missiles . . . It left John Burns digging around in his compendious brain for a 1945 quote from the father of the atomic bomb, Robert Oppenheimer. As best Burns could recall, Oppenheimer had said on the testing of his first bomb: 'I have become the destroyer of worlds.'

They came in rapid succession and we were especially glad to be in the grime of the Palestine Hotel as we watched missiles flash in the vicinity of the al-Rashid Hotel, a squarish box that sat on the skyline just beyond the angled, blazing remains of Saddam's executive office in the presidential compound. Obviously the warnings had been right. At 10.30pm I made a note that I had heard the sound of the first US aircraft flying low over Baghdad but, within milliseconds, a screeching, wheels-in-gravel sound and a fast-moving blur told me exactly how close a cruise missile had come to us, as it sought its target. Earplugs, for which my wife had demanded a special markets mission by Mohammed, stayed in my pocket—forgotten.

The downtown bombing trailed off in the early hours of this morning. And with just the occasional dull thump of explosions beyond the city Anderson, Burns and myself sat down to write our first 'Shock and Awe' pieces—Anderson worked at the desk, with a pink-tape-criss-crossed mirror in front of him; Burns had his laptop on a small TV table; and I tapped at my laptop on a low coffee table. We were wired, running on pure adrenalin. The weeks we had already spent in Baghdad had been a draining cocktail of crazed deadlines, no sleep, nervous tension and constant anxiety about our own safety and security. In the dead of night the only sound was the soft clacking of the three keyboards.

Despite the constant communications hassles and the eeriness of being cut off in Baghdad, we were witnessing war in the global village. During lunch we had a telephone message from colleagues in Britain, to tell us that the B-52 bombers had taken off from Fairford, a US airbase in the UK, and that they were headed in our direction. Minutes before the first strike, my wife rang from New York to say she had just been told that the first bombs would drop any tick of the clock now; and halfway through the barrage, a Sydney broadcaster called to say that the White House had warned of hundreds more to come. The bombs falling all around us were dropped by pilots who would be back at their British bases in good time to take their children to their usual Saturday morning sports fixtures.

It all left me wondering about Tariq Aziz's claim a few days earlier that the will of the people, not smart bombs, would decide the outcome of this war.

The will of the people was not doing a lot for the Iraqi side, and the fall-out from all the bombing—smart or otherwise, Iraqi or American—was a burgeoning workload for Baghdad's emergency services. When I arrived in the morning at the Yarmuk Hospital, to the west of the city centre, there was an ominous pile of stretchers stacked against the front wall and inside doctors who said that they had more than 200 civilian patients. These seemed to be victims of incoming US missiles and outgoing Iraqi anti-aircraft fire. I had a feeling of dread about what was to come.

Despite the US threats, we were still drawn back to the al-Rashid. We vainly attempted to ginger the staff into understanding their predicament. We stopped for lunch—the kebabs and Iraqi bread were good, and the freshly squeezed orange juice satisfied a particular need for the health-conscious Burns. While the al-Rashid was a good distance from the Palestine, our minders allowed us go there unaccompanied, so we had an opportunity to observe the impact of the US-led bombing without the hand of a minder on our shoulders.

But as we finished lunch, there was gut-wrenching news from the north—Paul Moran, a freelance cameraman working for the Australian Broadcasting Corporation, had died in a suicide-bomb attack at Gerdigo, near Halabja. ABC correspondent Eric Campbell was also injured when a man near a Kurdish militia checkpoint in north-eastern Iraq summoned him and Moran, and then detonated a car.

Gerdigo was a small town that had been occupied by units of Ansar al-Islam, a terrorist group said to include remnants of al-Qaeda, which had fled Afghanistan to the wilds of northern Iraq. Hundreds of journalists had poured into Kurdistan to cover the long-expected US push on Baghdad from the north— a plan which fell away when Turkey refused to allow US troops access to northern Iraq through Turkish territory. Witnesses said that the ABC crew had been with other foreign journalists on the outskirts of Gerdigo, interviewing people fleeing in the wake of a US cruise missile bombardment that had begun last night. Moran was still filming, but most of the other journalists had just left the scene when the explosion occurred.

I knew first-hand how dangerous this part of the world was. In November 2002 I had ventured into Iraqi Kurdistan to write a four-part series, partly about the victims of Saddam's running campaign of death and deprivation against the Kurds and partly about the Ansar al-Islam, as I tried to piece together what links there might be between them and Osama bin Laden's men. In Sulaymaniyah the atmosphere had literally choked you with fear. No journalist could go out unaccompanied and most got out of the area as quickly as they could.

We all felt stunned. This was the first journalist killed in the war—and we knew there'd be more. We paid the bill quickly and returned to the Palestine. Already we were suffering from a bewildering combination of not enough sleep and a near-overpowering sense of what-might-happen-now? If last night had been the curtain raiser to 'Shock and Awe', what could we expect tonight?

DAY FOUR

A State of Denial

Filed Sunday, March 23 at 6.30am   **Palestine Hotel**

In the face of punishing US-led attacks, the Iraqi regime is in crisis, denying the truth of the invasion forces' rapid advance towards Baghdad and issuing desperate appeals to the UN Security Council and Arab leaders for help. As a wearied Foreign Minister Naji Sabri was reduced to travelling by taxi to Damascus, in neighbouring Syria, to pitch a plea for Arab assistance, Information Minister Mohammed Saeed al-Sahhaf held a midnight press conference on a Baghdad kerbside at which he insisted that the regime was in full control of Iraq.

As the people of Baghdad ventured out for furtive glances at the damage wrought in Friday night's relentless attacks on the city, Iraqi forces lit a ring of fire around Baghdad, torching a series of oil-filled trenches in the vain hope that the blanket of thick smoke that now hangs over the city will frustrate the US targeting.

34

Throughout Saturday night, powerful explosions rolled in from the outskirts of the capital, shaking buildings and suggesting that units of the Republican Guard posted to fend off the advancing American-led forces might be taking a hammering. But the biggest hits on downtown Baghdad were psychological. Ordinary Baghdadis were able to see the precision nature of Friday night's strikes against regime targets, and Saddam's continued absence from local reporting of the war fuelled speculation on his fate and that of his henchmen.

The city's mosques, memorials and monuments were spared. Yet, near a main city intersection, the headquarters of one of the arms of Saddam's oppressive security establishment had been gutted from the inside, with sunlight shining through a hole in the roof to the floors that were sandwiched at ground level. But, with the exception of a few broken windows, two high-rise apartment blocks less than 50m away were unscathed.

The presidency office, Saddam's official suite in the presidential compound on the banks of the Tigris River, was a charred skeleton and the Sajida Palace, his newest which he had named after his wife, was a dishevelled wreck. Across the road from the Sajida Palace a sprawling intelligence complex lay in ruins. The city headquarters of the Air Defence Ministry also had been knocked out.

Yesterday the Information Ministry bureaucrats took foreign reporters to see civilian damage—first a mangled tourist resort on the Tigris and, late in the evening, a huge crater where eight houses had stood in al-Qadisiyah, a western suburb.

Houses around the crater, which was about 15m deep and maybe 35m in diameter, had been peeled open. But there was no neighbourhood crowd to interview and, though Information Minister Sahhaf said that the strike had happened only three hours earlier, there was no dust in the air. Metal in the debris was as cold as the night.

Asked if it might have been a deliberate strike, because the regime had located one of its hideouts in this civilian quarter (a tactic adopted by Saddam during the 1991 Gulf War), Mr Sahhaf said: 'That's a dirty lie, an unbased claim.' He could not say how many had been killed or injured by the missile strike.

Doctors at the run-down, short-supplied al-Yarmuk Teaching Hospital said that they had treated 101 casualties in the wake of Friday night's attacks, half of whom were in a serious condition and most of whom suffered shrapnel wounds. It was not possible to say whether they had been injured by incoming or outgoing fire, but some of them were pitiable cases.

They included five-year-old Wahed Kamal Hamid, who was so traumatised that he wept as he attempted to recount his cameo role in the Iraq War to some of the 200 foreign reporters bussed to the hospital by the Information Ministry. He said that, as his terrified family raced away from the bombing, seeking shelter in the home of a relative, flying shrapnel knifed into his lower legs, tearing at the flesh of both calves.

It was the same story in the next bed. Her face adorned in tribal tattoos, 50-year-old Amal Hassam was a stark contrast—white bandages against her black *abaya*. She was getting out of a taxi at the home of a relative when she was raked by a spray of shrapnel. She has severe cuts to her arms, chest and abdomen and needs surgery but, according to London-trained consulting surgeon Fadel Habib, she'll be alright.

Dr Habib believes that this war is about oil and it saddens him. 'This is what we have in the 21st Century? I was surprised by the force of the attacks but we expected them to use extra power to force us to their position. We have adapted to this, but it's difficult,' he said.

He provided what sounded like a genuine breakdown of the 101 war casualties in the hospital: half-and-half serious and minor injuries; 20 per cent women; mostly adult; and 80 per cent civilian. But then there was a ruckus. A burst of tribal dancing and pro-Saddam slogans announced the arrival of Health Minister Umid Midhat Mubarak, who had a different set of figures: 'We have received 215 casualties—all are civilian, mostly children and elderly cases.' He claimed three had died.

Manipulation and control is the order of the day in Baghdad. The regime has adopted the Stalinist model of information control—journalists' movements are controlled and information is held tightly. If the regime doesn't like the latest news from the front, it simply denies it. Journalists are appointed minders and some of them are watched by plain-clothes intelligence officers.

So when the press asked to see damage to civilian property in Baghdad, we were bussed to the banks of the Tigris River, to a mangled mess which, until Friday's bombing, had been an innocuous holiday resort. Shattered crockery and melted glassware and cutlery marked the remains of the kitchen; a twisted typewriter, a broken office chair and charred paperwork littered the remains of what had been a humble office.

It seemed like an act of vandalism, but the more time we spent at this 'civilian' establishment the more unanswered questions were raised. Why did a uniformed soldier block those of us who attempted to wander along the river bank from the resort? Why was there a series of sand-bagged dugouts in the grounds? Why was there such a solid concrete footing in the flooded foundations of what had been a 'small office complex'?

And why did the Americans strike here with such ferocity? Two missiles had ripped the place apart. We ended up speculating about who might have been recent guests at the resort. It was very close to Saddam's Republican Palace and might well be the sort of place that senior members of the regime would use to avoid the bunker-busting bombs that the US uses to peel open the places where Saddam and his cronies usually hide.

Earlier in the day, Information Minister Mohammed Saeed

al-Sahhaf held a press conference where he was quizzed on the progress of the war. Asked about the US-led invasion forces' capture of the southern port of Umm Qasr, he said: 'The fight is fierce, we have inflicted much damage on our stupid enemy; they are not making any penetration.' The Fao Peninsula, where the US was reported to be in control? He gave the same answer, adding: 'We have foiled that attack.'

Thousands of Iraqi soldiers had surrendered or been captured? 'The cowards and mercenaries who tell these stories have actually taken civilians as prisoners.' And in the face of reports that the Americans have advanced to the Shia shrine city of Najaf, only 160km from Baghdad, he undertook to take reporters to Iraqi-controlled Najaf this morning.

But even the polished Mr Sahhaf was rattled when he was quizzed about Saddam Hussein. Asked when Saddam would address the Iraqi people, he turned abruptly from the questioner, and said: 'Next?' And pressed later on whether he had seen Saddam in the last few days, he showed great irritation, saying only: 'Next! Next! Please ask me something reasonable.'

▲

Last night it was dark around the hole in the ground and as the TV lights bobbed on the shoulders of the cameramen, it was difficult to make out the speaker. But he was filled with anger and indignation as he accused the US of wanton civilian death and destruction. I noted his denial that the Iraqi leadership might have been using one of the now demolished homes to hide from the US attacks, and as the press pack dispersed, I chased after him to get his name. I caught up as his military-style vehicle was about to pull away and was saved from making an awful fool of myself by the timely arrival of John Burns.

'Excuse me, sir, could I please have your name?' I asked of the small man wearing a great coat and a black beret as he sat on the back seat. But before he could reply, Burns' voice boomed over my left shoulder: 'Ah, it's the Minister for Information . . .', at which point I was able to mask my embarrassment at not having recognised the public face of the regime, who previously I had only seen in civilian garb. I covered: 'But it's dark, sir; and I didn't recognise you in uniform.'

Looking out from the balcony this morning, I counted thirteen towering pillars of black smoke. The Iraqi military had been torching more oil-filled trenches and this had reduced Baghdad to a gloomy, permanent twilight. As the soot rubbed off from our bodies and clothing, it turned the greyish-white sheets on our beds to greyish-black. We were sleeping in our clothes, to enable us to run if it became necessary, and it was hard to know if we were grubbier than the beds.

Walk the corridors of the Palestine at night and you entered a journalists' world. You might find a French party—real wine in real glasses in a real war—while in another room you'd see the pained expression of the creative process on deadline. Not far away, you'd hear invective screamed at a failed piece of vital equipment; or from another room maybe, just maybe, the strains of a Bach prelude.

This was a weird hotel. In order to keep the fierce heat of summer at bay, half of what might have been a stunning panorama of the city and the river was blocked out by a creepy concrete cobweb. I had to peer through it to count the oil fires. The peep-hole on the door to our $US40-a-night room had been filled with wax and the door itself clearly had been on the move—physically, this was Room 905 but the only number on the door was 0 and on either side of it were marks that showed it used to be on Room 1208.

The seventeen-storey Palestine might once have been a great hotel—when it opened in 1982, it had five stars and French management. Now it was on autopilot and headed for the rocks. Most of the staff had stopped coming to work; most of the rooms were occupied by journalists, but half of these booked in the names of journalists who had fled before the start of the bombing; the lifts were inordinately slow and the coffee so bad that we had determined never to eat from the Palestine's Orient Express restaurant or its room service— if either should ever become available.

But in the history of world affairs, the Palestine had already earned its place, just as previously had the Commodore in Beirut and the Holiday Inn in Sarajevo. Its cockroach-infested and litter-strewn corridors had become home to the reporters covering the Iraq war. The persistent could still phone in to it by landline from abroad—Channel 9 and SBS in Sydney had managed to get through almost daily. I was now one of only two Australian reporters in Baghdad, which meant I was the target of an avalanche of interview requests—up to a dozen on high-demand days. It was impossible to convey the sense of mayhem to some people in Australia—amazingly some media organisations didn't understand that there was no mobile phone network in Iraq and that I couldn't pick up messages left on my New York mobile phone; and one idiot radio producer, who got through on the sat-phone, tried to take ten minutes of my time to complain about the quality of the line.

The hotel's barber shop was abandoned; its tennis courts were layered with mud and the slimy contents of its swimming pool were so thick I might have walked across it. The dusty dishevelment was completed by the 'e' that dangled forlornly from the end of the word 'Palestine' in the neon sign hanging above where the hawkers gathered, selling anything, from stolen cigarettes to a car ride to Amman for as much as $US2000.

The flat roof of the low-rise section of the hotel was a warren of tents, camera spots, generators and uplink dishes for the handful of TV stations that had decided to stay in Baghdad.

But most of the US networks had left and CNN had been thrown out after a brawl with the Information Ministry.

The ministry itself had now moved into the ground-floor lobby, which created a constant swirl of journalists looking for, or trying to lose, their minders. It also brought the presence of secret service agents, who made little or no pretence as they sidled up to listen to our conversations. Occasionally I'd turn on them, and yell: 'You speak English—don't you? What do you want? Who do you report to?' They'd stare back brazenly, before in time moving off to plonk themselves within earshot of another group of reporters.

The fact that American and British spin-doctors worked just as hard as our ministry minders to manipulate and twist news on the war was no consolation to us as we faced the refusal by the Iraqis to allow us to visit military or official targets around a city on which, on Friday night alone, the US had dropped missiles worth $US1.3 billion. Then the ministry said they would show us 'civilian' damage, and they put on four big buses to take us and our individual minders and translators to the western suburbs. I'd been up much of the night trying to piece events together in a meaningful way for Australian readers, so I was pretty well wiped out.

But when we alighted from our bus convoy, instead of the accidental hit we had expected, we were confronted by what seemed to have been a deliberate strike on a small riverside tourist resort. I walked around it with Matt McAllester, a crew-cut and slightly conspiratorial young British reporter who writes for *Newsday*. At first it all seemed quite innocuous, but the substantial fortifications in the resort grounds left me wondering whether this was the sort of nondescript place in which Saddam and others in the regime might have sought refuge from the US bombing.

Driving back to the city there was an eruption of anti-aircraft fire—overhead we could see US cruise missiles sailing in towards unknown targets in the first daylight bombing of Baghdad. But since Friday night's onslaught it had been relatively quiet, with the exception of a multiple-missile strike on the General Directorate of Security, east of central Baghdad. This had been an odious place, in which one of Saddam Hussein's more powerful security arms had jailed, tortured and executed Iraqis as it went about maintaining what had been dubbed the 'republic of fear'.

We were learning to take the US missile strikes in our stride. They were fearsome things, especially when we got to see the damage they caused, but we had a growing confidence that the US bomber pilots and mission planners knew the world's press was in the Palestine. This gave us some sense of personal safety, even if we were acutely aware that this was a luxury that the Iraqi population did not enjoy. But our equanimity did take a bit of a setback when we returned from the bombed-out tourist resort to the ministry's Press Centre, where the Sinak Bridge meets the west bank of the Tigris, and found colleagues standing out in the car park, looking skywards, apparently expecting an imminent air strike on the ministry's bunker-like building.

We were all troubled by veiled threats that the Pentagon might put us off the air—that the satellites serving our phones would be shut down or, worse, that the US would use its much-vaunted new generation e-bombs to fry the insides of our laptop computers and satellite phones. In the absence of any sensible technical advice, some were storing their sat-phones, computers and camera equipment in metal trunks or wrapping them in tinfoil. Others— including the *Newsday* duo, McAllester and Saman—took the advice of a British TV crew and went out and bought several microwave ovens. Their rationale was that, if the ovens were built to keep microwaves *in*, then it followed that the ovens would keep microwaves *out*—and therefore anything stored inside the ovens would be safe from weapons-generated microwaves.

Personal security was a constant and critical issue. Now that the streets of Baghdad were devoid of local traffic I got anxious at the prospect of going out in a single car. Where possible I insisted on two cars so that, if there was a problem with one, we could all pile into the other to get back to the hotel safely; or, if one vehicle was bailed up, the other could fetch help. It didn't help that we had had more bad news of journalist casualties—one ITV correspondent dead and two of his colleagues reportedly missing near Basra, in southern Iraq, apparently after coming under British fire.

The British news service ITN had reported on Saturday that Terry Lloyd, cameraman Fred Nerac and translator Hussein Othman had been fired upon in the town of Iman Anas. They had been travelling in clearly marked press vehicles—the only sensible way to travel in a war zone—but they were not embedded with either US or British forces. A second cameraman, Daniel Demoustier, had told the BBC that they had been chased by Iraqi troops, who might have been attempting to surrender to them, and that the incoming fire on their vehicles had come from US or British forces.

Demoustier said that he had been seated next to Lloyd in a vehicle that caught fire after crashing into a ditch and he had managed to escape, but he was not aware of the fate of the other three. A notice on ITN's website on the Sunday stated: 'There is now sufficient evidence to believe that ITV News Correspondent Terry Lloyd, 50, was killed in an incident on the Southern Iraq war front yesterday.' According to ITV, both Nerac and Othman were wearing multiple photographic press passes at the time of their disappearance. Nerac had three such passes—one American and two Kuwaiti. Othman was wearing exactly the same.

In a sombre mood we drove out of the city for lunch, over which we went around and around (again!) on the topic of how to stay alive if the regime turned on the foreign media, a constant but unresolvable fear. We were at the Latakia Restaurant in Karada, a few minutes south of the Palestine Hotel. We presumed the management had special blessings from the regime because, unlike other eateries, the Latakia was always open and still had plentiful supplies of most ingredients. This meant that, if we could get there, we could create our day's food routine around at least one square meal.

The fare was classic Arabic—lamb and chicken tikka or kebabs, flat rounds of leathery Iraqi bread and tasty mezza dishes . . . hummus and chickpeas, yogurt and eggplant, and a dozen other vegetable salads that came to the table with a flourish. Pepsi or 7—as Seven-Up is known here—was the extent of the drinks menu and we'd round out the meal with tiny glasses of sweet, black tea.

But this day, the first serve, when a group of us walked into the restaurant, was from the surly Uday al-Tai, the Director-General of the Information Ministry. We'd hardly washed our hands and faces before he barrelled in with a party of colleagues and some fawning French journalists who were forever hanging on, seeking official favours because of France's opposition to the war. As he sat down, al-Tai snarled loudly, to ensure that we'd hear from several tables away: 'We have two American pilots—we have them in Baghdad. These armies thought that coming to Iraq would be a picnic—cream cakes and crates of Pepsi. But you will see—they will be slaughtered.'

We put this outburst down as more Baghdad bluster and denial. There were constant Iraqi claims of US aircraft being shot down that could never be substantiated. Meanwhile, it seemed that the American-led invasion force was making good progress on the ground—this was only the fourth day of combat and the advance US units were already flanking the Shia shrine city of Najaf, just 160km south of Baghdad. And in the capital people were asking just one question: 'Where's Saddam?'

DAY FIVE

Monday, March 24

Saddam Hussein Addresses his People

Filed Monday, March 24 at 12.38pm   **Palestine Hotel**

To be shot down behind enemy lines is every fighter pilot's nightmare. But among the crowd that watched on the banks of the Tigris River yesterday, as Iraqi soldiers searched for a British pilot they believed had bailed out over Baghdad, some were willing him to safety.

Saddam Hussein was not among them. In a defiant and at times lurid speech televised in Iraq today, Saddam urged his people to destroy the 'open and pale-faced infidels' who were attempting to occupy Iraq.

Yesterday the rest of the world might have been focused on the increasingly feisty Iraqi resistance to the advancing US forces and on General Tommy Franks' efforts to provision and position his men for the battle for Baghdad. But this is a city

45

desperate for distractions, so the search for the pilot unfolded as a bleak, compulsive comedy. Not even an air-raid alert, renewed US bombing and bursts of anti-aircraft fire could send the crowd home.

That this happened on a day when Iraqi television paraded its first US prisoners of war and allowed cameras to pan across some of the first American war dead was gut-wrenching enough, but the life-or-death circumstances for the pilot—if he was there in the first place—made it almost unbearable to watch.

The TV images that zinged around the world were the brutal reality of war. The ten or more Americans who died in the battle for Nasiriyah were spread as trophies on a bare concrete floor; their bruised and bloodied faces were shown in close-up while an Iraqi medic smiled for the cameras as he carelessly rearranged one of the bodies.

The treatment of the captives was no better. The five seemed disoriented and terrified, eyes darting every which way as they became tools of Iraqi propaganda. Over and over, TV audiences saw an unseen interviewer mock the prisoners with questions that belittled US Vice-President Dick Cheney's recent prediction that Iraqis would welcome the invasion force with songs and flowers.

'Have Iraqis met you with flowers or with guns? Why have you come from Texas to Iraq?' the interviewer asked James Hudson. 'I follow orders,' the captive replied flatly.

The Geneva Convention, which the US had to be pushed into observing for the hundreds of prisoners it shipped from Afghanistan to a cage-like prison at Guantanamo Bay in Cuba, says that prisoners of war should not be treated as objects of public curiosity. But, just as Baghdad did last night, the Western media this week has been full of pictures of Iraqis captured by the US being paraded across the desert.

▼

One of the first who said he saw Baghdad anti-aircraft gunners hit the British aircraft on Sunday was 50-something Mohammed Abdul Salkah. Pointing to the west, he said: 'I saw the attack—the plane went that way and the pilot jumped into the river. I saw the soldiers find his parachute and helmet.'

The search focused on a long, narrow strip of bulrushes on the west bank, between the Sinak and Jumhuriyah Bridges, and it played out against an eerily lit skyline as the setting sun fought through clouds of dense black smoke from oil fires lit by the Iraqis to confuse US bombing missions. At first the searchers tried to smoke the pilot out—dousing the rushes in gallons of petrol, which they ignited. When that didn't work, they called in the Iraqi equivalent of navy SEALs—three overweight men in a dinghy, who wore swimmers and were obliged to share the one half-length wet suit.

When they failed, troops with sickles stomped through the rushes and, whenever they suspected they had the pilot cornered, more than 100 men with Kalashnikovs and pistols opened fire, pouring thousands of rounds into the rushes. Every now and again a shout would go up and the crowd would surge along the river bank, tumbling into the rushes before it was pushed back. '*Jibo, jibo,*' they yelled, which translates as 'Bring him, bring him.'

This exercise had a vital commercial element for the Iraqis— Saddam Hussein pays any Iraqi gunner who downs an enemy aircraft the equivalent of $US50 000. Those who bring him a live pilot get $US50 000 but, if the pilot is dead, the reward slips to $US25 000. At times the crowd broke into pro-Saddam chants but sitting on the levy one bearded Iraqi held back, saying: 'This is bad. I'm a pilot and I hate to see another pilot treated this way.'

Soon after that exchange I was joined by an Iraqi mute, who explained his view in animated sign language. At first he said that he wanted to go into the rushes, pull the pilot out and, after shaking him by the shoulders, he would punch him in the nose. But it seemed this was a response conditioned by the Saddam song sheet, which also played a part in the mob mentality of the crowd, because the mute thought about it for a while longer and then, with elaborate gestures, he showed he was capable of a more personal, more humane reaction.

Pointing at his brain to suggest intelligence, he said that the pilot would be hiding underwater; that he might be able to swim to the middle of the river and drift downstream to safety. This would be good, he said with a thumbs-up gesture. As sunset approached, he circled his watch with a finger to indicate the onset of darkness in an hour's time; he pinched his nose and used arm movements to demonstrate underwater swimming, away from the rushes; and he smiled a smile of great satisfaction.

Just before it was dark, there was wild cheering as the crowd saw a reed, standing vertically as it floated downstream near the rushes. Two soldiers stripped off and swam towards it but, as they neared it, the Kalashnikovs opened up again.

They scarpered . . . and the reed got away.

Wearing his military uniform and seated behind a desk for today's telecast appearance, Saddam appeared more composed in this, his first appearance since last Thursday morning, when he had seemed rattled and distracted as he addressed the nation only hours after the US attack-bombed a bunker where it believed he was hiding.

But, despite the jumpy editing of today's telecast, Saddam appeared fit and well. Singling out the people of Basra in the south, who are surrounded by invading forces, he urged them to be patient because they too would be victorious; and he warned the people of Baghdad, Mosul in the north and Muthanna in central Iraq that they were likely to be subjected to even greater bombardment by the US.

As heavy bombing continued, he read from a prepared text, saying: 'These are decisive days in which we will live or die. Our enemies are surprised at how we have responded, so strike them on the neck, the head and the heart. Though in most cases they will avoid engagement, they have put their troops within range of our weapons. We have them surrounded; we are firing at them after they belittled our abilities. We will inflict heavy casualties. Strike at the enemy with strength and precision and our victory will be final and clear.'

Saddam urged his forces to tire the invasion forces, urging them to understand that he was teaching the US and Britain a lesson so that they would never again attack Iraq. He said: 'God is disappointed with the enemy and he will support us. We pledge before God that we will pay with all that we have so that the enemy will go into the abyss.' Alluding to international anxiety about the war, he said: 'Those who were sleeping and deceived by our enemies in 1991 are now rising from their sleep.'

▲

Email to Pam:

Got in abt 20mins ago—will call soon . . . but v fearful of using sat-fone. New goons have been appointed to every floor of hotel. Cheers/love

I had filed my last news report for the day, but the search for the pilot—if, indeed, he ever existed—went on. Some time after midnight I was drawn to the balcony of Room 905 by rapid bursts of gunfire that seemed to come from just outside the hotel. The search had shifted downstream, to clumps of bulrushes just in front of the Palestine. Now more than a dozen excitable Iraqi gunmen were spraying the reeds with bullets.

But despite their sustained aggression, I was still amazed by the apparent goodwill towards the phantom pilot that had been displayed all day by ordinary Iraqis, particularly given that US and British aircraft were flying overhead during the river search. The detonation of the bombs they dropped could be heard by the crowd on the river bank and the bombed-out presidential compound—and all that it symbolised about Saddam's regime—was only 500m down the river.

But I had a more urgent concern of my own—my sat-phone. We could set the dish for Jon Lee Anderson's Mini-M sat-phone perfectly to connect with the satellites orbiting over the eastern Atlantic Ocean. When we thought it was safe to use it, the phone sat on the balcony wall, perched on several of the plastic boxes in which I carried small items of electrical equipment. Anderson's dog-eared copy of Joseph Conrad's *Heart of Darkness* kept the small, square dish tilted at a perfect angle. But our immediate worry was that the dish could be seen from the street; equally, any attempt to retrieve it amidst all the wild shooting might draw some of the gunfire in our direction. My own phone, a Nera World Communicator, had too big a dish to fit on the wall, and not being able to use it was driving me crazy.

Using the sat-phones in our rooms was illegal. To our utter frustration, almost everything about sat-phones in Baghdad was illegal. We had to agree that we would pay $US100 a day for the privilege of using a phone and make calls only from the Information Ministry's Press Centre, which the Pentagon had stipulated as high on its Baghdad target list. If we flouted these undertakings then we were breaking the law, and risking both confiscation and possibly our expulsion from the country. All of this got under my skin—I wanted to be able to use the phone from my hotel room and I didn't want to pay $US100 a day to bureaucrats who I knew were skimming the kitty. Sat-phones had been a sensitive issue in Iraq since the last Gulf War as the regime feared they would be used to communicate information to the US military.

The process of paranoia started the moment you entered the country. When reporters crossed into Iraq from Jordan, the Iraqi border guards would fix a lead seal to the zipper on sat-phone bags. As long as the bag remained sealed—and, quite clearly, unusable—we were not charged the $US100 and could keep them in our rooms. However, I quickly discovered that some gentle pressure with a pair of pliers allowed me to remove the seal from the zipper in a way that did not break the seal. So I was able to use the phone, at least under cover of darkness, and at the same time keep it officially sealed and unusable—by putting the lock and seal back in place on the bag whenever I left the room, in case of a ministry raiding party

But it wasn't quite as simple as that. To initiate a satellite connection, I needed good line of sight to the western horizon and that meant surreptitiously holding the dish—with a surface area almost as big as a broadsheet newspaper—out the window. During my first weeks at the al-Rashid there was no balcony—so I had to smuggle into the hotel the makings for a wooden shelf that protruded from the window, on which I could sit the dish without it blowing away. Once I had established a signal, I'd then discreetly bring the dish (and the shelf) back into the room. I would then position the dish in such a way that the guards, who sometimes swept the sides of the al-Rashid with searchlights, would not notice it. By day I'd hide the shelf under my bed, hoping that it would not raise suspicions during the daily security checks on my room.

All this stuff took hours, and the whole procedure had to be conducted under the relative safety of darkness and in a lather of perspiration precipitated by anxiety. Nevertheless, I had arrived in Baghdad early enough to have my pick of rooms and had asked for a west-facing room which I knew, from previous experience, picked up the best signal from the bird over the eastern Atlantic.

It's hard to overstate the level of fear generated by the Information Ministry's insistence that we work from its targeted office—there was little doubt that they wanted to use us as human shields. TV crews had such bulky equipment that they had no other choice than to buckle under the demands of the ministry; but print and radio reporters fought a harrowing game of hide-and-seek with minders, who sometimes would settle for cash if they uncovered an illicit sat-phone.

I spent one evening walking the dreary corridors of the al-Rashid, looking for a place in which to safely dispose of the normal cell phone I carried, which I could use in neighbouring Jordan, but not in Iraq. Even though there was no cell phone network here, they too were verboten. I slipped the phone's chip into my wallet, but I last saw the phone itself hidden in the folds of an emergency fire hose on the hotel's ninth floor. It had disappeared by the time I went back.

And on one crazy evening at the start of the war, the ministry minders confiscated a dozen sat-phones and there was physical violence on the Palestine's rooftop when the minders—and the thuggish spooks who shadowed them—set upon a group of photographers who were setting up to shoot the night's bombing. Blows were struck, a couple of photographers were thrown, or pushed, down a flight of stairs and several had expensive equipment dashed against a concrete floor.

We had to devise a system of coded, rat-a-tat-tat door knocks so that any of us using a sat-phone would know instantly if an unannounced visitor was friend or foe. Whenever we knew the minders were searching the hotel, colleagues would phone around on the hotel's internal phone system with warnings so we could hide the sat-phones in air-conditioning ducts, or in the housekeeping staff's corridor cupboards, or get one of the drivers to take them for a drive around the block. I took to burying mine deep inside the big box of MREs—meals ready-to-eat—that I'd been hauling around for weeks. Ann Garrels, of National Public Radio in the US, and Larry Kaplow, of the *Atlanta Journal-Constitution,* both confessed to working naked—in separate rooms—so that, when the knock came on the door, they would have time to feign having been asleep or, better still, would embarrass the minders by going to the door half-naked.

We were able to use the internet cafe at the al-Rashid Hotel until the day before the first bombing of Baghdad—when the staff moved in with a stack of cardboard boxes, into which they started packing all the terminals, announcing as they went that they'd be back after the war. At times we'd had to queue for an hour to get a terminal in the cafe and email sent from there was read by the Information Ministry—at least one colleague was called in by the ministry and confronted with a copy of his unguarded reference to the plight of the Kurds in what he had presumed was a private email that had vanished into the ether some days earlier. This reading of our emails, plus eavesdropping on our conversations, meant that we had to develop our own code—my sat-phone became my 'nail clippers' and using it became 'having a manicure'. My emails to office and home were filled with references to when I might be able to do my nails and whether or not my nail clippers were functioning.

The other big hassle, as the bombing campaign wore on, was the jamming of the satellites we used whenever missiles and US aircraft were in the skies over Baghdad. It was a disaster when this happened, plunging us into a complete communications black-hole. No phone or email, no online research or information from the outside world—unless some persistent soul managed to get through on the hotel telephone, which worked only intermittently. Sometimes, we could get and hold a data line to send email via the sat-phone, but not a voice line to make a call. The jamming was constant nearly every night and it drove us mad.

This was the sort of pressure that had helped reduce our numbers from 500 to about 130, maybe 150, in the space of a week. But there were two fears in particular that tipped the scales for those who were of a mind to leave—one was that in a flash this regime could turn on us; and the other was that we might get caught in the cross-fire of bloody street fighting in Baghdad, which the Iraqis were now insisting was the cornerstone of their defence plan.

Email to Pam:
Sorry I was ratty earlier . . . was on deadline for the arvo edition and had just rescued JL's sat-fone from hiding after sweep of hotel by spooks and had just taken call from Alan Jones and the other fone was ringing loudly while JL was sleeping so I had hung up on Jones' producer . . . so I was a nervous wreck. On top of that nothing happened at 2am and I have to write 1200 words by 8am. Sorry—that's why I was strung out. Nothing to do about fone except move rooms or move hotel—we do have a few options, but can't explore till tomorrow. Will just have to press on . . .

DAY SIX

Colleagues Disappear

Filed Tuesday, March 25 at 12.16pm   **Palestine Hotel**

Iraqi farmer Ali Obeid is the hero of the regime. When a fleet of 30 low-flying US Apache attack-helicopters rumbled over his fields on Monday, he pulled out an ancient Brno rifle and apparently managed to shoot one down. He's on Iraqi TV around the clock—with his trophy helicopter.

But Obeid is not alone. After days of confusion and uncertainty, the Iraqi regime has pulled itself together, just in time for the decisive battle for Baghdad.

The US-led invasion force is on the capital's doorstep and its high-altitude bombers are pummelling Republican Guard divisions that encircle the city. Since late on Sunday incessant explosions have rolled in to the centre of Baghdad, sometimes so powerful that they push you back on your feet.

The guards, the backbone of Saddam Hussein's defence, are being punished with 2000 pound guided JDAM bombs and

Tomahawk cruise missiles launched from B-52 aircraft flying out of Britain. Agile Apache attack-helicopters (less one, thanks to the wily Obeid), Harrier attack-jets and Warthog anti-tank aircraft try to nip in from the sides, attempting to smash the guards' air defences and command and control structure. Following Saddam Hussein's TV appearance on Monday, a phalanx of senior ministers is being wheeled out on a daily basis to brief the foreign press on the progress of the war, and to show that US claims that they have fractured the regime are untrue. Behind the layers of rhetoric and invective there's a determination that few analysts expected at this stage of the war.

In conventional terms it's too late—the coalition's technological superiority will win out. But winning means different things to both sides in this war. For George W. Bush, Saddam must be ousted—he cannot make the same mistake his father did in 1991. But Saddam only has to keep standing; for him survival in any form is winning.

This is the cleft in which they face-off for the showdown at Baghdad. Strategically and tactically Saddam can roam free, but Bush could be hamstrung—civilian death and destruction in Baghdad will play badly for him, internationally and in the minds of Iraqi people. A siege of Baghdad, because the US says it will not let Saddam lure it into urban combat, would create an appalling humanitarian disaster in a city of five million people.

This will be a war of nerves. Saddam is using the civilian population as a human shield; and the provision of chemical warfare suits to the Republican Guard suggests that he may have —and could use—chemical or biological weapons. In the last three nights his Baghdad anti-aircraft batteries have been virtually silent, suggesting that he is conserving ammunition for what could be a bloodier and more effective use of his AA-guns— as high-powered shooting platforms for street-fighting in the city.

The precision bombing of regime targets in Baghdad has been a powerful psychological tool for the US because, in the minds of some Iraqis, it serves to separate them from the regime and to jolt them into a reality check on its failings after decades of mind-warping domestic propaganda and control.

But Saddam is fighting back, with appeals to the Iraqis' very real sense of nationalism and with stories like that of Obeid, the Karbala farmer, and his Czech-made rifle. Each time Saddam speaks, he appeals to the entire nation—the Baath Party militia, the sons of the tribes and the civilian defence units—and not just his regular armed forces.

Many Iraqis yearn for a post-Saddam life. But there is great fear of the horror of this war and it won't take much for them to switch back to the devil they knew last week. I know a grandfather here who can't wait for the overthrow of Saddam but, during the bombing on Sunday, his pregnant daughter miscarried and he sees that as a direct consequence of the US attacks.

This is the context in which Deputy Prime Minister Tariq Aziz gave a detailed regime perspective on the war to date when he summoned reporters on Monday night. Unlike his colleagues, he avoided the Baghdad brand of invective. Instead, he calmly posed questions that, despite the Pentagon's supreme confidence, must be troubling US strategists as they prepare for the battle of Baghdad.

'They said that once the war started the leadership would collapse and that Iraqis would side with the aggressors; they talked of Iraqis welcoming them with music and flowers. They said that Saddam Hussein was isolated, with only the Republican Guard and the people of Tikrit, so he would have to fight alone.'

Then he turned to the fighting in what the regime now refers to as 'little' Umm Qasr, where Iraqi fighters are still resisting the invasion in a town of 600 people that should have been cleaned up in the first hours of this war. He said: 'There are no Republican Guards and there is no one from Tikrit in Umm Qasr. The fighters are ordinary Iraqi units who arrived in the town the night before the war—they didn't even have time to dig trenches.'

Mr Aziz challenged the US description of the fighting still taking place in Umm Qasr, Nasiriyah, al-Fao and Samawa as 'pockets of resistance' that might easily be dispatched. He said: 'The best way to resist invasion is to divide into pockets and these are very dangerous pockets for the enemy. Do they expect our officers to appear in marching columns to be picked off by their planes and helicopters? What is important is that we are firing to kill the enemy. And what of Division 51 and their claim that 8000 men had surrendered? They are still fighting and none of the fighters in the south are from the Republican Guard or from Tikrit.'

He ridiculed early US reports that the city of Nasiriyah— a crossing on the Euphrates River that is vital for the Americans to supply their units headed for Baghdad—had been captured. Then he made his point: 'If it takes them this long and they still don't have Umm Qasr and Nasiriyah, how long will it take them to get a city the size of Basra?'

Aziz joked about flowers and music. 'The farmer who shot down the helicopter welcomed the Americans with his gun. It is the only instrument he plays and he welcomed the Americans in the best Iraqi tradition. They say they will be ready for the battle of Baghdad by the weekend. But they will get the same welcome as they are getting at Umm Qasr and Nasiriyah—it will be the best music and the best flowers ever grown in Iraq. Our leadership is intact, except for the death of one Baath Party martyr at Najaf. The government is in good shape and US and British public opinion is about to learn that it has been dragged into a quagmire where it will learn huge lessons.'

The US policy of avoiding towns and cities leaves each one it passes as a virtual time bomb. Already at Basra, Iraq's second city, the defenders are trying to lure the invasion force into urban combat—and British units on the northern outskirts of the city are falling for it. On Monday they returned fire with artillery into a city in which the Iraqi defences are spread through the civilian quarters. A little more enticement from the Iraqis could easily draw them right into the city. And this is the mini version of what Saddam is planning for Baghdad.

The analysts' view that the war is bogging down is premature—the US-led advance to Baghdad has been remarkable. But it has been at the expense of leaving carefully planted units of Iraqi fighters in cities that might erupt at any time and which will always be nipping from the rear at the American, British and Australian troops.

Iraq's Defence Minister, Sultan Hashim, calls the US advance the 'Swerve and Stop' campaign. He says that the Americans are staying in the desert, always heading north. He said: 'They can keep going north for as long as they like, all the way to Europe if they want to. But if they want us, they will have to come into the cities; they will have to come into Baghdad.'

Cautious analysts have observed for months that the Iraqi forces are better than the US makes them out to be, and they are proving that point. The Republican Guard is well armed and equipped. It has rifles, machine-guns, hand grenades, anti-tank weapons and, most important, familiarity with the battlefield. And if it comes to a street fight in Baghdad, the US's technological superiority will be blunted.

The Iraqis see death in battle as honourable; the Americans see it as a political crisis at home. More importantly, the US has never captured a heavily defended city as big as Baghdad, which has a population of 4.5 million. And US successes in smaller cities like Hue in Vietnam in 1968 came at a cost of more than 1000 Americans dead or wounded and 9000 Viet-namese casualties.

The direst warnings are in the Pentagon's own Doctrine for Joint Urban Operations, which noted: 'Cities reduce the advantages of the technologically superior force. The physical terrain of cities tends to reduce line of sight, inhibits command, control and communications capability [and] makes aviation operations more difficult . . . It also degrades logistics, and often reduces ground operations to the level of small-unit combat.'

Aziz argued that the US-led troops entered Iraq at the peak of their psychological preparation in the belief that the regime would collapse in hours or days. 'Remember, they said "Shock and Awe"? But if they can't take Umm Qasr and the heavy casualties we are inflicting, you can imagine what the next seven days will be like.' Asked if, at this stage, a diplomatic solution might avoid more bloodshed, he added: 'I don't have candies to offer them, only bullets.'

Dr Aziz ended with an invitation to reporters. Asked how he thought the battle for Baghdad would play out, he didn't miss a beat: 'Stay in Baghdad and watch.'

▲

A violent *turab*, or dust storm, swallowed Baghdad on a horrible day in which bad news mixed with awkward news to drown out a bit of really good news. Briefly, four of our colleagues vanished from the hotel in the night and they included Matt and Moises from *Newsday*. Despite their early speed on the ground, the US-led invasion forces seemed to be bogging down on the road to Baghdad—creating new uncertainty about how long we might have to sit out the rising tension in the Iraqi capital. And, as I said, a morsel of good news that was drowned out: the Information Ministry caved in to a campaign of quiet but persistent lobbying, and agreed that henceforth we would be allowed to use sat-phones from our hotel rooms.

On tumultuous days like this we didn't need to be reminded that we were in the eye of the story. But to counter the Iraqis' Pollyanna version of the conflict, we leavened the Iraqi News Agency's coverage by monitoring a string of news websites that, even in the news-free zone of Saddam's Baghdad, were easily accessible through a laptop connected to a sat-phone—the BBC, Reuters, AP, CNN and the major US and British newspapers' websites. The only person in Baghdad who seemed not to be affected by the *turab* was the irrepressible Information Minister, Mohammed Saeed al-Sahhaf. We hadn't had a lot to do with him in recent months, but clearly he had been nominated by Saddam as the face of the regime for the war. Instead of the stolid diplomatic skills we had seen in Tariq Aziz, Baghdad's front man in 1990–91, Sahhaf would bound into his daily press briefings with a lopsided grin and a lopsided update on the fighting. He regularly reported fabulous feats by the Iraqis and never reported Iraqi military casualties.

It was only the sixth day of the war but, wherever we looked, the wheels seemed to be spinning on the great Bush crusade. The US was meeting such Iraqi resistance that it was slowing its northern advance to 'mop up' in the south; as this was happening inside Iraq, even Saddam's foes in the Arab world were proud of the fight he was putting up; British Prime Minister Tony Blair was headed for Camp David for talks that he hoped would ease the US rift with Europe; the CIA and the Pentagon were squabbling over which agency had made the right calls on how best to topple Saddam; and the US Army stood accused of failing to anticipate Saddam's guerrilla-style defence.

But, from where we sat in the bull's-eye, there was not a lot of upside for Saddam. Even as the *turab*'s yellowish dust combined with the black smoke from the flaming oil trenches to turn day into night, Saddam knew, and most of his people knew, that the bubble of his power was about to burst—that coming up the highway was a force that he could never counter, a force that could not be deterred by resorting to the old regime fallback of airing on Iraqi TV more vintage footage of the Hussein father and sons.

Nor was the smoke working as a deterrent. The dust had grounded US combat helicopters, but in and around Baghdad the bombs kept falling. The deep rumble of exploding munitions—dropped from high-altitude aircraft and launched from ships far away from the wrath of the *turab*—pushed in from the south-west, activating the anti-theft alarms on cars that couldn't be seen in the gloom. This wind disturbed and depressed the locals—the few who had previously stayed in the streets now retreated to their homes and there was no longer any trade for the few diehard shopkeepers who, up until now, had refused to be cowed into closing just because there was a war on.

The sudden disappearance of Matt McAllester and Moises Saman was very worrying. At various times I had worked quite closely with them, especially Matt. I had spent much of Sunday with him, watching the search for the phantom allied pilot from the banks of the Tigris. On Monday, like the rest of us, he had come back to the hotel and emailed his office to brief his foreign desk on the story he would be filing, before settling in to write into the early hours. But, as best we could tell, he had not actually filed to *Newsday* and, when some of his colleagues went looking for him about mid-morning, they found that the room he had shared with Moises—Room 1122—had been stripped of any sign of the two of them. This was alarming, playing as it did on our fear of being taken hostage by the regime or being co-opted as human shields.

But then came word that two others had also disappeared—Molly Bingham, a photographer and heiress to a US media fortune, who had tried to schmooze Jon Lee Anderson into believing that she had a gig to work for *The New Yorker* in Baghdad when neither he nor his New York desk knew anything about it; and a Danish photographer of whom we knew very little, Johan Rydeng Spanner, a freelancer who was shooting for the Danish daily *Jyllands-Posten*.

We knew all four had come into Iraq on dodgy visas and there was a feeling that, before we panicked, we should wait and see if they turned up in Jordan or Syria in the next few days—like several others who had been kicked out for having the wrong visas. Also there was speculation that Matt and Moises, in particular, might simply have decided to go underground. This was an option we all had considered when our visas were threatened, but it was dangerous and, if analysed properly, was not worth the risks. However, we had to allow that it was a call that Matt and Moises might have made, because they were desperate to cover the war and the Iraqis were keeping us on a knife-edge on the visa issue.

In the way of things in Baghdad, I was easily distracted from Matt and Moises' problem, because I had one of my own— the narrow balconies at the Palestine were set at such an angle that there was just enough room on the right-hand end of the balcony rail for Jon Lee Anderson's small satellite dish. But there was no way that my Nera World Communicator dish—twice as high and five times as wide—could pick up a working signal from the east Atlantic Ocean at such an angle. Up until now, Anderson had generously allowed me to use his phone to transmit my stories and to make some calls, but we might be here for months so I had to resolve the issue of the reception on my phone as a matter of urgency.

Officially, I did not exist at the Palestine—I was there as Mitch Potter, the Canadian reporter whose editor had ordered him to leave Iraq. Now I desperately needed an even-numbered room, on the hotel's south side, so I could pick up an Indian Ocean satellite. It took a $US250 bribe to acquire Room 830 but, and for reasons the hotel never explained, I was not permitted to sleep in it. So I was still double-bunked with Anderson in Room 905 and I would go down one flight of stairs and along the corridor to Room 830 when I needed to use my phone—the dish for which was now strapped tightly and openly to the balcony rail with a bright green baggage strap. I still wasn't paying $US100 a day to use the phone but, with the disappearance of our colleagues and a sense that the Baghdad story was coming down to the wire, I had a sudden urge to regularise all my affairs so that, if I came to the attention of the authorities for whatever reason, I'd not be sprung for an unregistered sat-phone.

But for now the Iraqis could not be sure who was staying in Room 830, which was my second case of mistaken identity. Arabic books start where ours finish—which is why the hotel receptionist had started working from the back of my passport and had checked me into Room 830 as Pam Williams, my wife, whose details as my next-of-kin appeared at the back of my passport. In Room 905 I was the clean-shaven, silver-haired Mitch Potter! The fixer, who had pocketed the $US250, wanted to know whether Room 905 was booked in Jon Lee's name or my name. When I explained that I was masquerading as Potter of the *Toronto Star*, he eyeballed me with a broad grin, saying: 'You Mafia!' To which I could only reply: 'Thank you, Mohammed. I learnt it all from your family.'

DAY SEVEN

Wednesday, March 26

Death in the Marketplace

Filed Thursday, March 27 at 2.27am   **Palestine Hotel**

The six cars that are bumper-to-bumper against the kerb in al-Shaab are carbonised—charred metal now devoid of all colour and fabric. The power of the blasts flipped another—all that is left of its tyres are the wire coils that ran through the rubber.

Yes, we're in a war zone. But al-Shaab is a civilian quarter, a maze of hard-working hole-in-the-wall mechanics and electricians. And the attacking US-led army promised it would spare civilians. The Pentagon says that it did not target the marketplace and it has left open the possibility that the two bombs that fell here on Wednesday morning could have been either American or Iraqi. But there is no way around the grotesque in this story.

There is no nice way to write about how 28-year-old Husam Madloon, a guard, found the severed head of his boss, Sermat the electrician, on the pavement. Nor of how one of his workmates thinks that a gnawed hand, severed at the wrist, might belong to Tahir, an expert on hot-water systems.

How can anyone tell whose are the brains found lying just near the door into one of the workshops? Or be able to recognise the remains of the mechanic who was working under one of the cars when it became a fireball? How will the news be broken to relatives that two American bombs meant for Saddam Hussein have obliterated a family of five because fate had them driving through this part of town at 11.30am on Wednesday?

This is a bad week in Baghdad. The talk outside may be that this war is starting to go badly for the Americans. But here minds focus on the sharp reality that the most powerful military force ever assembled is massing at the city gates. So fear and tension run high.

People are edgy and even the weather is appropriately apocalyptic. The whole country is in the grip of the *turab*, which translates as 'the desert moving' and is a violent sandstorm. Wild winds whip up sheets of abrasive dust and sand, streaked with thick black smoke that billows from the trenches of flaming oil, ignited to confuse the US bombers. At 2pm the daylight is a deep, burnished orange, eerie and luminescent. And, because of the tonnes of dust in the air, the rain falling on the scene of this disaster is actually mud.

But people like Sermat and Tahir keep going to work at the al-Shaab commercial district on the road north from Baghdad to Kirkuk, a poor area of grubby ground floor shops and tatty first-storey apartments. Madloon was asleep when we arrived, but 55-year-old Salah Yousif, who runs a kebab house and carries a walking stick, was walking up the street. He said: 'I heard the planes overhead and then, two bombs. Four seconds apart.'

In the city I heard the two short booms. By the time I got to al-Shaab, the last of the dead and injured had been taken away. Blood ran in the muddied street and the façade was ripped from many of the shops. Chunks of concrete dangled from lengths of reinforcing steel that refused to snap. Most of the seventeen people who died were in cars in the traffic; many of the 45 injured were pedestrians or local workers and residents.

Neighbours are dropping burnt bedding from an upstairs apartment where the front wall is on the verge of caving in. The door of the kitchen fridge has been blown off its hinges and a child's white teddy bear lies singed and abandoned under a ceiling fan, the blades of which are bent three ways.

The local response to this horror show is ritualistic and surprisingly passive. There is a crowd, mostly male—teenagers and young adults who could be expected to be combustible in the face of such an errant onslaught. Groups of young men, many brandishing Kalashnikovs and pistols, are dancing on the burnt-out cars, chanting slogans in praise of Saddam.

But there is no hostility when a busload of Western reporters, many from coalition countries, arrives on the scene. 'Welcome, welcome,' I'm told by Yousif the witness. He says: 'The Americans always claim they are defending us, but they do the opposite. That is why Saddam is on the right side, fighting this evil. He gives us strength and we give him strength.'

Madloon the guard, whose flip-flops are embossed with the word 'free', says that the pregnant woman who lives in this apartment is dead. And he says that the pavement was littered with body parts. He says: 'They said they would attack the army, but this is a civilian area. Why do they do it? Do they know that Iraqis don't change, that we are Iraqis and that we will not change for America?'

The law of averages in war times says that the US was always going to present the Iraqis with this propaganda gift. Nonetheless, journalists have come away from some of their bus tours of civilian damage around Baghdad with more questions than answers. For example, most of the patients in the hospital they took us to after the first night of bombing in Baghdad seemed to have been injured by Iraqi anti-aircraft fire, and the orphanage they took us to yesterday—before the errant al-Shaab bombing—didn't quite add up.

The Iraq Family Village is home to more than 500 orphans of all ages who were bussed to the care of relatives as war approached. But the complex is a huge sprawling place, with several walled and wired compounds within it and one building that stood apart from the rest because of what looked like inordinately large air-conditioning units on the roof. Five days ago the orphanage laundry was bombed.

But the al-Shaab bombing is the sort of mistake that will play on the minds of Iraqis who might be on the verge of breaking with Saddam. They expect brutality from him—if they step out of line. But they were all minding their own business yesterday when they got it from the US.

At the al-Kindi Hospital Dr Sabah Hassan, director of the general surgery unit, is utterly professional. There was neither politics nor sloganeering as he outlined the hospital's response to the emergency.

One of his younger colleagues, 42-year-old Dr Abdul Razak, is among the Iraqis who might be expected to be receptive to the Bush democracy doctrine—educated, aspiring and capable of free thought. But he is living proof of the risks for the US. After dealing with the hospital's share of the al-Shaab deaths and injuries, he says: 'I have changed my mind about the US because of what they have done. Now I would like to kill an American soldier.'

Army Major-General Stanley McChrystal, US Joint Staff Vice-Director for Operations, told a Pentagon briefing: 'Coalition forces did not target a marketplace nor were any bombs or missiles dropped or fired in that district. We don't know for a fact whether it was US or Iraqi. We'll continue to look and see if we missed anything. Another possibility is that Iraqi anti-aircraft artillery or an Iraqi anti-aircraft missile falling back to earth was responsible.'

However, US Central Command confirmed the US was working the Baghdad area at about 11am, seeking out nine Iraqi surface-to-surface missile launch sites, most of which were within 100m of civilian homes. But a spokesman said that none of Wednesday morning's targets was in the vicinity of al-Shaab.

▲

In this war, there were the lucky and then there were the Iraqi. I was among the lucky—sickeningly so, it seemed. Reporters were in Baghdad by choice and we had safeguards and protections of which ordinary Iraqis could only dream. For starters, until now the Americans seemed to be going out of their way to avoid killing us—we were getting precisely worded emails from a committee of senior US media executives who liaised with the Pentagon, warning us when not to go near particular parts of the Iraqi capital, even down to the time of day and particular buildings that should be avoided.

Two were referred to constantly. One was the fabled al-Rashid Hotel, home at one time or another to just about every journalist and diplomat who had visited Iraq in the last twenty years. Now we were told the Pentagon had identified it as one of its most important non-military targets in the city. We watched every night, waiting for something to happen. The other building, on the west bank of the Tigris and two blocks away from the al-Rashid, was the Information Ministry headquarters from which we were ordered by our ministry minders to do most of our work. This was the bunker at which they insisted foreign TV networks must position their uplink dishes and do their telecasts; it was also the place where we had been ordered to deposit our sat-phones until the day they agreed to allow us to have them in our hotel rooms.

There could be no doubt the ministry was a target—it was the nerve centre of the Iraqi propaganda operation and yesterday a series of missiles coming in from the north had caused convulsions in the adjacent headquarters of Iraqi TV. Television screens across the country went black for several hours, before the Iraqi network could wheel in the mobile, back-up transmission units that it had confiscated from foreign networks over the years.

In the late morning we moved around the city in the golden half-light of the *turab*, now in its second day—but filled with just as much anger as when it blasted in from the west on the previous day. On the strength of the latest and most strident warnings from Washington, we headed for the al-Rashid Hotel, to warn a stubborn last handful of guests—mostly journalists—and hotel staff that the US appeared determined to destroy whatever it believed was under the hotel. The desk staff was aware of journalists staying on the third, ninth and eleventh floors—they gave us the room numbers.

A near-empty hotel is a sad place. The usual corridor bustle had evaporated; the suited men who spied on us were gone; and, as we waited for the lift on the ninth floor, a phone rang somewhere. And rang and rang and rang. On the eighth floor we found a journalist—an elderly Italian who took a while to grasp what Burns, Anderson and myself were saying. He said he'd shift out, and the hotel staff undertook to inform other guests. But they then alerted us to a complication—as the warning to stay away from the al-Rashid had percolated through the Palestine Hotel press pack, some Spanish and Greek news crews had got it back to front, and now they were starting to arrive at the al-Rashid, looking for rooms.

In the accommodation stakes we three still actually had a bob each way, because we had not surrendered our rooms in the al-Rashid. However, in the past we had failed to get the staff there to understand the risk they faced by remaining on the premises. I made a last attempt to get the duty manager at least to acknowledge what we were saying as I went through the whole business one more time. But it was only from the way in which he blinked back at me that I at last understood where his resistance came from—this was a regime hotel and the staff took their orders from the regime, not from a foreign reporter. All he said to me was: 'Sir will pay his bill?'

We had lunch at the Latakia Restaurant—mezza; lamb chops, spiced and grilled; flat breads; and Pepsi. And in the afternoon I learnt some hard lessons about how the Iraqis didn't get a warning of impending attack—even when they might have had one.

We had thought little of two muffled blasts that had come from the north-west corner of the city late in the morning. But, as we drove past the Press Centre after lunch, the buses were lining up and reporters were piling in for who knew what. The ministry always studiously ignored our requests to be taken to military targets that had been attacked by the US and revealed little about where we were being taken, until we got there. A couple of times in the past we had been taken to see no more than a hole in the ground. Sometimes these were big holes, in which the missile that had caused them had had a fearsome impact, but, in the overall context of a war, they were of little moment.

On this day our four buses drove through the wrongly-timed twilight and occasionally through utter blackness as our route took us past some of the oil-trench fires. As we got closer to the al-Shaab district on the road to Kirkuk, traffic ground to a halt and even the ambulances, with sirens blaring, were stuck.

There had been no warning—two missiles had wrecked the marketplace, and the people who lived and worked and shopped there were trying to pick up the pieces of their lives after confronting mass death and injury. The Americans said it wasn't them, and indignant Iraqi officials said the missiles weren't theirs. And, as local Baath Party officials went through the motions of attempting to turn grief into a pro-Saddam rally, it didn't seem to matter. War was war, the grotesque was still grotesque and nothing could quite prepare us for the exercise in heartlessness that would be revealed in the coming hours.

Such was the ferocity of the Washington warnings about an attack on the Information Ministry that one of the foreign reporters in Baghdad quite sensibly took it upon himself to pass on the warning to Uday al-Tai, the Director-General of the ministry. It made sense—foreign TV crews were still using the building and ministry staff still operated from it.

Twelve hours after the breakfast meeting at which al-Tai had thus been informed that his office bunker was a prime target, none of his executive staff could be found in the building—but the junior staff were working away, oblivious to the risk they faced. With a colleague, I then went through the Press Centre telling the Iraqi staff to get out and, as we went, hearing pitiable arguments from some of them that they had nowhere to go in the city, that they could not reach distant homes because of the war and that they had intended to sleep in the building. 'Get out!' we yelled at them.

We went to the sprawling third-floor roof terrace that had been home to more than 50 TV networks for weeks. Most had evacuated and, as the dregs of the *turab* meshed with the night, we were confronted by a scene of utter desolation. The wind had shredded the makeshift canvas offices that the networks had built, whole temporary buildings had been up-ended and a handful of brave souls were attempting to file their last reports. Yes, yes, they had had the warning. The pity was that the ministry's junior Iraqi staff had not.

As usual, I was up writing in the middle of the night. The days in Baghdad vanished with energy-sapping haste. The hours felt like minutes, but the days felt like years. By the time we scrambled to get the news of the day, took a reading on security, touched base with colleagues or contacts to make sure that we had a grasp of what was happening, and watched the bombing as it exploded around us, there wasn't a minute left spare. When the city was under attack, it was impossible to write without jumping to your feet after each detonation to see what might have been hit. And when the bombing started, so too did the phones—at one stage or another, it seemed, every Australian TV and radio station wanted an interview.

But there was no news on the story we most needed to hear—what had become of Matt and Moises.

DAY EIGHT

Thursday, March 27

A Lull Before the Expected Siege

Filed Friday, March 28 at 10.43am   **Palestine Hotel**

The Americans lost a lot more than a few days on the road to Baghdad this week. As new waves of missiles slammed into downtown Baghdad overnight Thursday, defenceless Iraqis cowering in their homes will have been ticking off the score sheet for the first week of battle, and asking what was in it for them. Waiting for the lift on the ninth floor of the Palestine Hotel, a tall, lean Iraqi was cheerfully singing a national song. Why? 'We're winning against the American,' he said.

The day before, there was more singing on the banks of the Tigris. As a wild dust storm engulfed the city, its regime-approved artists assembled by the river to record songs they hoped would inspire the people. Leading this chorus was the well-known Daoud al-Kassi—open-faced, smiling and looking like anything but an entertainer in his Baath Party military fatigues. He had a pistol on his hip.

They were just a short walk upstream from a corner of the presidential compound that is being pulverised in the US bombing raids, but Kassi was unfazed. He said: 'I fought in Iran and Kuwait, and I will fight in Baghdad.' Kassi is one of those Iraqis who might never break with Saddam. When I referred to the fighting around Basra, he said: 'There is no fighting at Basra; the ground war has not started.'

Well, what about the fighting at Umm Qasr? Nasiriyah? Samawa? Najaf? 'There are no US soldiers in Iraq—we've held them at the border. There is no fighting in those cities. This is just US propaganda.'

I listened to their rousing music and, as I melted away into the dust that had reduced the city to a beige-on-beige monochrome, one of Kassi's colleagues called after me: 'We will drink their blood!'

This weather they call the *turab* does funny things to people. They become tense and anxious, as though they didn't already have enough on their plates. But, even as the gloomy statue of Saddam Hussein in Arbaatash Ramadan Square was lost in the dust, some Baghdadis were trying to push the 'normal' button.

The fires have gone out in the traditional *masgoof* restaurants that face the Tigris River along tree-lined Abu Nawas Street. Here you used to get fabulous spiced and barbequed river fish and a cold beer. The beer went in Saddam's campaign for secular Iraq to be more Muslim and war has doused the fires. But a band of public works labourers was back on Saadoun Street today, digging the hole they started last week. And the gasman, who goes door-to-door on a mangy donkey-dray laden with cylinders of cooking gas, was back in harness, belting a metal rod on the empty cylinders behind him to announce his arrival in the neighbourhood.

Chicken and currency exchange shops were open; as were the baggage merchant, a jeweller, some barber shops and a lot of pharmacies. At the Pyramid Grocer's on Saadoun Street, owner Ahmed Ismail said that the bombing troubled his children in their sleep: 'When my two-year-old daughter heard the first bomb, she yelled "Down, Bush, down!" and my older sons go up to the roof of the house to watch the bombing.' He laughed at that, before telling me: 'No one here supports the US; even the people who are against Saddam are more against the US.'

The bombing goes on. The payloads being dropped on the Republican Guards' lines 30 to 40km south-east of the city are so powerful that the reverberations activate the anti-theft alarms on cars parked in central city streets. One of Thursday night's munitions was so powerful it shook the Palestine Hotel, lifting my chair off the floor.

A taxi driver who was driving near the Sajida Palace when it was bombed again on Thursday afternoon said that the force of the blast lifted his Mercedes Benz more than 20cm off the roadway. A donkey tethered near the Palestine Hotel brays with each explosion. Late at night the mosque muezzins broadcast sung prayers from one minaret to the next across the city as each missile smashes another Saddam edifice.

Practical government has almost collapsed. But the essential element of Saddam's regime is still in place—fear. The Americans have acknowledged that his command structures still function and that his air defences, which were to be wiped out in the first 48 hours of battle, are still operating. There is enough evidence that a sizeable portion of the population wants regime change and the Bush Democracy Doctrine, but this is where we get to the week's score sheet.

The early bombing was a powerful reminder to Iraqis that it was the regime, not them, that was being punished. This was demonstrated by the confidence with which many came out to watch the bombs dropping and by the fact that the lights are on, there's water in the taps and the phones are working.

But, in the battle for the hearts and minds of Iraqis, the Pentagon's unvarnished surprise at the fierce resistance they've met has convinced Iraqis that the Americans don't understand their country and its people. The fact that the coalition is bogged down and now talking about a months-long campaign means that the much-touted 'dawdle in the desert' has become a dangerous waiting game. And Wednesday's accidental killing of seventeen people in the al-Shaab marketplace, be it the fault of the Americans or Iraqis, has become a powerful propaganda tool in the hands of the regime.

So when Iraqis read that Donald Rumsfeld, the man who promised minimum civilian casualties, is now proposing to besiege Baghdad and to call on the city's ill-equipped Shia population to revolt against Saddam and to do the job that he came to do, they will be sickened.

The Americans came to Iraq dismissing the abilities of the Fedayeen Saddam, the guerrilla force that is spearheading the resistance. One of the war planners reportedly described them as insignificant riffraff and late last year a Pentagon official was quoted as claiming that 'the Fedayeen will run with their tails between their legs' at the first sign of trouble. But this week a military intelligence officer said: 'The intelligence we gathered before the war accurately reflected what the troops are seeing out there now. The question is whether the war planners and policy makers took adequate notice of it in preparing the plan.'

American complaints about the nature of the fighting suggest that they anticipated the Iraqis would work from the same West Point and Sandhurst military manuals carried by the Bush coalition. But the chances are that the dictator president has learnt from the Palestinians, the IRA and the Serbs in Kosovo on how to mess with big military machines when you are outmanned and outgunned. They can't win, but they can play for time.

If the Shia of the south had given the invasion the much-hyped 'flowers and songs' welcome the Americans expected, spirits might have lifted among supporters of the US in Baghdad. Spare a thought for 21-year-old US Marine Corporal James Lis, who told a reporter in the south this week: 'When we came here, we were told everybody wants to surrender, nobody wants to fight. Now [Iraqi civilians] wave at me, and I wave back through my rifle sight.'

In the north, an Iraqi Kurdish fighter made the same point more powerfully: 'America must smash the Iraqis, bomb them hard, without stopping! You can't let them think for a moment that Saddam Hussein is going to live. Until America goes all out, the Iraqis will fear Saddam more than the Americans.'

But there is deep anxiety that the Iraqi resistance in the desert is just a foretaste of what could unfold in the battle for Baghdad. Multiplied proportionately in the capital, this would mean a high civilian cost for liberation. The Americans fully expected the Shia south to be on their side, but it hasn't happened quite that way. As Deputy Prime Minister Tariq Aziz said this week: 'The greatest percentage of people in the cities where the resistance is strongest is Shia.'

This does not preclude the suggestion that Saddam has moved fighters into the cities but, with the exception of a disturbance in Basra on Tuesday, the absence of overt support is hardly surprising. In 1991 the US stood back when the Shia and the Kurds in the north rebelled in response to the urging of then president George H. Bush, and did nothing while Saddam brought the rebellion to a brutal halt. Likewise Iraqis are fed a steady diet of news on the plight of the Palestinians and the failure of the US to take a more middle-of-the-road approach to resolving that crisis.

So when Iraqis see the faltering American performance on their own doorstep this week, many have been left wondering if the US will be able to follow through and deliver as promised. The prospect of a long wait and then a drawn-out battle means that few would risk any support for the US till after the Stars and Stripes are flying over Baghdad.

Shock and Awe has become the grunt and groan they said it would not become. That worries a lot of people here.

▲

There was real worry now about the fate of the four who had disappeared—Matt McAllester, Moises Saman, Molly Bingham and Johan Spanner. They'd been gone for three days—long enough to have surfaced in Amman or Damascus if they had simply been expelled from Iraq. Were they in prison, or worse? We had no way of finding out and the whole thing was incredibly ominous as reports surfaced outside Iraq that someone had seen them or spoken to them, just before they disappeared, and they had made no mention of leaving. Some journalists in Baghdad wanted to brush aside the issue, arguing that, because they were all on funny visas, it should be no surprise if they had been asked to leave abruptly. They expected that the four of them would soon turn up.

I knew that, when Matt and Moises were unable to get a formal Iraqi press visa, they had piggy-backed with members of the human shield who had volunteered to occupy facilities like water treatment plants and power plants in the hope of deterring US bombing. Their strategy had been to write a few stories on the shields, but to plan to break away and regularise their credentials once they were in Iraq.

They knew it was a risk. But what they may not have known, as they hopped from hotel to hotel around the city in the weeks before they applied for—and were granted— Information Ministry press accreditation, was that they were being watched very closely. Secret agents were hidden among the staff of every hotel in the city, as part of Saddam Hussein's security apparatus. These smart-looking young Westerners would have stood out so much that those monitoring their movements would have built a fat file on each of them.

The reality was that, simply by being in Baghdad, we had all put ourselves within the grasp of a regime we knew was capable of anything.

Larry Kaplow, from the *Atlanta Journal-Constitution*, generously became the Baghdad anchor for an international campaign for the release of the four. Much of the strategising was done on the run, but on this particular Thursday we met in *Guardian* reporter Suzanne Goldberg's suite to consider the options. On the one hand, we feared that, if they did not have proper credentials, they might have been delivered to a much harsher arm of the regime than the Information Ministry; on the other hand, we were all the time conscious that, if we did not handle this matter with some delicacy, we might expose them to further risk and at the same time suck into the same vortex any colleagues agitating for their release.

Al-Sahhaf, the Information Minister, was at the lectern for his daily press briefings on the war. It was tempting to confront him, but we decided against it, on the grounds that it would be counter-productive. Instead, we would gather what information we could in Baghdad and feed it to a range of politicians and others whom *Newsday* executives were asking to press their case to the Iraqi regime—including the Iraqi mission at the UN in New York, the Vatican (which did not close its Baghdad diplomatic post during the war), Yassar Arafat (Moises Saman was a Palestinian) and a number of British and American politicians who might be able to ask the regime for a favour.

Speculation persisted that there had been a visa blitz on the hotel in the early hours of Tuesday and the pair had already been bussed out of the country. The scary truth was—we didn't have a clue.

DAY NINE

More Bombs, No Candles

Filed Saturday, March 29 at 1.30am   **Palestine Hotel**

Silver stars and red tracer-fire lit the sky as the people of al-Shuala washed the bodies of their dead—as many as 58 of them who were slaughtered when a bomb exploded in their pitiable little marketplace.

Some carried blanket-draped coffins through dreary, darkened alleyways on their shoulders, lighting their way with candles and kerosene lamps. Others strapped their coffins to the roofs of battered cars. But from all houses the same teary cries drifted into the chilly night: 'There is no god but God.'

As each family group left the Musa al-Kadhimain mosque, the men lined up to face Mecca in prayer and the lights of passing cars etched the outline of their women, standing in tight knots off to the side, their black *chadors* revealing only the pain in their faces.

Iraqi officials insist this bomb, the second in 48 hours to hit a civilian market, was dropped by a US or British fighter jet that witnesses said headed south. The Americans are investigating; they say they don't know. But the suffering and the grief radiating from a small crater in this impoverished Shia neighbourhood in the north-west of Baghdad will make it more difficult for ordinary Iraqis to see the US-led invasion force as an army of liberation, rather than one of conquest.

At the al-Noor General Hospital, 500m from the marketplace, tearful men wrapped each other in their arms as distraught women yelled the names of the dead. A man sobbing with grief yelled over and over: 'That man! That man!' Relatives said he was referring to George W. Bush, who in Washington appeared to be warning of more setbacks before victory, when he said: 'We are now fighting the most desperate units of the dictator's army. The fierce fighting under way will demand further courage and further sacrifice, yet we know the outcome of this battle.'

In the face of stiffer-than-expected resistance from Iraqi fighters and chronic frontline supply problems—security and logistical—US commanders have now decided on a pause of up to six days in their advance on Baghdad. The al-Shuala carnage came at the end of a day in which the US seemed to put aside its undertaking not to damage Iraq's civilian infrastructure. Waves of strikes, including the first confirmed use of 4700lb bunker-buster bombs, destroyed much of Baghdad's telephone system after direct hits on at least three telephone exchanges.

In al-Shuala, it was 6.30pm on the Muslim Sabbath and people were busy shopping in the crowded market. Ghannun Hussein was in his home, waiting for the return of his 59-year-old father with vegetables for their evening meal, when he heard the whoosh of a missile. Standing by his father's hospital bed, he said through an interpreter: 'Then I heard the explosion.

I ran. All the people were on the ground—people's arms and legs were cut off, there was too much blood...'

Najin Abdula, who works at the hospital, raced to the scene: 'There was the body of a man with no head. I stopped cars in the traffic to get them to bring the injured to the hospital.' Then he opened the door of a blood-soaked morgue refrigerator for me. Inside, there were five bodies on bunk-like trays. One young man had half his head blown away; the nose of another was gone and his flesh and clothing were ripped and torn; another stared back from eyes that were wide open in a mud-caked face.

As family members and hospital staff, many of them in tears, feverishly worked the wards, survivors who could talk spoke of their split-second encounter with war. Khalid Jabar Hussein, 49, who had shrapnel embedded in his arm, wrist and right leg, said: 'First I heard an aircraft and then the missile coming at us...and I don't know anything after that. I fell down.'

Five-year-old Sajaja Jaafur, one of five members of her family who were injured, lay in her bed, arms waving distractedly and crying in pain as she tried to turn her body to face her mother. She was the picture of innocence—her lovely olive skin torn by shrapnel or debris, a tube in her nose, a bandaged head and a blood-stained dressing around her abdomen.

Samaan Kadhim, 52, in need of pain-killers for the bad gash on his back, said: 'This was a civilian area, there were no soldiers. It was just a market.' He had been out with his daughter and grandson to buy a TV antenna. Speaking in a low whisper, he said: 'They slaughtered us.'

In the midst of all this Dr Ahmed Sufian lashed out: 'Our floors are covered with the blood of our people, the walls are splashed with blood. Why, why, why? Why all this blood? I'm a doctor, but I can't understand such things. They say they come to free us? Is this freedom?'

Families quickly retrieved the dead. They brought home-made coffins to the hospital, which they then took to the mosque, opposite the marketplace, for ritual bathing and shrouding in white cotton, ahead of burial ceremonies that were to start at dawn on Saturday. In a country of slogans and chants, this Shia mosque, adorned with black flags and portraits of Imam Hussein, the grandson of Muhammad the Prophet, was a place of pained tranquillity.

There was no overt support for Saddam Hussein but all blamed the US for the marketplace bombing. And there was no hostility towards Western reporters, who were invited by the families to witness their rituals and their grief. 'America did this to us,' said 50-year-old Kadhim Ali, pulling his grey cloak tight against the cold. 'Why does it hate the Iraqi people?'

But for the most part families waited patiently for their turn in the washing room, sitting and praying by their coffins. 'God forbid, God forbid,' an old man mumbled over and over. Old women placed the body of a nine-year-old girl on a cement slab to sponge the blood and dirt from her as her mother's coffin took the next place in the queue.

A turbaned Shia cleric prayed with the waiting families: 'We pray to Muhammad and to his descendants, and to the Prophet Abraham, revered by all Muslims, Christians and Jews. We pray for the Muslims who have died, and for those who still cling to life. We say that we depend on God, and only God, to save us. And we pray that he will lead the Americans and the British to go away, and leave us in our land of Iraq. Lastly, we pray for the spirits of the departed to go to Paradise.'

▲

Three hours sleep last night. The minders had a fit of the jitters as they prepared for something they obviously thought to be very important. They would say nothing, but at about 8pm they began herding reporters from the bleak lobbies of the Palestine Hotel towards a block-house style ballroom where, bizarre and all as it sounds, the only gesture to softness was a big, gilt-framed portrait of Saddam Hussein—resplendent in the uniform of a field marshal.

Press conferences in this part of the world are chaotic, a hit-and-run news-gathering process where TV cameramen are so possessed by the notion that *they* must capture every second of what is happening that, if we let them, they'd steamroll right over all the hapless print reporters before we could say *notebook and pen*. (Or, in the quaint practice of my colleagues from *The New Yorker* and *The New York Times*, Messrs Anderson and Burns, *pencils*—for which each always seems to carry a sharpener in his pocket.)

But in Baghdad, because a few of us had taken to standing our ground, pushing back and barking louder in the face of the stampeding cameras and wrecker tripods, the Information Ministry had set down some civilising rules—correspondents sat on chairs in front of the lectern and the cameramen set up *behind* them, shooting over their heads and using the very sophisticated technology of the lens to get as far up the nose of the speaker as they liked—without marching up our vertebrae to get there.

A few days before the first US strike on Baghdad, the cameras drove me mad when Saddam's white-clad 'martyr' squads marched in a military parade in the city. My efforts to interview squad members had been interrupted three times, once by the sharp edge of a camera firmly between my shoulder blades, when CBS correspondent Lara Logan and her crew hove into view demanding that I move so that she could do her 'stand-up'—the bit where the reporter speaks to the camera—right where I was standing. I let fly: 'Fuck off!' We traded invective for a while, but she accepted my point and, finally, we swapped apologies.

Now, in the Palestine Hotel's ballroom there was a rising sense of anticipation. But suddenly it was Mr Kadhim who breasted the lectern to announce that we had assembled at the wrong venue and could we please exit the Palestine, cross the street to the Sheraton Hotel and take our seats in the ballroom there.

This was instructive—normally they wanted all of us seated before a press conference so that they could then throw a heavy security cordon around the room—the entire hotel even—before a minister or a regime heavy would slip into our midst. And usually, when it came time for the official to leave the premises, they would lock the doors to the conference room—holding us inside, till the official was clear of the building. But last night's last-minute scramble between venues allowed us to snatch glances at an intense, heavily-armed security operation.

The surprise speaker last night was the lugubrious General Sultan Hashim, Saddam Hussein's Defence Minister. He walked us around a map of the Iraq battlefield, which was propped up on an easel, before making what I thought was a big call—he expected the Americans to encircle 'great parts of Baghdad' within the next five to ten days but street-by-street fighting for control of the capital to last for months. It was a telling prediction because, despite the surprisingly fierce Iraqi resistance, he was conceding the south; at the same time he was expecting a speedy US recovery from the chaos of this week.

It was past 10pm when the general had finished. We then headed back to Room 905—chatting, talking and straggling along the way before sitting at the coffee table to wolf down the now-cold kebabs and bread that Sabah the driver had run to ground somewhere out in the city. And *then*, as midnight approached, it was time to start the day's work—check-in telephone calls to home and office; interviews for steam radio and morning current affairs TV shows that were about to go to air in Australia; mapping out the story to be filed early the next morning, and going through notes and research material (we each hauled around an extensive library). After that I grabbed a few hours of bomb-interrupted kip, before rising in the pre-dawn darkness for some of the heaviest allied bombing of Baghdad as I juggled writing and another round of radio and TV interview requests for the evening bulletins that soon would go to air in Australia.

As the war went on and the number of foreign reporters in Baghdad fell away, we all were inundated with interview requests from around the globe. Reporting to opposite ends of the world meant that, invariably, Anderson was sprawled asleep fully clothed on one of the mattresses while I was working, and vice versa. The early hours were fuelled by instant coffee, but sometime around 8am there was the blessed relief of Sabah arriving with a flask of 'Madam Sabah's' prized Turkish coffee and her tortilla-like circles of rice bread on which I would spread soft cheese and perhaps a hard-boiled egg. Usually the only other meal for the day would be a restaurant stop in the mid- or late-afternoon or whatever Sabah or Mohammed could find, if it was safe enough for them to go foraging in the evening.

In the wake of the civilian deaths in the al-Shaab market-place on Wednesday, the US military campaign seemed to be in the grip of a terrible madness. It was as if Rumsfeld and his team were taking out on the people of Baghdad their frustrations over the slowing of their march to the capital and rising criticism of their tactics. Before the war, there had been clear commitments to protect the civilian population, but al-Shaab breached that; and they had said they would spare the nation's civilian infrastructure, but the wave of missile strikes on telephone exchanges across the city seems to have put paid to that.

I filed to the *Herald* and when I got downstairs the buses were out the front. As we boarded for another grim outing, National Public Radio's Ann Garrels attempted a spot of black humour, revealing that my reputation preceded me. Feigning her fear of bad luck, she protested: 'You're not coming on this bus, are you?' It was a reference to an incident in the 2001 Afghanistan War, in which I survived a Taliban ambush on a Northern Alliance armoured personnel carrier in which three of my colleagues died. I got on the bus and what unfolded was a classic, wearying Baghdad kind of day.

We were guided from one bombed-out telephone exchange to the next—first the trashed remains of the al-Weiya exchange, in the inner east, which served more than 25 per cent of metropolitan Baghdad; and then the al-Rashid International Exchange, in the heart of the city, which to my untrained eye seemed to have survived two bunker-buster bombs. But several of us had the urge to flee from here, because a lack of shrapnel damage at what appeared to be the point of impact left us wondering if, somewhere deep in the ground beneath us, there might be close to 10 000lbs of unstable, unexploded bomb.

The third facility was the al-Mamoon exchange, set on one of the symbolic crossroads of power in Baghdad's eastern suburbs. On one side of the intersection where it stood were the shattered remains of the Sajida Palace, said to have been the one most favoured by the dictator in Baghdad, and on the other side the towering Saddam Communications Complex. It was hard not to conclude that before us lay all the smart-bomb brilliance and all the human madness of war. The Americans destroyed this communications tower in the 1991 Gulf War, so Saddam had it rebuilt—to more than twice its original height. After last night's raids the tower was still standing, but only 30m away the vital innards of the huge, aluminium-clad al-Mamoon exchange had been ripped out much as a ghoulish hand might scoop away the heart of a watermelon.

The buses delivered us back to the Palestine. Sabah, unaware of where we had been and what we had seen, was even more excitable than usual. As we waited an hour for a press briefing, which then was cancelled, he spoke to Jon Lee Anderson in hushed tones. When we got up to Room 905 I understood why—on the coffee table was a big cake with the words 'Happy Birthday, Mr Paul' piped out in icing, a bottle of Findlater's scotch and a tray of fresh fruit and sweets. They had done a ring-around and the plan was for Burns and Richard Downs of RTE, the Irish national broadcaster, and a few others to drop in at 9.30pm for cake and scotch. As Anderson said in an email to my wife back in New York: 'We'll have ourselves a little *fin de siècle* birthday party.' I was 49.

But there was to be no party that night. At about 9.20pm we got a call about the bombing of the al-Shuala marketplace, about 25km north-west from the city centre. The minders abandoned any procedural notion that we should go by bus and we drove out, piling into whichever car was ready to leave the hotel as we tumbled from the lobby. There was a surreal numbness about the evening—the hospital that couldn't cope; the morgue and its mangled bodies; the impoverished Shia neighbourhood which least deserved to suffer such a bomb attack, errant or otherwise; and the sense I got from these people that there were greater forces at work in their humble lives, that despite their suffering and oppression, neither Saddam Hussein nor George W. Bush really mattered to them.

It was about 1am and we were looking vainly for a taxi when a local youngster called out to us—Anderson; Caroline Cole, a photographer from the *Los Angeles Times*; and me. The boy recognised us because he was on the housekeeping staff at the al-Rashid Hotel and he escorted us on foot to the edge of al-Shuala, where a giant expressway knifed through the district. He flagged down a 'safe' car that would deliver us all the way back to the city.

It's during such moments, spent standing on a median strip waiting for an unknown ride in an unknown city in the middle of the night, that you sometimes wonder about this job. Why? And I looked at Jon Lee's chiselled features and at dark-haired Caroline buried under her photographer's swag, and I was filled with an overpowering sense that somebody from the outside world had to be in al-Shuala this night; someone had to be bearing witness. But I would have felt so much safer if Matt and Moises had been there too.

DAY TEN

Ministry of Misinformation Takes a Direct Hit

Filed Saturday, March 29 at 10.44am   **Palestine Hotel**

It is the early hours in a city suspended in darkness, and now it is being cut to pieces again. First there is the sound of US aircraft, but then an incoming missile drowns the sound of the jets and an ear-splitting explosion signals another barrage hurled at Saddam Hussein.

I don't know what the target is. But minutes later, in a phone call from New York—which manages to navigate the increasingly shattered circuitry of the Baghdad phone network—I'm told that CNN has just aired footage of the missile striking Saddam's propaganda nerve centre, the Information Ministry.

In the morning the jets are still prowling when I arrive at the ministry. Most of the windows are blown out; the blast has made colanders of the roof-top communications dishes and edgy, armed soldiers make it clear there will be no press inspection of the internal damage.

But there is a party. Rousing music blares from a giant mobile sound system and more than 500 Iraqi artists and entertainers are singing, dancing and swaying on the roof of the lower section of this bunker-like building. A man in a suit—white hair and wrap-around sunglasses—is swirling the national flag. A soldier with a big gut and a droopy moustache brandishes his Kalashnikov as he joins the chorus, from which the dapper Hadi al-Shati emerges to inform me that he is a famous singer.

It needs to be understood that all this prancing and dancing is a deliberate act of defiance, that these people are daring the US to strike the building again. They could have stayed at home, and not answered the telephone round-up for this protest. But as the sun dazzles on Shati's ensemble—dark-blue tie, shiny blue shirt and blue hunter's jacket—he tells me: 'We are not frightened to be on this target.'

The tail section of the missile that struck the ministry building is brought in and the crowd becomes ecstatic, raising it above their heads and singing with even more gusto as they give the Saddam salute in time to the music.

In Baghdad we journalists make a careful study of this salute—right arm thrust into the air with a clenched fist. Desperate to divine private thoughts in a country in which people can't air them, we have concluded that the energy that goes into this gesture of loyalty and the accompanying slogans is indicative of support for the regime. The singers are with Saddam.

But eight hours earlier there had been no singing or saluting the leader as the Shia of al-Shuala buried their dead. These people have suffered long and cruelly at the hands of Saddam, and Washington desperately hopes they will rise in revolt, thereby legitimising its invasion of Iraq and making the final stage of war easier for the Americans, who are keen to avoid street fighting that will inevitably lead to the loss of more American lives.

But while the Shia, the majority religious group in Iraq, have nothing good to say about Saddam, so far they are sitting on their hands. Instead of appealing for the US to get on with the business of decapitating the regime, they plead only for a halt to the war. Only one mourner dares to criticise the regime, and then chooses words that are a back-handed lash at the US: 'Why don't they go and bomb Saddam's palaces?' she asks.

Perhaps the Iraqi sense of reality—their truth in this conflict, if you like—lies somewhere between the singers and the Shia. Saddam is not the glue that holds them together; but in this crisis maybe being Iraqi is. And in tumultuous times their nationalism is accentuated. They know of no life other than under Saddam. Ten years of Western efforts to contain Saddam with sanctions has left them with little positive sentiment about the place that Iraqis often refer to as 'outside'—the rest of the world and, in particular, the US.

This may be the key to understanding the working of the national psychology at this time. A regime of fear keeps them in line, but they know their place and they know that within the confines of that place they are relatively safe as long as they abide by Saddam's rules.

Take the twenty-something Iraqis. Since their early teens they have known only the Gulf War, regular foreign bombing of targets in the no-fly zones imposed on Saddam after that war, and sanctions. The older generations, brought up under the dictatorship or the rickety regimes that preceded it, might even have some fond memories of what, by comparison, may have been an easier time—under British colonial rule. But, after decades of Saddam's hyper-nationalism, these people have been marginalised. So there's a void. The Iraqis have been exposed to no useful links with the West—there have been no cultural centres, no lending libraries, nothing much of social or cultural value beyond the beloved Chevrolet Caprice.

Now, as the West bombs them around the clock, a few Iraqis get a sense of what the conflict is about through the BBC or Voice of America. But, for most, it is Saddam's state-run media that fills their media space, filtering most of what they know about the US and the rest of the world.

In the old days, the nicotine-stained al-Zahawi coffee house on Rashid Street was a hotbed of free thought and was frequented by Saddam Hussein when he was a young revolutionary. One night last week I asked Ahmed, a world-travelled businessman, if the all-male crowd talked about anything other than, as they would say in Northern Ireland, the troubles. 'No; we talk about it all the time,' he said. 'Well, the debate must be interesting,' I said. 'No—we agree with each other all the time,' he replied.

Foreigners arriving in Baghdad bring their own reference points, so they see a demonic construct that is repugnant. There is certainly hunger for change among Iraqis, but many ordinary Iraqis have great difficulty in seeing how they might get to any new, alternative existence.

So, all the performers on the roof of the Information Ministry can do is sing in defiance of the US. For them it is safer to be in a system and a philosophy that has been drummed into them for years. Which is why, when I asked the blue-clad Hadi al-Shati what sort of people were in the crowd, he told me: 'We are the artists of this ministry.'

It all still revolves around Saddam Hussein. Had he been killed in the first strike there would have been a fracturing at the heart of the regime. But while he remains, no one dares to step out of their place in the controlling concentric circles of their existence. Shatter the system and you shatter their lives.

Seen from Baghdad, what Washington is offering is no guarantee of security—if they are to respond to US prompting, Iraqis must be able to see the other side. Instead, what they are getting is great insecurity—bombs shake their homes all night and they hear about American 'massacres' when they turn on the radio or TV in the morning. Their children cry in the night and their daughters miscarry. And now that the US has set about destroying the telephone system, they can't call an ambulance in an emergency or each other when they need reassurance.

Parents can't go to work to earn their weekly pittance and children can't go to their neglected schools. Their highway median strips have been dug up for soldiers to dig in and the internal security vice that clamps them into Saddam's world has tightened.

You might be able to rationalise this war if it had been a swift and brilliant strike under the aegis of the UN and had removed the oppressor without plunging the nation into devastation. The prospect of Saddam having been winged with the opening shot was tantalising, but only during the vacuum of the few days when the leadership went to ground.

But then the regime quickly re-emerged. It had confiscated enough TV uplink dishes from the foreign media to be able to get a blurry Iraqi TV back on the air after it was bombed. And it is now pumping out its version of Iraqi triumph as the great US bogs down, runs out of food and fuel at the front line, and has to call in an extra 100 000 troops.

Perplexing images are streaming across the world of the Iraqis, who were safe in their homes two weeks ago but are now being bombed and shot at by young troops who often can't tell the 'enemy' from civilians. There are images of young women and small children, their lacerated bodies being wrapped for burial, years before their time. One of the more chilling quotes to date was from a US soldier, explaining the death of an Iraqi woman: 'The chick got in the way.'

With the US in a quagmire of its own making, ten days after the start of the war, many of our preconceptions of Iraq and its people are becoming more nuanced. So where does this leave George W. Bush and Donald Rumsfeld, as they move their little tanks and toy soldiers around the map-top table in a distant White House war room?

America desperately needs an Iraqi revolt but, with the Iraqi intelligentsia in exile and Saddam's security forces very much in place, there are no voices of criticism at this crucial time. Indeed it was the British who up-ended the statues of Saddam in Basra at the weekend, not the Iraqis. As the bombing continues, Saddam's survival becomes less relevant in the minds of the people because, as the US falters and they get saturation reports on 'criminal massacres' by the US, the Baghdadis see themselves in the bull's-eye along with Saddam.

Again Iraqi nationalism kicks in. It's a national duty to defend your country, to fight back and to resent those you believe are trying to kill you—but the US doesn't seem to have factored the possibility of such sentiment into its war plan at all.

Whatever their private feelings about the regime, many Iraqis are going through the motions of defending their country—and Saddam has ways of making those who feel half-hearted about it get themselves to the front in a hurry. This is the position the US has placed them in through its failure to take its war games beyond the most superficial elicitation of the Iraqi character and culture. In these circumstances many Iraqis simply want the war to stop; to be able to go back to work and get on with the abject lives they know.

There is an old man here whose mood swings I observe on a daily basis. He has no love for Saddam, but this week his chest is out with shy pride over reports of Iraqis knocking out US helicopters and tanks. It all feeds into Iraq's warrior history. It's all a part of the national mythology, which Saddam has been cultivating and re-shaping to his own end for years. And now it's paying dividends.

These forces push and pull violently at all Iraqis. Each has an inner mechanism that oscillates according to the news of the day. But for many the bottom line could be that the ruined life they have is more acceptable than the ruined nation the regime tells them would come with American 'liberation'.

Saddam made a strategic error by going into Kuwait in 1990. But if his people—all 25 million of them, who have paid the price ever since—have been willing the coalition to push him over the precipice now, it does not appear to be working. This time the US-led coalition doesn't have the world behind it and it doesn't have a broadly accepted justification.

War sometimes can be justified on the basis of human rights. There was no great objection throughout the world to the Bosnian or East Timor wars. But while this doctrine is valid in some circumstances, Washington has come to it late and only as a fig leaf for its own faltering agenda, which was articulated in too many shifting forms—from the elimination of weapons of mass destruction through to claimed links to al-Qaeda, the need for regime change, proposals for the introduction of US-style democracy to the Middle East and the protection of the American homeland from Saddam. Its claim to be restoring human rights lost all credibility.

Probably the single biggest reason there has been no Iraqi uprising is a lack of trust in the ultimate intentions of the US—with so much ducking and weaving, no one is sure anymore what this war is about, least of all the Iraqis. The regime is pulling together. Whatever is occurring in the dark heart of Saddam's empire, outwardly we now see determination, exemplified best by the calculatedly urbane Information Minister, Mohammed Saeed al-Sahhaf.

He is perhaps the only adult male in Iraq who does not have a Saddam-style moustache (some women in the press pack insist that he dyes his eyebrows). Each day he briefs the foreign press with a dash that is reminiscent of one of Donald Rumsfeld's cockier briefings in the lead-up to the war. Mr Sahhaf arrives with a pistol on one hip and two spare ammunition clips on the other. He laughs at his own asides. Yesterday he evidently enjoyed his own wit—he referred to George Bush as 'the president of Zaire'—then, after a brief lecture on ancient Roman history, he offered reporters a loan of the relevant text from his personal library.

Even on the day his own ministry was bombed, Mr Sahhaf fronted as usual, in an annexe adjacent to his hammered headquarters. And when three heavy bombs dropped nearby, causing the plastic chair in which I sat to vibrate under me, the minister didn't miss a beat. He continued his review of the pause in the US war effort.

The braggadocio of Mr Sahhaf and other members of the regime could evaporate as quickly as it has been re-asserted if the US suddenly secured a psychological and military advantage. But for now the Information Ministry is making itself heard in the propaganda war. Al-Sahhaf may be the public face of a regime that has been barbaric towards it own people, but his demeanour in the face of America's overwhelming might is playing well to Iraqi pride and nationalism.

▲

The pretence of normality sometimes was staggering. As we arrived at the Latakia Restaurant for lunch, a labourer was hunched on the pavement, ladling runny cement from an old bucket as he filled a broad crack in the footpath. With bombs going off close by, there was no guarantee his handiwork would ever get to dry.

The restaurant's own wartime regime was a little more pragmatic. The menu was getting pared back as key ingredients became more difficult to find, and the Latakia would stop serving each day once it ran out of the greatest of Arab staples, bread.

The temperature in Baghdad was rising—it was now in the mid-twenties Celsius. Weeks ago, when it was much cooler and we were still ensconced in the al-Rashid Hotel, I had organised a drill, during which Anderson, the London *Daily Telegraph*'s David Blair and Heathcliff O'Malley, and myself practised getting our chemical warfare suits on in a hurry. The instructions said that, if there was the slightest prospect of a gas attack, we should don the full-body suit, which was made of a sailcloth-like fabric called Tyvek. Anderson had had a bit of a problem taking part in this drill because he couldn't get his chemsuit out of his suitcase—he had forgotten the code for the combination lock. So he just used a gas mask and his drill was confined to getting the gas mask out of its storage pouch and over his head in less than the prescribed nine seconds.

After a few trial runs, the rest of us mastered the full procedure. But, recalling the discomfort of spending just a few minutes in the chemsuit in the cool of a mid-February evening, I did spare a thought for our colleagues embedded with the US military, having to be in their chemical suits day and night as they raced across the desert in the spikier heat of March.

After the desolation of the early days of the bombing, bigger crowds were now back onto the streets of Baghdad. The city's vegetable growers were opening small pavement markets, at which they charged exorbitant prices for vegetables that had been in storage for so long that they were on the turn. Most of this produce would have been picked before the start of the war, ten days ago. Chicken farmers were selling eggs and live chickens from the backs of trucks. During our travels this particular morning, we passed one such market next to an Iraqi military complex. As we did, a missile exploded nearby. Soldiers came pouring out of the barracks, stumbling in an unruly rabble as they sought the protection of foxholes dug into the median strip on the road along which we were travelling.

As we kept driving, the person sitting next to me shared an interesting story. The staff of a key Iraqi government agency had been trucking voluminous files from its city office complex to be hidden out of harm's way in nondescript buildings on the campus of the University of Baghdad. But the removal operation had not gone unnoticed—the task had hardly been completed before the new document store became the target of a US missile attack. Furious that information was being passed to the US, Saddam's Mukhabarat security service swept the neighbourhood, embarking on a house-by-house search that rounded up five well-equipped, Iran-based Iraqi opposition fighters. This story confirmed several things: The US had fast-acting human intelligence agents on the ground; Iraq's vile security apparatus was still at work; and the exiled Iraqi opposition forces were coming home to fight.

We spent a considerable amount of time observing and analysing the local people. It's hard to generalise, but the Iraqis are a proud, conservative people—many of the women wear the black head-to-toe *abaya* and the men wear traditional dress in muted tones or very conservative Western dress. They considered most of us—journalists, human shields and aid workers—as quite mad. But they were polite about it. They responded to our explanations as to why we were in Iraq at such a time by asking further questions, about our wives and families. Then they would close the conversation with '*al hamdulillah*'—as much a prayer as a philosophical declaration that the fate of us all was in greater hands. *'Alhamdulillah'* or 'Glory to God'.

But they were goggle-eyed when John Burns marked the first really hot day by stepping out in his Bombay bloomers; and Khalid, a fixer I used from time to time, was more admiring of the brightness of the shirts I wore than were Australian TV audiences. I had left home with strict instructions from my wife, who had spent some time as a TV producer, that, if I did any television interviews, I should wear 'the blue shirt'. But, with war closing in and ABC-TV's Kerry O'Brien wanting an interview at short notice, I didn't give a thought to what I was wearing as I headed up onto the roof of the Information Ministry office for a live cross to the *7.30 Report*. There was no significant public reaction to the content of what I had to say but my wife received a torrent of emails from Australia, all remarking on the brightness of the orange shirt I was wearing. It was a somewhat *incandescent* orange. On the other hand, as many of my colleagues in Baghdad absorbed items of local dress into their wardrobe, especially the chequered scarf, it was hard to tell whether they were imitating the movies—or if the movies were imitating them with their stereotypical presentation of correspondents in neck-scarves and multi-pocketed hunter's jackets.

The Iraqis had to come to terms with some fine 'feral' types among the hundreds of human shields who passed through Baghdad. We media workers were nervy, but the locals seemed to take in their stride the dozens of *jihadists*—volunteer fighters from other Arab countries—who hung around the Palestine Hotel. And they were perfectly at home with Neville Watson, a beaky-nosed 73-year-old clergyman from Perth, who was a casual and comforting pastor for most who spoke to him.

But even the Iraqis were confused by the surreal tableau beneath the jacaranda trees on Abu Nuwas Street, where a Turkish protester named Salam Adin Tellioglu had chained himself to the trunk of one of the trees. He wore white robes and a crocheted skullcap; in the branches above him he had hung many white pillows, each decorated with an anti-war slogan. But it wasn't as though he'd thrown away the key or anything like that—quite often he'd unlock himself and wander back to the hotel, sitting on the leather sofas in the lobby, still wrapped in chains. When I passed the jacarandas in a taxi one day, I looked at the driver and he looked at me. 'Crazy,' is all he said.

And some Baghdadis were perplexed by the black-clad, 50-something Patrick Dillon. An Irish-American and a Vietnam veteran, he was a sometime filmmaker, sometime aid worker, who had adorned his shiny-shaven skull with a tattoo of a bull's-eye. It was he who had given Conrad's *Heart of Darkness* to Jon Lee Anderson; in an interview for *The New Yorker* he told Anderson that, since Vietnam, he had been obsessed by death.

The banks of the Tigris in front of the Palestine Hotel were a shady, inviting strip that the locals knew to avoid because it was a no-go security area for the presidential compound on the opposite bank. But Dillon wasn't to know that and when he blundered in, armed with his cameras as he always was, he found himself being strip-searched in public with a pistol held to his head. A few days later he was arrested and thrown out of the country when he wandered too close to where some American bombs had landed. He told Anderson: 'I love death. I know it's wrong, but I do. Don't you? Isn't that why you're here?'

I was often asked this last question. And the answer certainly wasn't about death. I had a strong belief in the notion that it was the duty of the media to cover international crises. The journalists who cover stories like Iraq tend to fall into two categories—there are those who write *down* into the issues by looking at the national leaders and their decision- and policy-making; and there are others who hit the road, and write *up* into the issues through the eyes of the people affected by that decision- and policy-making. If you were in the latter group, you wanted to be in Baghdad.

The other question I was asked repeatedly dealt with my own safety. I would argue that there were many safe places between the exploding bombs shown close-up and in narrow focus on TV, and that it was always possible to find somewhere to lie low. This argument did acknowledge that, simply by being in a war zone, we were at risk but, as I chipped away at the extent of that risk and as I qualified the potential dangers, I'd conclude by saying, probably too patly: 'So you see, the risk is no greater than being run over by a bus on Fifth Avenue.'

The chat over a recent lunch had got around to what old correspondents should do as they got even older. I told the others about my fury back in 1992 when Milton Cockburn, then a *Herald* deputy editor, had telephoned me in London to say that my term as the paper's European correspondent was up and I would be re-assigned to domestic reporting in Australia. I argued hotly for the right to exercise an option in my contract to have another year in the post, claiming that I'd earned that through my coverage of the first Gulf Crisis and later the Balkan Wars. But Cockburn cut me off. 'Mate, you've had your trips!' he snapped.

Burns had been dining out on this story ever since. Whenever the talk had turned to travel, difficult postings or what any of us might do as we got older, Burns would cut us off, saying 'Mate, you've had your trips,' and then burst out laughing. Burns regaled us with stories of reporters aged 60-plus breasting the bar in various war zones and of some of them not being a pretty sight anymore. The conversation had its own urgency for him—he would be 60 next year.

Of course, we journalists wouldn't be journalists if we didn't dissect a few of our colleagues. I was curious about Burns' colleague Neil MacFarquhar, who had covered Baghdad in the days up to Burns' arrival a couple of weeks before the war. One day I had encountered MacFarquhar standing on the marble steps of the al-Rashid Hotel and he had told me that he needed to leave before the war because he had health problems—on which he did not elaborate.

Talking to Burns now gave me the opportunity to ask about his predecessor's health. 'They filled his body with metal pins after he was run over by a bus . . . on Fifth Avenue,' Burns said.

DAY ELEVEN

Sunday, March 30

Suicide Bombs

Filed Sunday, March 30 at 11.34am   **Sheraton Hotel**

Iraq yesterday promised a wave of suicide bombers on the battlefield and throughout the world after awarding hero's medals to one of its soldiers who killed four Americans when he detonated an explosive-laden taxi near Najaf, a shrine city for Iraq's majority Shia.

Hours later Iraqi Vice-President Taha Yassin Ramadan, one of Saddam Hussein's closest associates, made clear that the bombing was part of a deliberate new campaign supported by 'columns of volunteers from the Arab lands' who were prepared to become 'martyrs'. And he called on all Arabs to 'turn every country into a battlefield'.

In an impatient and defiant address to foreign reporters in Baghdad, Mr Ramadan said: 'They bring their B-52 bombers, which can kill 500 people or more at a time. Do they expect us to wait till the Arabs can make bombs to counter that? I'm sure operations by our freedom fighters will be able to kill 5000 people.'

Iraq's resort to guerrilla tactics to rattle and delay the US-led advance on Baghdad has wrong-footed American-led forces in a country in which they fully expected an immediate welcome as an army of liberation. This escalation, at a time when the US has decided to delay its advance for almost a week—in the hope of buying time to deal with serious manning, security and logistic problems—will heighten battlefield tension. Security will have to be much tighter and all Iraqis will be suspect in their eyes. 'It looks and feels like terrorism,' said Major-General Stanley McChrystal, US Joint Staff Vice-Director for Operations. 'It doesn't affect the operation at large. But, to protect our soldiers, it clearly requires great care.'

The car-bomb deaths bring the US toll in the war to at least 32; 104 have been wounded; seven taken prisoner and fifteen are missing in action. The official British death toll is twenty, only five of whom were killed in combat. The Iraqi toll is estimated to be more than 1000 dead and more than 4000 taken prisoner.

The explosion happened at about 11.30am on Saturday. The taxi is said to have approached a checkpoint with a non-commissioned Iraqi officer, Ali Jaafar al-Noamani, apparently in civilian dress, at the wheel. He called to the American soldiers, indicating that the car had broken down, and, as they approached, he detonated a hidden cache of explosives.

The American forces have until now been allowing the free movement of civilians through these checkpoints, which are guarded by armoured vehicles and infantry soldiers. A sign in Arabic orders all vehicles to stop. But the security implications for the Americans and the harsh consequences for Iraqis as a result of this incident were immediately clear—three other taxis, approaching another army checkpoint on the outskirts of encircled Najaf, were attacked by Bradley armoured vehicles. An unknown number of Iraqis were killed.

Colonel William F. Grimsley, the Commander of the US First Brigade, whose Third Division is stationed at Najaf, later conceded that the three vehicles—painted white with orange corner panels, which is typical of Baghdad's battered taxi fleet—seemed not to have been rigged as bombs. But the fear that will have haunted the Americans on the ground was that they could have been part of a coordinated strike at the division's anxious defences. 'It certainly happened near simultaneously,' he said.

Without referring specifically to Saturday's suicide attack, Information Minister Mohammed Saeed al-Sahhaf accused US soldiers in the Najaf area of reacting 'hysterically to what is happening to them'. He accused them of opening fire on seven civilian cars and killing all passengers; shooting a woman walking to her house; killing three civilians on a bridge on the road to Kufa; and killing four men at Abasya. 'They are in retreat,' Mr Sahhaf said. 'Shooting people because they are Iraqis, as if they are avenging what has happened to them.'

Mr Ramadan claimed that 'battalions' of Arab militants were coming to Iraq to join the paramilitaries known as Fedayeen Saddam, or Martyrs for God. He said that the Fedayeen, who are led by Saddam's older son Uday, and the foreign volunteers would enthusiastically emulate Ali Jaafar al-Noamani.

Asked if Iraq would accept offers of assistance from Osama bin Laden, he replied: 'I will not answer that question because it might help the objectives of the aggressors. But we will encourage anyone who stands up to the aggressors. These are not suicide fighters. Those who commit suicide are desperate people; they are not filled, as the martyrs are, with faith and confidence in the Arab nation and in their homeland. They have not reached the state of sublimeness. I say to the United States administration that it will turn the whole world into people who are willing to die for their nations.'

▲

This waiting was terrible for the people of Baghdad. The US bombing had become remorseless and defeat seemed inevitable— unless, that is, you were listening to the words of Information Minister Sahhaf. Here was a man who seemed more pleased with himself the more all around him was crumbling. On this day he would have had us believe that he didn't even notice that the Palestine Hotel was shaking from bombing runs as little as 20km away. After he'd walked us through a minor skirmish in the south, he insisted that the American 'snake is in a quagmire now'.

But for us the waiting was a heaven-sent opportunity— a lull in the story that meant that we could move hotels. Too many people—journalists, minders, security agents, human shields and suspected *jihadists*—were again squeezed into the Palestine. It was set to burst. The lifts were getting slower and more crowded. But virtually none of the staff could get to work. It was becoming almost impossible for Anderson and me to move about in Room 905, where thick layers of *turab* dust were starting to weld all that we had into something that an artist down on his luck might call an installation. My birthday cake, untouched, still sat there, watched over by a crestfallen Sabah still hoping that we'd get a party together before it went off. I was continually up and down the stairs to Room 830, where I had my sat-phone tuned in to the Indian Ocean satellite. I used 830 as a place to write and to make telephone calls, but it was a nuisance not to be living and working in the same area.

Then, out of the blue, the Information Ministry late on Saturday night made it known, almost by accident, that foreign journalists would henceforth be allowed to stay at the Sheraton

Hotel, just across the street from the Palestine. Jon Lee had Sabah, his driver, primed so that first thing on the Sunday morning Sabah was in the office of the Sheraton's manager, doing whatever deals needed to be done. We wanted a suite—and we got it. We wanted panoramic views of the city—we got them. Separate sleeping and working areas—yep. An extra desk—you got it.

When Sabah and Mohammed Izzedine, my driver, moved our gear across the street it was as though half of the tension went from our lives—suddenly I relaxed a bit. We tended not to notice how tired we were, probably because we were so far beyond tiredness that we were in another zone. We were managing on three or four hours sleep somewhere in the 24-hour cycle, and we had already been here for more than a month. When I hit the pillow in the early hours of our first morning at the Sheraton, I fell into an instant deep sleep. So deep that, when the phone rang minutes later, I sat bolt upright, picked up the alarm clock and spoke into it.

Jon Lee's driver, Sabah, is the 'old man' or the 'silver-haired man' that I referred to from time to time in my news reports from Baghdad, using him as a bellwether for the mood of the city as the regime continued its delusional dalliance in the face of inevitable defeat. To have identified him before now would have been upsetting for him, possibly even dangerous. In many ways he was a classic example of an Iraqi who had carved out a relatively secure space for himself in the nightmare world of Saddam's Iraq. He knew there were tight boundaries on his daily existence, but he managed to live within them. For more than twenty years his life had revolved around his work as a driver for guests at the al-Rashid Hotel—a regime institution at which state security officials had absolute sway over whether he could be a hotel driver and, consequently, whether or not his family could exist.

Sabah's big dream up to now had been to own a GMC four-wheel drive, the vehicle most commonly used on the overland drive from Baghdad to Amman, the Jordanian capital. Sadly it may have to stay a dream. During the last twelve years, UN sanctions have made the overland route a necessity, but in that time Sabah could not earn enough to buy the GMC with which he could exploit this trade. If the Iraqi economy revives in the next few years he might be able to earn enough to buy a GMC, but the lifting of UN sanctions and the resumption of commercial air travel into Baghdad will offer the best paying customers—the diplomats and journalists, who will be joined by an aid and business army—a cheaper and more convenient alternative to the traditional overland route.

Even on our first day at the Sheraton, Sabah was a man transformed. Jon Lee and I immediately managed to spread our mess around the suite, but Sabah was making up for the time he had lost during our sojourn at the Palestine, where things were so cramped that he could not assert himself. He quickly had our stores neatly divided up between the suite—Rooms 1208 and 1209—and his adjoining room, 1210.

Mohammed, my driver, was anxious about his young family, so he returned to the suburbs every evening. But Sabah? These were our rooms but, in a flash, they became Sabah's empire. Like a shadow, he was perpetually behind us—cleaning up, providing food, getting laundry done and watching out for us. When he couldn't get food from a restaurant, he would get 'Madam Sabah' to cook and he would ferry it in to us at the hotel; and if 'Madam' was indisposed, then Sabah cooked—sometimes on a hotplate in the room. If the commercial laundry was closed, Sabah did the laundry. He was scrupulous with costs and all the time he spoke an inverted pidgin English that was as frustrating as it was endearing. Anderson knew him well and often had to translate for me. 'Me take him . . . ' meant 'I give you . . . '.

There still was no word on Matt and Moises, the *Newsday* team who by tomorrow would have been gone for a week. We still thought it would be best if questions about them, and the other two missing journalists, came from high-profile voices outside Iraq, rather than from us inside the country. *Newsday* was based on Long Island, near Manhattan. But because Matt was English, efforts were being made to enlist the lobbying assistance of British MPs like George Galloway, who had access to Saddam Hussein. Likewise, African-American rights campaigner Jesse Jackson had been asked to help find the four— in 1990 Saddam stage-managed the release of some of the American hostages he held after the invasion of Kuwait to coincide with one of Jackson's visits to Baghdad.

Then came more disturbing news from the north—Gaby Rado, a much-liked and highly regarded correspondent for Britain's Channel 4 News, was found dead in the car park of the hotel in which he was staying in Sulaymaniyah, the second city in Iraqi Kurdistan. There was speculation that his death might have been an accident and ITN, producers of the Channel 4 News, said in a statement: '[There] appears to be no direct connection with any military action.'

Rado's distraught colleagues said that he had recently been through a tough marriage breakdown, but they ruled out suicide on the grounds that the man was blissed out in a new relationship. Yet it was hard to fathom how someone who had survived Bosnia, Afghanistan, Bucharest and the West Bank could be found dead in mysterious circumstances—it seemed he had fallen from the roof of Sulaymaniyah's Abu Sanaa Hotel—as a war was going on around him.

Tributes to dead journalists often concentrate on their coverage of cataclysmic or courageous events. But when Rado's Channel 4 colleague Jon Snow wrote of him in *The Guardian*, he fondly retold the story of a potato:

' . . . serious and sensitive, [Gaby] was also blessed with a wonderful sense of humour. Amid the dog days of one Muscovite autumn, he came up with the idea of reporting on a day in the life of that vital Russian staple, the potato. Being television, his news desk wanted it that very day. He and his crew set out from Moscow, without a clue as to where they would start their tale. On the way out of the city he glimpsed a babushka and her husband digging spuds at the roadside. After they had filmed the scene, the old woman informed the crew that the potatoes were destined for a nearby school. The school turned out to be a private English language establishment. Thus rare English interviews were available on tap.

'Then one of the pupils announced she had an uncle with a potato farm. So off they went, to film rows of Russian women pulling up the potatoes, and then, because the region was so poor, being paid in them. The final touch was some dance music lifted from one of Boris Yeltsin's recent crazy presidential market-dance routines. In five hours Gaby had constructed both an informative and amusing insight into the lives of impoverished rural folk in the emerging Russian Federation. The story when it aired that night was a classic example of Gaby's luck and intuition.'

We were moving up in accommodation, but our small Baghdad world was shrinking. We now had to ask the media minders for permission just to go a few blocks down the road to see Karim the barber. Sabah had been going to him for decades and he had introduced Jon Lee, who in turn had brought me along for a tidy-up to Karim's shop in the Christian Quarter. It was a sobering measure of the tension in our lives that we had to ask a thug in a suit if we could go down the street to have a shave.

We even had to think twice before crossing the square outside the hotels to go to the mosque, in order to find the man responsible for the mournfully sung prayers that emanated from the minaret speakers within seconds of the opening of every US bombing raid. Day or night, the voice of Muthana Mohammed Saleh, the 33-year-old son of the imam, would waft across the neighbourhood, managing to make itself heard between the detonations and so providing a balm for fractured nerves and frightened hearts. Some nights it was reassuring to hear other mosques take up his dirge-like chant—'*Allahu akbar*'—and send it on from mosque to mosque around the city. Near the hotel there was also a donkey that brayed whenever the bombing started. Curiosity about this donkey had been eating away at Anderson, but we had not yet found the time to track down the beast and its owner.

After weeks of threats, the Americans finally pulverised the Iraqi Information Ministry in the early hours of Saturday. Like the TV network's bunker next door, the fourteen-storey propaganda complex had to be abandoned. On Sunday, the ministry started moving into the Palestine Hotel where till now it had simply had a desk in the lobby.

Last night I counted lights in only fifteen rooms in the al-Rashid but this morning it seemed that, in the wake of the bombing of the ministry, the hotel's staff had finally figured that it was time to close. Many of us still had back-up rooms booked there—Jon Lee Anderson and I still had our much-loved, but little-used, suite on the eighth floor. I had stayed at the al-Rashid countless times over the years; indeed, when the ministry ordered me to leave Baghdad and Iraq during the US bombing of the city in 1991, the ministry minders were so certain in their prediction that I would be able to return within a matter of days, that they said there was no need for me to pay my hotel bill—which by then was more than $US3000. This, they said, was a matter that could be attended to on my return. But it was several years before I was allowed to return and the matter of the unpaid bill was never raised.

This time it was going to be different. Many of us owed mere hundreds of dollars and the al-Rashid cashiers knew they had us cornered. There was only one functioning exit door from the lobby of the Palestine Hotel and that was precisely where Salam, the al-Rashid cashier, set up his ledgers, while his colleagues roamed the lobby, hauling all malfeasants before him. At least they were prepared to accept US dollars instead of Iraqi dinars, which had to be delivered by the sackful if the bill was for the likes of a TV crew, who might have been in town for weeks.

Salam stripped us of our room keys—even the keys to our safety deposit boxes. Burns of *The New York Times* stood to one side and observed the efficiency of this little operation before offering some wry words of advice, paraphrasing Mr Micawber: 'Never settle your debts with someone in poor health.'

DAY TWELVE

A Guerrilla War in the Offing

Filed Monday, March 31 at 1am   **Sheraton Hotel**

The Iraqi resort to suicide bombing is hardly surprising, but the dumbfounded response from US commanders is another sign of their lack of preparedness for war in this region. The swagger is gone from the 'Shock and Awe' campaign; instead of being welcomed by flag-waving and cheering Iraqis, President George W. Bush is confronted with the ugliness of asymmetrical war— brazen Iraqi units and individuals who can nip through gaps in the most technologically superior force ever sent into battle.

It does not mean that the US-led forces will lose the war. But it does mean that the ground rules have changed dramatically, handicapping Washington and, to use Saddam's words, increasing the blood-price that the US will pay for victory. The Iraqi resistance is as much a measure of Saddam's fear-driven control of his military and civilian populations as it is of the doubt that many ordinary Iraqis harbour about American intentions.

It's ugly now and it promises to get uglier. The media here and elsewhere in the world is filled with images of civilian grief and damage that now is spreading beyond what were described as 'regime targets'. In the early hours of Saturday several of Baghdad's telephone exchanges were bombed, further isolating civilian Iraqis by denying them local calls in a time of great stress.

As Saturday's suicide bombing took place, Information Ministry officials in Baghdad were handing out video-cassettes of the most appalling images of death and destruction, which they blamed on the Americans. The footage showed several buses and cars that had been incinerated on the road between Najaf and Baghdad, and which were riddled with machine-gun fire. There were long lingering shots of the skeletal, charred remains of passengers. When the images are telecast, particularly in the Arab world, US claims that Iraqi fighters have been using public transport to get through American lines will count for little.

The US came here apparently in the belief that chemical or biological attacks were the only unconventional attacks they might face. But Iraqi militiamen dressed as civilians mount hit-and-run attacks and then meld into anonymous local crowds; they scoot around with ease on public transport, springing ambushes; they hide their big guns in civilian quarters. And the most remarkable aspect of it all is the shocked surprise by US commanders in the field and at the Pentagon.

Iraqi rhetoric is threat-laden and blood-soaked at the best of times, but the timing of the Najaf suicide bomb and Vice-President Taha Yassir Ramadan's self-congratulatory press conference in Baghdad on Saturday night has to be taken as an unambiguous warning of worse to come. This is the regime that eulogises the suicide bombers of the West Bank and the Gaza Strip, paying $25 000 rewards to the families of Palestinian suicide bombers, and there were echoes of the Palestinian justification for their methods of war against the Israelis when Mr Ramadan said: 'Any method that stops or kills the enemy will be used.'

Observers, the foreign press included, have been watching and waiting, confused by an apparent lack of war planning across Iraq. But with the war now in its second week, the explanation is clear—this is shaping as a guerrilla war, like we saw in Vietnam, Northern Ireland, Somalia and a dozen other battlefields. Already the majority of American casualties have been in guerrilla strikes in and around Nasiriyah.

At Najaf, Captain Andrew J. Valles, the US First Brigade's civil and military affairs officer, was quoted as saying: 'I don't know what motivated this guy to kill himself. To me, this is not an act of war, it is terrorism.' But in Baghdad it was just war.

▲

Email to Pam: We just had Cruise missiles going in four different directions around the hotel. Amazing!

Reply: If you both are not wearing earplugs you are very stupid.

Email to Pam: Not that close. I always have the plugs in my pocket.

Reply: Yes, but never in your ears.

Email to Pam: When I need them, that's exactly where they will be.

I was trying to get by on the sleep I could grab during the night. But, desperate for rest, I fell back on the mattress once I had filed my report this morning. It was a waste of time—in the space of an hour I was interrupted five times by the phone ringing or by a knock on the door. The last of these was John Burns with a crew from CBS's *60 Minutes* in tow, filming for a segment on 'the most dangerous man in Baghdad', as information supremo Uday al-Tai had taken to calling the *NYT*'s man, even in public. I had to jump up to take a role in a stilted conversation on 'the situation' for the cameras, after which Burns and crew departed—leaving me fully awake but reluctant to get on with the business of the day.

And, after his first night in a Sheraton bed, Anderson was not too happy either. He woke up, declaring: 'What is this joint—a 1965 shag palace? There's sure been a lot of rumpy-pumpy in this bed; but all I've got is a sore back.' And with that he despatched Sabah to search for any of the housekeeping staff who might be able to insert a sheet of hardboard between his mattress and bed base.

By now we were virtually prisoners of the Information Ministry—not allowed to go anywhere, pretty well not allowed to see anyone. We were performing our journalism under almost impossible conditions. We got to see what was happening in the city and suburbs only when the ministry buses took us to destinations the ministry believed would produce their kind of story. Or only when we went to a ministry-approved hospital (there were three of them) or to a ministry-approved restaurant (also three). Special pleading would occasionally produce a permit to go by car to a normally unauthorised destination and Anderson was using the ruse of a back ailment to get to see a medical professional who was one of his contacts. Otherwise we were becoming reduced to binoculars on the balcony.

This day's bus outing was absurd—it was another that posed more questions than it answered. There was a big bomb crater on the campus of the University of Baghdad, just near an imposing gate to the university into which had been incorporated a huge image of Saddam Hussein—wearing a mortar board. Windows were shattered in the surrounding buildings, but none of the ministry minders could explain why this corner of the campus, which housed the College of Women's Education, needed sandbags or what kind of heavy vehicles had recently churned the earth near where the bomb had struck.

My most pressing problem, yet again, was what to do about my sat-phone. I was still relying on my secret zipper seal, which by now had saved my newspaper Information Ministry fees in excess of $US4000. But, as the Baghdad tension rose, I was anxious to eliminate any aspect of my operation that the authorities could use against me if I should fall under the same spotlight as Matt and Moises had done. So I dismantled the phone, packed it in its carry case and resealed it, so that a member of the ministry's 'technology committee' could officially unseal it for me.

Burns went off to have his woolly hair cut—for *60 Minutes*. Here was a man who, days earlier, had told us of the pact he had with a hairdresser in London—for old family reasons, only she would ever cut his hair. Now, because *60 Minutes* wanted actuality for its report on Burns of Baghdad, he was off to the nearest barber.

On his return we had to deal with another looming crisis, the fact that we were running out of cash. The Iraqi dinar was shot—when I first came here in 1990, I paid $US3 for one dinar but today I could get 3500 dinars for $US1. Cheques were no good; there were no credit cards. The only reliable tender was the greenback. When you handed them over, notes were held to the light with great suspicion and often they were rejected for reasons that were never clear. And if I was paying Information Ministry fees in $US100 notes, I was obliged to record on a piece of paper the serial number for each note and that document then became part of my departmental file.

The dilemma we faced—Burns, Anderson, Tyler Hicks and myself—was that, with the risk of a US siege of Baghdad, we could become bogged down in the city for however long US forces were bogged down outside it. And the longer Baghdad was closed off, the more our daily costs—now running at about $US800 a day—would rise. It seemed that, just as we had a closing window of opportunity to get *out* of Baghdad before the war started, we now had a closing window of opportunity to get money *in* before a siege began. The roads to Jordan and Syria were under the control of US troops, but they had not yet been closed to traffic. We knew of foolhardy but trustworthy Jordanian and Iraqi couriers who were still prepared to make the desert dash from Amman to Baghdad and, for the right fee, they would bring anything to us.

What then unfolded was a rather extraordinary wartime currency movement. Coordinating between our three head offices—*The New York Times* and *The New Yorker* in Manhattan and *The Sydney Morning Herald* in Sydney—we set in train a cash transfer to the most cut-off and most dangerous capital in the world and it looked as though it would be done more quickly than any bank transfer I had organised between Australia and the US in the last two years.

The amount was $US100 000, to be shared between four of us. This then was the deal we worked out, as Baghdad came under renewed and ferocious bombing: The *NYT* would act as lead banker, putting up the full amount in the knowledge that the *The New Yorker* and the *SMH* would settle for their shares of the total as soon as practicable. Burns' wife, Jane Scott-Long, would be the chief courier—the money would be signed over to her in London; she would fly to Abu Dhabi and then back-track to Amman, where she would link up with one of Burns' *NYT* colleagues; and together they would pass the money to the local couriers.

Burns concluded his account of the plan to his foreign editor with a frank, but utterly alarming, email that warned: 'Having looked at this problem from every point of view, we see no alternative. The Iraqi couriers we use have been 100 per cent reliable in the past; they are amply rewarded for what they do, and will remain on our "payroll" here in the days and weeks ahead, giving them the incentive to fly straight and level. Any losses that may be incurred, God forbid, will be borne respectively by the news organizations involved; ie, from the moment the money begins its journey from London, it will be at the risk of the *NYT*, *The New Yorker* and *The Sydney Morning Herald* in proportion to their weight in the courier package.' And so the money train began.

We were so chuffed with this arrangement that the news-pack news of the day almost passed us by: NBC had sacked Peter Arnett, who, because of his and CNN's performance during the 1991 Gulf War, was probably the most high-profile correspondent in Baghdad. During the first war they were the only broadcasters allowed by the Iraqis to cover the entire conflict from Baghdad and some—including myself—still harboured a grudge because CNN, as the favoured network, had not fought then for the right of other news organisations to stay on in Baghdad, a move that would have enhanced its credibility considerably. There had been only five or six of us left in the country in '91, apart from CNN. But in the end we were expelled on the third or fourth day of the war, leaving the whole pitch to CNN and a lone Spanish newspaper reporter, who was hiding out in the suburbs.

But since the first Gulf War, Arnett had parted acrimoniously from CNN after the cable network retracted a controversial Arnett report that had accused the US of using sarin nerve gas in Laos during the Vietnam War, and this time in Baghdad the tension between the reporter and his former employer was palpable. And other old hands were heard to mutter 'you're as good as your next story, not your last' as young European and Asian reporters in particular queued up on a daily basis to interview Arnett in the weeks before the war.

Time for payback seemed to come when the Iraqi authorities kicked the entire CNN crew out of Baghdad only hours before the start of this war, claiming the network was biased in favour of the US. Overnight, Arnett seemed to grow a foot taller and he took to publicly lecturing CNN on its shortcomings, arguing that they lacked the political skills needed to deal with the Iraqi authorities. Twisting the knife, he told other reporters: 'It's nothing they did particularly that the Iraqis were irritated at. A degree of diplomatic and personal relationships gets you through in a place like Baghdad.'

Arnett could have been sitting pretty. But by yesterday his second chance for TV stardom in Baghdad was in tatters. In the face of protests in the US over an impromptu interview he gave to Iraqi TV, NBC at first defended him but, as the protests intensified, the network sacked him. Arnett told his Iraqi interviewer more or less what analysts in the US were saying about the conduct of the war. But, his critics said and he later agreed, it had been a gross error of judgment to appear on the 'enemy' network.

However, there was something else that was very troubling for those of us who worried about journalists' security in Baghdad, something that made many of us pause—and then decline—when we were asked to sign a petition against his sacking that was to be sent to NBC. A big international campaign was being mounted for the release of the four journalists, who we now were certain were in Iraqi custody. So it didn't make sense that Arnett—a member of the board of the Committee to Protect Journalists, which was deeply involved in this campaign—would actually go on local TV and praise the Iraqi authorities for their treatment of foreign journalists.

The Arnett petition was posted on the Information Ministry's noticeboard in the lobby of the Palestine Hotel. I read it as I waited to have my sat-phone formally unsealed. But, after waiting for a couple of hours, I decided that I had a story to write and that I'd go back and sort things out on the sat-phone front later. When I left the lobby to return to the Sheraton, there were about a dozen signatures on the petition.

DAY THIRTEEN

Marking Time

No story filed this day   **Sheraton Hotel**

Our life in Baghdad by now seemed to have developed its own chaotic rhythm. It would still be dark when I tumbled from the mattress, still in yesterday's clothes, to grasp at a ringing telephone. The first callers usually were TV and radio producers in Australia, on whom I'd imposed a simple discipline—I'd talk if it didn't interfere with my *Sydney Morning Herald* deadlines and so long as I was not put on hold for more than 30 seconds. If they kept me waiting I'd hang up, because waiting on the line for an ad break or a news bulletin really blew my concentration. The interviews themselves didn't take long—maybe 30 minutes in all at either end of the day.

But the producers had to take pot luck that I'd be in the hotel when they called. It was impossible for me to plan around their programming schedules and, besides, I never knew when the satellites might be jammed, which meant I'd have no line at all—voice or data. This jamming, especially close to our deadlines for filing, really ratcheted up the tension. Anxious and spraying invective, Anderson and I were often forced to spend hours on and off tapping at the 'connect' button on our sat-phone software. Then we would both use whichever phone got a connection first.

We could never understand why sometimes one of our phones would work while the other one, all of six metres away from it, would not—possibly it was because he worked through the Atlantic satellites and my dish was pointed towards the Indian Ocean. Of course, no phone signal meant no email or internet, which meant that at such times we were totally in the dark in terms of what our foreign desks wanted, and what was happening in the war and the world beyond Baghdad.

The war outside our window made us tense enough. We'd somehow adjusted to the incessant bombing, though it was impossible to sleep through it and there were days when we were living on pure adrenalin. We'd even got over being intimidated by the US propaganda machine.

A few weeks before this, our families were distressed—although most of us hadn't seen it—when the US allowed the media to film its testing of the world's biggest non-nuclear weapon, a 21 000lb MOAB bomb. You could almost hear the boffins' brains clunk as they contrived to call it a *Massive Ordnance Air Blast,* in the hope that headline writers would hear the acronymic echo of Saddam Hussein's *Mother Of All Battles* threat against the US in 1990. We hadn't seen any MOABs—yet. And we'd forgotten about the threatened use of e-bombs—these were the microwave munitions with which the Pentagon would fry the insides of our laptop computers and sat-phones.

This particular morning I had a breakfast of Madam Sabah's rice-bread sandwiches and Turkish coffee, before setting out across the road to the lobby of the Palestine Hotel to make my peace with the Information Ministry's Technology Committee. For once I was not in a great rush, because I wasn't quite sure where the story was going today.

I detoured through a press conference with the Foreign Minister, Naji Sabri, whose bodyguards were armed with polished-metal Kalashnikovs. But I was distracted because *Newsweek*'s Melinda Liu was telling me in a stage whisper that the only other Australian reporter in Baghdad had just been ordered to leave the country. John Burns came into the conference late, took a seat beside me and passed a pencil-written note, that was as brief as it was informative, about the imminent departure of Ian McPhedran, my only Baghdad-based competitor in the Australian news market: 'Unapproved trip to see Info Min—with South African; spotted by Mr U; both out!'

Later I found a forlorn McPhedran. It was only the previous evening that we had been warned about going unescorted to sites that had been targeted by the American bombers; but, he said, his minder had assured him that it would be okay to have a look at the bomb damage to the Information Ministry. He had gone to the cratered building with a South African colleague, but there they'd had the misfortune of being sprung by the ministry's Director-General, Uday al-Tai, as he was making his own humiliating inspection of his shattered domain. The DG snarled at them and withdrew their press accreditation on the spot, ordering them to head for the border within 24 hours.

I was still on the lookout for the Technology Committee. Finally two men greeted me on the leather sofas in the lobby of the Palestine Hotel. They examined the case in which I carried the sat-phone—failing to notice that the only part of this bag that had crossed the border with me, when I entered

Iraq six weeks earlier, had been the two tiny zipper tabs you pulled in opposite directions to open the bag, and the string-and-lead seal with which they were tied together.

The Iraqi border guards had originally tied these tabs together so that, when the two zipper mechanisms ran up and down the zip together, the bag didn't open and the phone it contained could not be used. To prevent me untying this string, they had clamped a lead seal on it. If that seal had been tampered with in any way, the men of the Technology Committee would have had me thrown out of the country. But in my nightly efforts to open the zipper and gain access to my sat-phone, by prising off the sliding mechanism without disturbing the seal, I had broken the brittle cast metal three times. So three times I'd had to go to the markets to buy a new bag, to which I would affix the sealed zipper tabs from the original bag.

The men from the Technology Committee studiously made an entry in their book; then they signed and dated my paperwork, to inform the ministry cashier that my phone was unsealed on this date and that from April 1 I'd be paying $US100 a day for the pleasure of using it. It had been a risky gamble, but it had saved a lot of money and I hoped that the bean counters back at home would appreciate my effort at cost containment. It had also given me immense pleasure to thwart the robbers at the Information Ministry.

Suddenly there was some really big news and it had nothing to do with the diatribe we had sat through with Naji Sabri. Someone yelled across the lobby that Matt and Moises had surfaced in Jordan. They had apparently crossed the border and were driving to Amman. The other two—Molly Bingham and Johan Rydeng Spanner—had also been released. A tidal wave of relief washed over the pack. But, rather than prompting cheers and backslapping in the lobby, their release was simply factored in as a badly needed positive in a sea of swirling negatives.

Their story would come to us in dribs and drabs, but in time we came to know all of its chilling detail—how they were seized and how, as they entered the infamous Abu Ghraib, about 40km west of Baghdad, Matt had informed his fellow captives: 'We're in the worst prison in the Middle East.'

The pair of them had been accosted in Room 1122 at the Palestine at about 1am on March 25, but it took time for Matt to realise the extent of their predicament—first he thought it was a sat-phone sweep that he'd be able to buy his way out of; and then he assumed it was a visa violation, for which they would be bussed to the Syrian border. It was 7am before they were ordered to pack up every item they had, pay their bills and exit the hotel via the service lift, which is where they had been seen by the last witnesses before they disappeared. It was as he was being handcuffed to Moises to be taken away that Matt realised their very real danger—'That was the first time I worried about being killed,' he recounted later.

And he had very serious concern indeed when the only word he understood from the exchange between his guards and the man at the prison gatehouse was the very ominous 'Mukhabarat'. This mention of Saddam's feared security apparatus dispelled any lingering doubt in him that power had shifted. They had gone from the jurisdiction of what the hard men of the regime saw as the limp-wristed team at the Information Ministry to the bare-knuckled brigade, for whom torture and murder were as frequent as bread with their meals.

Matt's account of their week in Abu Ghraib—the first taste of which we were able to read online—varies from terror to indignity to humiliation. But throughout it there is always a gnawing sense of impotence. They took from him everything except his boxer shorts and issued him with prison pyjamas and slippers. Like the rest of us he had done the hostile environment training course, and now its lecture on how to assess your survival chances had thundered back in his head. He recalled: '"Be worried if your captors let you see their faces. Be worried if they don't blindfold you or put your head in a bag. That means they don't care if you see their faces—it means they might already be planning to kill you." I could see their faces and I could see where we were.'

Matt was living our worst nightmare: 'To begin with, I couldn't control my panic . . . my whole being throbbed with fear . . . they suspected us of spying . . . they could kill us at any minute . . . they could torture us, which I felt would lead to execution . . . overall, I calculated, we had a five per cent chance of getting out and a 95 per cent chance of dying. Nothing was in our favour.'

At first he couldn't sleep and, when he did, his dreams were filled with faceless men dismembering human beings. Whichever way he looked at their circumstances, they didn't improve—he was British and Tony Blair's troops were a part of the invasion force then closing on Baghdad; Moises, Palestinian by birth, was a Spanish citizen and his government was continental Europe's most voluble supporter of war against Iraq. Matt thought: 'How can I kill myself? It's a better option than suffering days of torture that likely would end with a firing squad or a hanging—the choice of someone else, not my choice, not my will.' And then the moments of clarity: 'I told myself I have no power. There's nothing I can do. If they take me to kill me, I will walk easily and stand there and accept it. I have lived 33 years and I've been in love. I've had great friends and I've loved my work. Everyone dies at some stage. If it happens to me now, that's okay. It's okay.'

Matt and Moises had entered Iraq on dubious visas and they had tried to avoid using the ministry minders, but the questioning in their interrogation revealed that the Iraqis knew a good deal about them and their movements. When they quizzed him on his career, Matt managed to gloss over having been stationed in Jerusalem for four years—the country most hated by the regime. But then they turned up his Palm Pilot—filled with the names and numbers of contacts in Israel and the Occupied Territories. Finally, after a week of hell and with no knowledge of the international campaign being waged for their release, they were told they could go. They were taken to the border crossing at Trebil, robbed of their last $US14 000 and dumped into Jordan. As word of their release swept the world, there was a consensus that it was the work of Yasser Arafat and the Vatican that had finally unlocked the door for them.

Impossible as it seemed, the story of the war in Baghdad on this Tuesday seemed to be marking time. So, after about twenty hours a day, seven days a week for six weeks straight, I decided not to file.

Burns had taken a room at the Sheraton at the same time as we did, but so far he had not moved across. I intended to catch up with him later, but in the meantime Anderson and I chewed over the story of Matt and Moises as Sabah took us to Karim for our ministry-approved shave.

The Christian Quarter is an endearing relic of the old Baghdad. It is a hodge-podge of once-elegant riverside villas from the Ottoman centuries, which survived in pockets of decay and collapse even as Saddam and his Baathist regime poured oceans of concrete to shape the sterile, even heartless monumental architecture that is today's Baghdad. But back here, in the nooks and crannies of the old city, there are still the latticed curves and the romantic over-hanging balconies of another time. One-third of the way along a grubby side-street that runs between Saadoun and Abu Nuwas streets is Karim's glass-fronted shop—it was the only one that was open at this time.

It was small. Karim saw the world through black-framed Coke-bottle glasses, but he said little about what he saw. He didn't talk. Instead of a walrus-like Saddam moustache, his was pencil-thin. European landscapes hung on the walls and by the washbasin a small-framed photograph of Saddam seemed to be little more than a token observance of the regulations than a display of fealty to his leader. Three potted plants were dying of thirst in a corner. Karim had one chair and a set of electric clippers that I'd never seen him use. Neighbourhood boys brought Turkish coffee—medium sugar—for the three of us, and for Anderson a nargile, an elegant water pipe in which apple-flavoured tobacco burnt under a bed of red-hot coals.

Karim took fifteen minutes to give me a shave, and then he used an ancient process that left my skin feeling scalded. It involved a length of cotton, which he looped between his hands and his teeth and which required him to come at me with his head bobbing, much like a pecking chicken, in such a way that the thread behaved like a pair of fine-bladed clippers on even the finest of facial hair. This was a classic Baghdad trim, enjoyed by all men as part of their vain pursuit of a hairless face—apart from the mandatory moustache and, for many, the regular dying of their hair and eyebrows. Such was the heat in my face that I thought I was on fire—and that was the point at which Karim doused me with cold water!

The visit to Karim's was a wonderful respite from war and work, but it was all too brief. Sabah delivered us back to the hotel and then spent much of the evening fussing over us. Often he would bustle about, making us a last Turkish coffee for the night, wearing full-length traditional robes or else bare-chested, except for his white singlet. He would come into our rooms four or five times in the space of a couple of hours, to dust and tidy our desktops as we worked. But on this night he was still unhappy about the fate of the cake—as was my wife in New

York. So we put a candle in it and Jon Lee snapped pictures of me blowing it out while Sabah looked on.

This was the night we threw the cake out and it was the night we got confirmation that the Mukhabarat were like cockroaches, preferring to move in the dark. One week before, they had come for Matt and Moises at 1am; around midnight this night, they came for John Burns.

DAY FOURTEEN

Cat-and-Mouse

Filed Wednesday, April 2 at 1.42pm   **Sheraton Hotel**

A lethal game of cat-and-mouse in the skies over Baghdad implicates the US as much as Iraqi forces in the errant missile strikes that claimed the lives of almost 80 civilian shoppers in suburban markets in Baghdad last week. Both sides were quick to blame the other for the death of 17 innocent non-combatants at the al-Shaab market place on Wednesday and, 48 hours later, the death of 62 people in the predominantly Shia shantytown of al-Shuala.

As the war progresses, the risk of death or injury to Iraqi civilians has risen dramatically. First, there is the shrapnel and debris from the cruise and Tomahawk missile strikes, and the fall to earth of the Iraqi anti-aircraft fire they provoked. Then there are the errant missiles. Finally, in the wake of the suicide attack that killed four American soldiers on Saturday, there is the adoption by the US of a shoot-to-kill policy for even mildly suspect Iraqi non-combatants.

On any given day now, hundreds of cruise and Tomahawk missiles cut through the city skies. On Monday night they were flying in four different directions around the press hotels on the banks of the Tigris. The many thousands of rounds of Iraqi anti-aircraft fire that go up must come down and an unknown number of Iraqi surface-to-air missiles are fired from Baghdad.

Precise figures are not available; however, Iraqi authorities say that since the war started more than 600 civilians have died and thousands have been injured. But reporters who were allowed to visit the marketplaces several hours after the blasts came away puzzled. They anticipated the major structural damage that a powerful cruise or Tomahawk warhead might cause. Instead they found high casualty figures, but surprisingly small impact craters and minimal structural damage to buildings in each area.

So they came away unknowingly susceptible to US denials that these were caused by American strikes and counter-claims by the Pentagon that errant Iraqi surface-to-air missiles were a more likely cause of the blasts. Allegations also came from within the exiled Iraqi community that Saddam Hussein was capable of attacking his own people for the propaganda advantage of blaming the carnage on the US. In the face of such allegations, Iraqi officials erupted with anger, vowing that the 'criminal' US-led bombardment of the city and the nation was the only wrongdoing that warrants examination.

However, damage at the blast scenes is consistent with the small, high-speed missiles used by the US to strike against Iraqi air-defence radars and mobile missile launchers. They are known as HARMs—high-speed anti-radiation missiles—and they cost $US284 000 each.

In a confused coalition response to the al-Shaab strike, the

US initially denied that it had aircraft in the area and Downing Street accused Iraqi officials of 'sanitising' the area before allowing foreign journalists in, lest they conclude that Iraqi missiles had been the cause of the tragedy.

But later the US said that it did have aircraft over Baghdad, hunting nine mobile missile units, and US Brigadier-General Vincent Brooks said that there had been an Iraqi missile battery in the neighbourhood, suggesting it may have been an outgoing Iraqi shot that landed in the marketplace rather than an incoming American shot. The American use of HARMs—with their knowledge of the Iraqi strategy for dealing with them—could make it difficult for the Pentagon to absolve itself of responsibility for the marketplace deaths.

Material published by the maker of HARMs, Raytheon, says that the missiles were first used in combat against Libya in 1986. In 1991, during Desert Storm, more than 2000 HARMs all but silenced the Iraqi radar threat. 'HARM was acknowledged as being the combat planners' weapon of choice in the suppression of enemy air defence radars,' it says.

Iraqi defence officials reportedly claimed early in 2000 that they could render HARMs impotent, thereby shielding from American attacks their air defence system, which is rated as one of the most dense in the world. The HARM is a semi-guided weapon—it seeks its radar target only while the radar is active. Adopting a practice used to good effect by the Serbians during Operation Allied Force in Yugoslavia in 1999, the Iraqis have opted to keep their radar switched off for much of the time.

When the radars are turned on, a HARM can be launched at them, homing in on the radar's signal. But if the radar is switched off after the missile is launched, the HARM can go out of control, losing its ability to steer accurately to the target. Also, when US pilots establish that a radar has locked on their aircraft, they are required to respond in an instant—attack or be attacked. This gives the crew little time to think about the precise location within the city of the radar that has a fix on them.

The HARM's 68kg warhead is designed to fragment into tiny pieces to tear apart radar dishes and other fragile electronic equipment. That is not inconsistent with the effect on the Baghdad marketplaces. Frail human bodies were torn apart, and buildings and other structures were charred and their contents scattered, but they were not demolished. At the time, Brigadier-General Brooks told reporters: 'We did have an air mission that attacked some targets, not in that area but in another area, and they did encounter some surface-to-air missile fire.'

Despite US claims that it would take some time—and possibly not until the US-led forces were in control of Baghdad and thus able to inspect the scenes—before an investigation could be carried out, I was told that it would be a relatively simple process to establish if HARMs were involved. It needed only for the exact time when any HARMs were fired to be established and compared with the time of the marketplace strikes. These missiles take only seconds to arrive at their target.

And when they explode they leave a shrapnel trail. After the al-Shuala tragedy an old man who lived within 100m of the impact point handed a piece of shrapnel to British reporter Robert Fisk. It bore the serial number thought to read 30003–704ASB 7492, but the B was scratched and conceivably is an H. Then there was a lot number: MFR 96214 09.

Research by one of Fisk's colleagues found that the weapon had been manufactured in Texas by Raytheon, the world's biggest maker of so-called smart-bombs. And that the buyer of the lot that included the al-Shuala missile was the procurement arm of the US Navy.

▲

Email to Pam:
Chaotic day here—all safe and well, just frazzled and in need of sleep. Will call when I can—lines been very difficult all morning because of the bombing; if can't call will email.

It was not quite the whole story, for today we imposed a news blackout of our own.

As we piled onto the buses this morning for a ministry outing, Sabah was giving me a hard time about Mohammed, my driver, and Firas, the fixer I'd been using on this and on earlier Baghdad assignments. All of us had trigger points for tantrums in Baghdad, and Sabah's was the arrival on the scene of *anyone* who he thought did not perform as well as he did; who charged more than he did; who wasn't available at all hours of the day, as he was; who didn't have a car as good as the Mercedes Benz that he used and of which he was a half-owner; or who didn't have a wife who made coffee quite like Madam Sabah's.

And in his anxiety he could never wait to be thanked. I'd be doing a live interview by sat-phone with ABC-TV in Australia and Sabah would be dancing about in front of me, holding up a wet pair of trousers and demanding my attention so that I would acknowledge, there and then, that he had washed them and done a good job. Or I'd be belting the keyboard as a deadline loomed and Sabah would insist on taking ten or fifteen minutes to explain, in that wonderful language of his, why a receipt was for $US10 instead of $US11. He had previously become very upset when Jon Lee spoke to him about $US5000 that had disappeared from his satchel—Jon Lee had merely been looking for information but, because of the language difficulty, Sabah thought he was being accused. Our punishment after this episode was that every financial transaction had to be explained in mind-numbing detail, causing Jon Lee to explode one night: 'Sabah, you make my head *majnoon* [crazy]!'

Firas the fixer worked full-time for CBS but he worked for others on the side—finding drivers and translators, getting hotel rooms over the objection of front-desk staff and sometimes pushing the right buttons to get a visa. Sabah was outraged that Firas took a slice of whatever fees were paid for the deals in which he played middleman. But, because I had done Firas a favour last year—introducing him to a crew from ABC Australia at a time when the transport mafia at the al-Rashid was trying to cut him out of the business when he was desperate for work—he believed he was in my debt and willingly helped with any curly issues.

The broadcast networks always snaffled the best fixers and Firas loved to prove his commercial connection with CBS by flashing the keycard to a permanently booked room CBS held at the Intercontinental Hotel in Amman, to which Firas had access as he went back and forth to Jordan. But this only infuriated Sabah more. Whenever he saw Firas, he'd spit: 'Mafia!'

It didn't seem to matter what time of day it was, the lobby of the Palestine Hotel was always packed, with a stream of people constantly heading out through a door off to the right between the cashier's desk and the lifts. These were the stairs to a third-floor terrace, a great outdoor area from which the twenty or so TV networks that remained in Baghdad beamed to the world. First there was generator alley—a narrow walkway where the teevs, as the networks were sometimes referred to collectively, had their own power source—dozens of noisy machines that guaranteed them independent and secure power at all times. Around a corner, there was a maze of tents, each identified by a network logo from somewhere in the world; and each with its own path to an area about three-metres square at the edge of the roof. These squares were marked off in spray paint and from within each the network logos again radiated as a huge 'no-go' sign. Each of these spots had a view of the mosque across Firdos Square, which was the backdrop that most of the teevs used for their Baghdad broadcasts.

John Fisher Burns was someone you could normally pick out easily in the crowd milling in the hotel lobby or straggling towards the buses—he was far taller than most and his magnificent shag-pile hair was like a beacon. But it wasn't particularly surprising that he was nowhere to be seen this morning—to meet New York deadlines he often worked through the Baghdad night, sometimes falling into bed at 5am or 6am for a few hours sleep. However, young Tyler Hicks, who had something of a father–son relationship with Burns, after working closely with him first in Afghanistan and now in Iraq, was on our bus and he was worried. Actually Tyler was very worried.

Tyler explained to us that, around midnight, Burns had been settling in to his all-night ritual of research and writing when there had been a knock on the door of Room 808 at the Palestine Hotel. When Burns opened the door, a team of men in suits and ties marched into the room, headed by the man who had up to now been masquerading as Burns' minder, but who had given himself away in that earlier encounter with Burns at the al-Rashid, when he had declared: 'You know who we are . . . '

This was Saad Muthanna—a bad-tempered, barrel-chested man, who invariably wore a scowl and really made little pretence of maintaining his cover as a media minder for the journalist in our midst who fascinated the regime the most. Burns, a two-time Pulitzer prize winner, was the very self-assured and wily Baghdad correspondent for the single most influential newspaper in America—the country mounting the death-or-exile attack on the Iraqi regime. Later in the war I visited Wamid Nadhme, a professor of political science at Baghdad University whom Burns had visited weeks earlier. The professor was full of questions about Muthanna, the minder who had accompanied Burns to his home on that occasion. Nadhme told me: 'He was security. He told me in Arabic what I could tell you and what I should not say; and when I asked him about people at the Press Centre he didn't know any of them . . .'

So, on Tuesday night, when Muthanna marched his team into Room 808 at the Palestine, where Burns still maintained his lodging despite our urging to move across to the Sheraton with us, there was absolutely no pretence at all. According to Tyler, Muthanna identified his team as intelligence agents. Indeed, some of them had the obvious bulge of a weapon beneath their jackets. Muthanna got straight to the point— they'd known for a long time, he announced, that Burns was a CIA agent so he was now under arrest and any failure by him to 'cooperate' would lead to more serious consequences. 'For you, it will be the end,' Muthanna warned. 'Where we will take you, you will not return.' And when Burns protested that the Information Ministry had approved his presence in the country, Muthanna turned on him and confirmed what I'd always suspected about Mr Kadhim, the interloper in the Press Office: 'Don't worry about Mr Kadhim—he works for me.'

The agents, who had loitered threateningly, then set about going through all of Burns' and Hicks' gear. What unfolded was a bizarre display of human behaviour, even for a regime in which brawn and unquestioning loyalty often triumphed over education or a considered response to events—the product of what Burns later angrily described as a regime that consisted of 'peasants in suits'. The agents stripped him of his ability to work—confiscating four laptop computers, a satellite telephone, two cameras and a printer. Then they demanded money— helping themselves to $US6000, which Burns kept in a zip-lock plastic bag.

But it was the chocolate Smarties that enthralled them. As the agents went through the *NYT*'s food stores, they found a tube of Smarties with a plastic Disney character on the lid. 'They tried desperately to open it,' Burns told us later. 'And when they couldn't, they punctured the bottom and the first man started to pour them down his throat. Then the others demanded a share, and each poured some down his throat till it was empty. And then they asked for more. They left, ordering me to remain in my room until "more senior" intelligence men arrived.'

Tyler had witnessed much of this, and on the bus the story tumbled out. The implications were huge. There was a tremendous immediate risk for Burns and a possible risk to us all while we stayed in the country; there was also the very likely prospect that our editors would stampede to pull us all out of Baghdad if someone of Burns' standing was detained.

The bus was headed south-west towards al-Hillah, a small town near the ancient hanging gardens of Babylon. We were being taken to a local hospital which was grappling with the aftermath of US attacks—a truly shocking visit with dreadful casualties that would form part of my report for the next day. This 200km round trip also took us down a highway that we expected to be filled with Iraqi military traffic. Given the regime's claim that Baghdad would be its last stand and that the US would pay in blood for daring to invade Iraq, we fully expected at least glimpses of the Republican Guards' supply lines and, at best, the military might of Iraq on the move.

Instead we saw very little—a railway siding where the Americans had bombed several tanks before they could be unloaded from a train; a few tanks and other fighting vehicles hidden under brushwood and in groves, near major intersections; and a few cannons, either set up for battle or on the move, behind trucks. And when we combined what we were seeing here with the very little we were seeing in Baghdad, disturbing questions emerged about the price that Saddam was asking the people of Iraq to pay. He apparently demanded that they suffer a war that he seemed to have no serious intention of fighting.

The Americans had pulled out of the trough and were now bearing down on Baghdad at breakneck speed. This day they were within a mere 30km of the capital and coming from two directions—the army from the west; the marines from the east. There had been virtually no challenge from the Republican Guards, whom the Americans had been pounding mercilessly from the air; allegedly, what was supposedly left of them was retreating towards Baghdad.

Ordinarily this would have completely absorbed us all, but now we were preoccupied. Burns' safety was a pressing issue. He had been on a knife-edge since he entered the country in the days before the war, but now the way he played this new game of roulette would have a bearing on us all.

That he'd had the guts even to come to Iraq spoke much of the man. The risks were huge—this was a regime that knew no limits—but he had an almost naïve faith in the protection offered by a venerable masthead, *The New York Times*, which he saw as his personal suit of armour. 'They wouldn't dare . . .' he'd say, late at night, without quite finishing his own sentence. But he was no one's fool—he had already spent time in a Chinese prison years before, accused of spying by yet another paranoid regime. The stage had now been set for a tug-of-war, in which the outcome might ultimately depend on when the marines made it into Baghdad.

Burns is a powerful and provocative writer. In Baghdad he more often produced an essay than a news report; he deftly cross-stitched the events of the day, plucking threads of a perfect shade from layers of history or from the understanding he had amassed after spending decades observing regimes in Moscow,

Beijing and a dozen other societies that had changed or were changing reluctantly.

The Iraqis made little pretence of the fact that he had originally been blacklisted for writing a series of articles late last year that unambiguously made the link that a lot of correspondents reporting from Baghdad were reluctant to make—it was state terror, and not much else, that sustained the regime of Saddam Hussein. When Burns finally wanted to enter the country and required a visa, he used contacts to get around the Information Ministry's veto.

When he did turn up in Baghdad, he thought long and hard about going underground; but instead, he requested a meeting with the ministry's Director-General, Uday al-Tai. Burns told me how he was made to cool his heels for three day before he was summonsed to al-Tai's eighth-floor office, whereupon the DG raised the issue of Burns' reports that dealt with torture and killing in Iraq's jails. He recalled every detail of al-Tai's remarks: 'You have written a great deal about killing in Iraq, and this is good. This is a shame for Iraq. But now America will be killing Iraqis. Will you write about that?' When Burns insisted that, yes, he would, al-Tai clasped his hand and undertook to have the necessary papers issued to allow him to report from Iraq. A visa won us entry to the country, but on arrival we were required to report to the ministry to be registered and to be issued a formal press pass to work as journalists.

But within days of Burns' arrival in the capital a whispering campaign had begun about the man who, like most Europeans, was known by his given names, as is the local custom. The drivers and minders were asking questions: 'How long is Mr John Fisher staying in Baghdad?' And giving warnings: 'It is dangerous to be talking with John Fisher.' And Burns was getting unvarnished warnings from within the Information Ministry. He told me later: 'A couple of the others at the ministry have been warning me that it's a ruse [al-Tai's undertaking to give him accreditation], and that the intelligence agencies have taken over my case.'

Sometimes when we were chatting—over a cup of tea—Burns would reveal his anxiety about what he was writing, pulling out a copy of what he had filed in the early hours of that morning, seeking a second opinion, even though he knew it was too late. Pressed about his views later by another reporter, he said: 'Nobody wants to forfeit his position immediately or put his head on the chopping block. [But] the overriding issue was that every moment of the day [in Iraq] there was terror and fear. If you didn't write about it, or attempt to write about it, you simply weren't doing your job. If you got thrown out, at least you got thrown out with your head up.'

On our return from al-Hillah I immediately went looking for Burns. I found him in one of his boltholes. He explained how he had sat in his room for a while after the agents left, but then had looked out the door. He was supposed to be under arrest but a guard had not yet been posted at his door. He took this as his cue to get out and he headed first for a darkened stairwell, where he collected his wits, and then set off, up into the higher floors of the Palestine, where the first of a group of colleagues allowed him to hide out.

While we had been at al-Hillah, he had been back to see the Information Ministry boss, al-Tai. 'Mr U told me straight up that they can't protect me anymore,' he said. We discussed the options he had and whether the one that was still least attractive to him—leaving Baghdad—was possible anymore: people who were driving west towards Amman in Jordan on their own were now being held up and robbed or detained, or both. The drive would take him straight past the Abu Ghraib prison, where Matt and Moises and the other two abducted journalists had been held—and that scared him visibly.

We knew that American troops were on the road to the west so we explored the possibility of him getting to them and then being able to go down the US supply line to Kuwait.

His life seemed to be flashing before him—in particular, he vividly recalled a life-threatening illness that had hit him here in Baghdad in 1990–91, at the time when he and I first met, and from which he subsequently recovered. He said: 'I remember standing in a room in a New York hospital, looking out the window at a man in the street buying a newspaper and then posting a letter and thinking that I might never do either of these simple tasks again.'

But, as we talked, he rallied. His clash with Muthanna's thugs had been devastating—he had been threatened with imprisonment or worse; he had lost all the tools of his trade and the ability to move around to report. But his sense of humour did not fail him—suddenly he chortled quietly and declaimed in a seemingly portentous manner: 'I'll have you know that I have not always been as you see me now.' Then he roared with laughter as he provided me with the context of this quote—Peter Sellers playing the role of a failed doctor who, having just used his fountain pen to write a prescription for a bemused patient, picked up the surgery cat and used it as a blotter to dry the ink on the prescription.

My memory of the rest of the day is a blur. I remember a lot of short tempers. On the bus to al-Hillah, as we were trying to make sense of Tyler's dreadful news, a German reporter rather abruptly asked Jon Lee Anderson to close the window. Anderson refused and, when the German complained, Anderson blew a fuse: 'You're a German, aren't you? You're a German! True to character . . . ' he shouted. And then he threw up his hands in disgust, without explaining the source of his fury.

In the evening Sabah produced a meal of kebabs and bread, but we bickered over the fact that he and Mohammed had managed to get our emergency generator past the front desk and up to the twelfth floor of the Sheraton—it was now on our balcony—but they hadn't managed to lug any fuel up from our 600 litre emergency store, which Firas had organised to be hidden in a nearby home.

And the Information Ministry was sending us insane, trying to rake in the cash again. Their ploy to make us pay more fees this time was to cancel the 'pink' press cards that had been issued a couple of weeks before and to replace them with 'yellow' cards. But to get the 'yellow' card you had to produce your receipts from the cashier, who was Jamal, the man with no fingernails. Because we were in Iraq, no one dared ask him why he had no fingernails but nevertheless he took $US3350 off me to cover the last four weeks and, because of the scam I had run with the seal on my sat-phone, only $US200 of this latest impost was a phone fee.

The jostling in the queue at Jamal's desk was heavy; those of us who had waited patiently for hours hurled abuse at a steady stream of would-be queue jumpers. I chipped a French woman about trying to get ahead of Tyler Hicks and me. She was one of the group who had lunched with Uday al-Tai the day he harangued us across the tables at the Latakia Restaurant about the Americans thinking that an invasion of Iraq would be a cake-and-Pepsi picnic. Challenged now, she turned on me: 'I'm French and you are British and we are in Iraq, so you don't matter; you just go back to your fucking country!!!' she spat. She was so ferocious that I didn't have the nerve to show her my Irish passport, which might have pushed the fight further. But others cheered when I stood up to her and she finally flounced off.

And then there was more sad news—another casualty. Kaveh Golestan, an Iranian freelance cameraman who was on assignment for the BBC, was killed when he stepped on a landmine as he alighted from a car in northern Iraq. And two News Ltd journalists from Australia—Peter Wilson and John Feder—and their interpreter, Stewart Innes, were placed under hotel arrest in Baghdad with about a dozen other journalists who also had entered Iraq without visas.

As the US taunted Baghdad with its 'psych-ops' effort to convince the Iraqi military and civilians that Saddam was injured or dead or had fled, the ever-confident Information Minister Sahhaf was wheeled out on local TV to read a speech in the name of a leader who seemed to have disappeared. The network ran old footage of Saddam and reported that he was busy—meeting with his generals and his sons, Uday and Qusay.

Meanwhile, across the world, readers of *The New York Times* would have been puzzled by the absence from the April 2 edition, for the first time since the start of the war, of a report from Baghdad by John F. Burns. But we decided that we would keep the story of his predicament quiet; that we would watch it play out a bit, before families and foreign desks were informed.

DAY FIFTEEN

Thursday, April 3

Trying to Find Tranquillity

Filed Thursday, April 3 at 11.14am   **Sheraton Hotel**

I wanted to write about the last pockets of tranquillity in a besieged city.

About the barber's shop in the Christian Quarter, where 65-year-old Karim deftly wields his cut-throat razor, saying little but oozing warmth and a welcome as he tidies us up. He smokes as he works, invariably signalling the job is done by stubbing his cigarette into the puddle of lather he has removed from my face.

About the peacefulness of the al-Jundi al-Majhul Mosque, an extravagant Ottoman creation that stands apart from box-like modern Baghdad, where the aged and frizzy-bearded Mullah Mohammed Sale cradles his walking stick as he talks quietly about Islam and the world.

About Ahmed's Chicken Inn Restaurant, a laminex and vinyl kebab house on Saadoun Street, where the wartime menu is pared back to just one dish—chicken, rice and Pepsi. Somehow

147

Ahmed managed to keep the nervous tension of the city beyond his fly-spotted windows.

But it's too late. No one lingers over lunch anymore and Karim the barber is a ball of nerves. The sanctuary silence in the mosque is shattered because the mullah's son, Muthanna, is forever rushing to the microphone for the minaret speakers to sing a dirge-like prayer to counter the latest wave of missiles: '*Allahu akbar, Allahu akbar . . .*', which means 'God is great, God is great'.

Baghdad went to bed on Tuesday night hearing reports that the US-led invasion forces were a day's march from the city. Yesterday morning the BBC claimed they were only hours away. The bombing is round the clock and has become increasingly more powerful. The planes return to pulverise buildings they previously put out of commission and which they know have been abandoned.

The al-Rashid International Telephone Exchange, on the banks of the Tigris, still stands. But it is a death trap for anyone who wanders within blocks of the twenty-storey tower. After the third strike in as many days, four or five floors in the middle of the building are gone and the upper floors are supported only by fragile corner columns.

Another suburban phone exchange which has been disembowelled continues to emit an eerie sound—the noise of thousands of phones left of the hook. And near a third bombed-out exchange, layers of dust and shards of glass coat one of Saddam Hussein's memorials to his 'victory' in the 1991 Gulf War—a larger-than-life bronze of himself and tiny busts of George Bush snr, Maggie Thatcher, Helmut Kohl and other leaders of the coalition of that time, which are strewn mockingly at his feet.

After punching a great hole through the Air Defence Ministry on Saadoun Street last week, the American and British bombers have been back to smash it completely. All that remains now is a flat pile of rubble and, out the front, a column on which a statue of Saddam is still standing. It's the same at the Republican Palace—they keep blasting it. The dome is gone but four huge busts of Saddam remain standing—one with a drunken lurch—and the Iraqi flag still flutters on a parapet flagpole.

On Thursday morning Mohammed, my driver, was coming through one of the better suburbs, Mansur, when four missiles landed around him. Stunned, he watched the force of the blasts crush a bus 'like a cigarette packet' and wreck a dozen cars. He fled on foot as windows shattered for blocks around and about a dozen substantial buildings were levelled in the Baghdad International Trade Fair complex close by. Seven motorists died, 25 were injured and a nearby Red Crescent maternity hospital had to be evacuated. Mohammed himself is fine; he was able to go back and retrieve the undamaged Toyota that is his livelihood.

The jets fly lower now, a sign that the US believes it has destroyed Iraq's air defence system. And many of the over-flights seem to be surveillance—they rumble across the city without dropping munitions. At night huge fireballs erupt in the smoke-mired downtown area and blinding flashes of light belt in from the south-western skyline, where Republican Guards positions are being bombed constantly.

The commercial districts are shuttered and a lot of building owners have taken to bricking up their doors and front windows. The al-Safir Hotel, where I had booked a back-up room, is now sealed with cinder blocks and cement. Business-men and shopkeepers worry about damage and looting. With a wary eye on the sky, the city's market gardeners sell vege-tables on the pavement and eggs are sold from the backs of trucks parked for a fast get-away.

The Information Ministry has been forced to abandon its gutted headquarters and has set up shop where the journalists are—in the abutting Palestine and Sheraton hotels. Even the shoeshine boys who used to work the ministry car park are here, among them the foul-mouthed Khalid, who uses his repertoire of disgusting English-spoken epithets to lure customers.

The small city of al-Hillah might have been another pocket of tranquillity. Despite its location, 60km south-west of Baghdad, it seemed to be thriving yesterday—the markets were bustling and most shops were open. But at the local hospital there was chaos and too much pain. Its lobbies were crowded with gurneys; every patient seemed to be a new amputee— men, women and children with blood-soaked bandages on the stumps of what had been complete limbs.

In the operating theatre, doctors fought to save three lives— a woman with serious head and facial injuries; a man who had holes the size of bread-and-butter plates in his abdomen; and a man who lay there with much of his abdominal organs beside him on the operating table. Dr Saad al-Falluji, an Edinburgh-trained surgeon, said that in 24 hours the hospital had received 33 corpses and more than 180 people injured from two incidents—what he said was a cluster bomb attack on a village and a mysterious tank attack on a bus headed for Najaf.

Hussain Ali Hussain, 26, said that a US tank had fired at his car four days earlier. He had not been able to get immediate medical treatment, so his right leg had to be removed below the knee. He said: 'We believed the US when it said civilians would be safe. I went back to my home to get food and some of our furniture—I saw the tank and I saw the shot. The US has changed everything—they used to come here as tourists, but now they come to occupy our land and to control us.'

In the next bed was Basan Hoiq, 38, who was one of 34 passengers on a bus bound for Najaf—his left arm, gone from just above his elbow, is bandaged, but gaping wounds on his legs are in need of urgent treatment. He had fled his home in strife-torn Najaf, but decided to return after being away for only a day. He said: 'I could see the American flag on the tank 500m down the road from us. There was no warning. There was a noise and a lot of shouting on the bus—then people's heads seemed to snap away from their bodies and many of them were dead.'

His wife, Samia, sits blank-faced at the end of his bed, clutching a two-month-old baby to her chest. His brother-in-law, Hiderj Abid Hamza, explains that Basan Hoiq's mother, Najia Hussain, was among the eighteen civilians who died in the attack. He said: 'When we heard about the attack we came to the hospital. We found Basan in one of the wards and his mother in the freezer. We had to bury her without her arm because we did not know how to match all the body parts for the different families. We still wonder about what happened. The bus did not explode and there were no burn marks, but the floor and the inside of the roof were layered with human flesh and the seats were soaked in blood.'

Dr al-Falluji said: 'We don't know what kind of weapon did this. The bodies were completely destroyed, but the bus wasn't. People's heads were severed and the viscera were outside their bodies; their limbs were cut off. It was a horrible thing to see.' Asked how he felt about his war-imposed workload, he said: 'Angry. I feel very angry about this situation. Don't you feel angry about it too?'

There is no tranquillity in Iraq today.

▲

Email to Pam:
We're fine; but worried that the last fireball might have been the al-Rashid—hard to get a fix on the location because city is blacked out.

The war had been going for two weeks now and we had been in Baghdad for seven; I was so tired that the backs of my eyeballs were starting to prickle in the day. The marines were storming Saddam International Airport, only 20km from the centre of the city. But Information Minister Sahhaf rattled on today as though a skirmish between the Republican Guards and US forces near al-Kut, about 160km south-east of the capital, was going to save the day. As American artillery rocked the city's outskirts, he ranted: 'They have been bitterly defeated.'

We were still getting a decent meal once a day. With the new tempo in the American advance, it was going to be a race now to see which got to Baghdad first—the marines or our money. The $US100 000 we were couriering in had arrived safely in Amman with Burns' wife last night.

The nights were warming up. But there was no air-conditioning in the hotel so we would leave open the sliding doors to the balconies that faced west from each of our rooms. The downside to this was having the dust and smoke and noise of war in our rooms.

I checked in on Burns this morning. He had decided simply to lie low for a few days. If the Iraqis wanted to order him out of the country that was fine, but they would have to find him first as he room-hopped through the upper reaches of the Palestine Hotel. For now he'd be confined to barracks, using colleagues' phones and laptops to file his reports. What he banked on most was a belief that the war was virtually over. He was anxious, but he was still driven by a determination to see this story through.

He and I had first come here in 1990–91 and now in his mind he had invented what he called 'the four-leaf cluster' — this was his imaginary journalism award, simply for having been in Baghdad for the duration of the war. We figured that somewhere between 130 and 150 journalists would be getting the cluster. Privately, I also thought there were a couple of special cases warranting at least a three-leaf cluster. Nick Farrow, a producer with Australia's Nine Network, had been so determined to see this story through that, in the days before the war, he flew home to Australia for the caesarean birth of his daughter and then returned to Baghdad—just in time to be evacuated from Iraq on an edict from Sydney. And then there was the Chinese reporter who had a war, but had no one to report his observations to when the Shanghai paper for which he worked was shut down by the Chinese authorities because of the tone of its political commentary.

When Jon Lee logged on to his email today and got news of the death of Michael Kelly he stared at the screen, frozen in disbelief. When he announced it to the small group of us sitting around in the room, there was a shocked silence. The pug-faced Kelly was well-known to many of us in Baghdad. Anderson admired what he described as Kelly's acute prose, clear-mindedness and superb writing ability; Sharon DeLano, Jon Lee's editor at *The New Yorker* in Manhattan, had edited Kelly's much acclaimed *Martyrs' Day*, a book on the first Gulf War. I knew Kelly from that war too—the pair of us liked to brag that we were the only two reporters who had covered both the bombing of Baghdad and the liberation of Kuwait back in 1991.

In the last few years Kelly had starred on executive row in American magazine journalism—first as a controversial editor of *The New Republic* and then as a much admired and respected editor of *The Atlantic Monthly*. As a columnist for *The Washington Post* and the *New York Post*, he was witty, acid-tongued and a real enemy of the Left; but at the helm of the *Atlantic* he was lauded for his broad-church thinking, his championship of good writing and an infectious and well-placed self-confidence. Kelly was the hero guy and he was the first American reporter to die in the Iraq War. As best could be told at this stage, he was a passenger in a Humvee travelling with the US Army's Third Infantry Division when it came under Iraqi fire, south of Saddam International Airport. The soldier driving the vehicle took evasive action, crashed into an irrigation canal and both he and Kelly drowned before they could be rescued.

This morning I had to visit Mr Kadhim at the Press Centre. When I showed him the receipt for last night's payment to Jamal-without-the-fingernails, he took my pink press pass and issued me with a new yellow document. While I was completing this exercise, I went several times to check on the well-being of the two new Australian arrivals—they were chaffing at being confined to the hotel and the removal of their gear, but otherwise they were fine.

At different stages in this crisis crews from nearly every other Australian media company had been and gone in Baghdad—News Ltd, Channels 9 and 7 and the ABC. I'd spent a bit of time with the crew from Nine—we had the odd pleasant drink in the early weeks as we swapped security information. But the Australian I really missed was my photographer colleague, Jason South. Personal reasons had drawn him home, but in the first month of this assignment he was dependable, reliable, inventive and damn good company.

News from home did intrude briefly tonight. My wife let me know that the executive who had fired me two years previously as editor of the *SMH* would himself be made to walk the plank. With bombs dropping all around, office politics didn't seem to matter—so I just danced a small jig. Later, I spoke with the editor of the Saturday *SMH*, Lis Sterel, but I didn't raise it with her, because I wanted to keep *her* focused on *my* story. Later, she confessed that she hadn't raised it with me because she wanted *me* to focus on *her* deadline. In the end it was John Burns who got the best rise out of it. When I told him, he chortled: 'Mate, he's had his trips.'

I thought of Jason again this morning as I chivvied Sabah and Mohammed about getting fuel for the generator up to our rooms. Jason had been the master of the generator. He had gone head-to-head with the management of the al-Rashid when they refused to allow us to have the machines in our rooms and I was certain that, if he had been here now, we would not have had this nonsense of not being allowed to store fuel in our room. The Sheraton staff was even refusing bribes on this one.

As luck would have it, we were hit by our first blackout tonight. The timing was appalling—I had written only the first five words of a big report—'By Paul McGEOUGH in Baghdad' was all I had on the screen. Anderson was finessing one of his weekly dispatches. As our suite faded to black, I knew that I had only a couple of hours battery life in my computer and sat-phone but I had a good six hours work ahead of me. I stumbled around, looking for the torches that should have been strategically located in the room for this eventuality. I went out on to my balcony and watched the last lights fade as the blackout rolled across the city.

In the twelfth-floor lobby I discovered that the hotel did have back-up power, but it lit only one globe—which happened to be right outside our adjoining doors. Desperate, I went to work. Removing the globe from its socket, I smashed it without damaging the two metal prongs inside; I then cut the plug from the cord on one of our power-boards, exposed the wires and joined them to the two prongs of the globe. Anderson watched aghast. Terrified that I might kill myself, I was in a lather of perspiration as I used a set of pliers to screw what was left of the broken globe back into the light socket outside the door.

We couldn't believe it. The red activity lights on the power-board came on; when we plugged a bedside lamp into the power-board, we had light; and when we hooked in the sat-phones and computers, everything was charging and working. I looked out from the balcony again and Rooms 1208 and 1209 were the only ones with any light in the Sheraton this night. I was triumphant.

But it was too good to last. I worked till about 3am, at which point I thought a cup of coffee would carry me through what I expected would be another hour's work. Jon Lee had crashed by this point, so I filled the electric kettle and plugged it in to the power-board. There was a flash and suddenly I was in darkness again. I'd forgotten that the kettle would draw so much power and, as it did, it fused and wrecked our emergency power system. Defeated and roundly abusing the sleeping Anderson, whose kettle it was, I fell into bed.

On top of all the Iraqi deaths and injuries we were witnessing every day, the Kelly death had upset us both—me because it was in Baghdad that I had first met Kelly and, in a way, it was because of Baghdad that we had not caught up when we might have earlier this year. Kelly lived in Boston, where the *The Atlantic Monthly* published, and I was in New York. When I heard in December that he was going back on the road as a writer, we exchanged emails with the subject line: *We never caught up.* The telemovie on CNN's first Gulf War had just been on TV and we swapped acerbic memories of the behaviour of some in the CNN crew that was at odds with the heroics we had seen on HBO.

We talked about lunch or dinner and Kelly had the last word: 'Let's fix that. I get down to NY semi-regularly. I'll write in advance next time and we'll get together. I'd love to see you— any chance of you getting up here? I was just thinking about the old days, in my irritation at the moviefication-lionization of those bastards at CNN.'

DAY SIXTEEN

Friday, April 4

People Pour from the City

Filed Friday, April 4 at 1.11pm   Sheraton Hotel

At eight o'clock the city was plunged into darkness.

The blackout started in the centre, rolling out like a blanket until the last to fade were the floodlights on the Tomb of the Unknown Soldier, on the west bank of the Tigris River. Apart from the odd game motorist, the only illumination was the roiling flames from dozens of trenches of burning oil and daggers of white light that flashed from heavy battles on the edges of the city.

All night the incessant thump of distant heavy artillery could be heard and more than a dozen huge explosions rocked central Baghdad, causing several high-rise buildings to erupt into flames.

Haunted by the imminent threat of street-by-street fighting, people are fleeing Baghdad in the thousands. All day crowded buses, taxis and cars stacked with personal baggage—and one with a coffin strapped to the roof—poured out of the city. They headed north and south to join relatives in the country and, in the case of the desperate, to surrender to the advancing US-led forces.

At times there was a sense of faux normality—a man washing his Suzuki soft-top at the kerb; a policeman nabbing a motorcyclist for running a red light; and sections of the markets bustling, but only for survival items such as food and water tanks.

Those who can't leave are double-bunking in whichever family home they think is the safest. A doctor explained that the house in which his family of six lived was now home to seventeen members of his extended family.

But Ali Ismail is going nowhere. He's a beautiful twelve-year-old with a head of fine black hair, piercing brown eyes and three cheeky freckles. He has the lithe body of a sportsman, except that Ali has no arms—they were burnt to the bone when what the Iraqis say was a US missile crashed into al-Zaafaraniyah, his family's neighbourhood south of Baghdad. And Ali doesn't have a family anymore. His mother and father and his six brothers and sisters died in the explosion, which killed a total of seventeen people and injured dozens more.

In a drab, spartan office at Baghdad's al-Kindi Hospital, Dr Osama Saleh coached me for my meeting with Ali with a deeply disturbing photographic display of al-Zaafaraniyah's dead and injured. 'These are the pieces of his family,' he said of a picture on the computer screen, which was so grotesque that his assistant gasped, before averting her eyes. It was a collection of charred, bleeding body parts. He went on: 'This is a piece of leg . . . this is part of a head . . . this is a child . . . this is Ali's sister . . . this is his mother and over by the doorjamb is her hair.'

These people had been hacked apart. And in their midst was the agonised face of a man in his 40s, locked in the horror of his own death. Dr Saleh said: 'He is shouting in pain. Look at his eyes. His mouth is open.'

Then he called up a picture of Ali as he had arrived at al-Kindi. The bones in his little arms were burnt back to the elbow and the flesh was gnawed raw. His chest was burnt black at the centre, spreading to livid red on his flanks. Dr Saleh became terribly distressed: 'I can't express my feelings anymore. These are simple, poor people; they were civilians. It is possible for any one of us—our wives, our children, our parents—to end up like this. In the last week the casualty numbers have been increasing steadily—now we get as many as 60 a day. But if there is street fighting in Baghdad the casualties will be massive.'

These are dangerous, perplexing moments in the Iraq war. The Americans are at the gates of Baghdad, ancient setting for *Ali Baba and the Forty Thieves* and other tales from *The Thousand and One Nights*, once the centre of the old Abbasid Empire that stretched from North Africa to the edges of China. And, before that, of the ancient Sumerian and Babylonian civilisations. But General Tommy Franks, the bluff US commander, has yet to reveal his next step.

To avoid Saddam Hussein's declared intention of luring the invasion force into urban combat, Franks will be tempted to lay siege to the capital in the hope that the regime will collapse from within. Or he might be tempted to get on the front foot, after two weeks of international criticism and internal questioning of his war plan, by mounting a dramatic entry to Baghdad.

Reports yesterday suggested the latter. Pentagon sources said that once he had secured Saddam International Airport, 20km from downtown Baghdad, Franks would order the seizure of the ten bridges that span the Tigris as it flows south through the city. That would leave his men fighting from the inside out and from the outside in.

But whatever he does, it's fraught. He comes long after previous invading armies of Arabs, Mongols, Ottoman Turks and the British tried to tame Baghdad, which for about 2800 years has sat on the sprawling flood plains, on a U-shaped bend in the Tigris River. Today there are none of the tower and wall fortifications of its medieval past and Franks' men can drive into Saddam's city on six-lane highways. But they still don't quite know what to expect.

They didn't expect resistance in the south of Iraq, but they got it and it was fierce; they expected it from the Republican Guards on the outskirts of Baghdad, but they seem to be pushing through unimpeded. Resistance in Baghdad at this stage is an unknown quantity. Those of us who have been here for the last couple of months are perplexed by the absence of a consolidated and obvious military force in the city.

But the regime, from Saddam down, insists there will be a fight. Deputy Prime Minister Tariq Aziz told Lebanese TV this week: 'It's best not to fight them in the desert but to lure them into the cities and towns and to populated areas, the areas where planes can't work with great competence.' Key buildings and intersections have been sandbagged and there are as many as a dozen soldiers with Kalashnikovs dug in at regular intervals on median strips.

Some of the anti-aircraft batteries atop city buildings have survived the last two weeks of bombing and they are capable of being turned on the US-led forces as they come into the city. And on a 60km-drive south towards Karbala this week, I could see a small number of tanks and multiple rocket launchers ill-disguised under shrubbery or hidden in groves, but not in sufficient numbers to suggest a conventional defence of Baghdad.

But, given the unconventional guerrilla tactics adopted by Iraqi fighters in the south of the country, the chances are that Saddam will use the same strategy in Baghdad. If the weapons and men are there, perhaps they are concealed in the factories and shanty towns of the distant suburbs to await the

Americans. That makes the civilian population a human shield and confronts Washington with the prospect of an unacceptably high death toll.

Franks is also coming in the footsteps of those who previously attempted to seize Stalingrad, Manila, Seoul, Beirut, Grozny and Mogadishu, all of which feature in the ugly history of urban combat and at their time demonstrated how difficult it is to minimise what inevitably becomes massive civilian and military casualties. Mogadishu seared the US psyche, as did the excruciating battle for the central Vietnamese city of Hue in 1968, during which, after four weeks, the US seized control of just seven city blocks.

Baghdad promises the same. Its flat geography, its narrow alleys and its dense structures give the advantage to those who know the terrain—in this case, the Iraqis. That knowledge puts the US at a psychological disadvantage. In American training exercises soldiers playing the enemy regularly 'kill' or 'injure' 60 per cent of the invading force.

This time they say they are willing to learn from the British experience in Northern Ireland. This required a city to be taken as a series of bite-sized strips of territory. Each time the invading army seizes a strip, it digs in before leap-frogging to the next one. But this dilutes superior firepower rapidly, forcing the attacker to resort to artillery or air strikes. As a senior British military trainer told reporters: 'It's rifles and bayonets stuff. Troops get tired fighting at this sort of intensity. It's not just physically exhausting; it's mentally exhausting.'

In the past invading generals have not given undertakings to minimise civilian casualties. But, if it sticks to its undertaking in this regard, the US will have one hand tied behind its back. It will not be fighting on the same terms as its enemy.

The outcome of the battle will be revealed in due course. But in the meantime Ali has already asked his doctors if he can have artificial arms. His left arm was amputated at the shoulder; no more than 10cm of his right arm remains.

And he is not alone. Up the al-Kindi Hospital corridor there is seven-year-old Miriam, whose left leg is severely damaged and fractured. In the next bed is her four-year-old sister, Abas, who suffered nasty shrapnel wounds. Then there is six-year-old Heideri, also with leg fractures that are held together with steel rods.

In the nearby bed is her neighbour from the village, Fatima, whose two brothers died in the blast and whose surviving brother is in another ward. Next to Heideri is another Fatima, a cousin of Miriam and Abas, whose right leg has been amputated just below her knee. Dr Saleh thinks aloud: 'How will she live and marry with that?'

Someone still has to find the courage to tell Ali that he is alone in the world. And then they will have to explain to all these children what this word 'liberation' means.

▲

Somebody dobbed me in. A knock on the door early this morning was from the hotel engineer, appalled by what he had found dangling from the light socket outside my door. But this brief chat was enough to be an icebreaker and we did a deal—$US20 to connect our suite into the Sheraton's emergency electrical supply. As long as the hotel's generator was going—and we could hear it thumping away below our balconies—we would have light and we would have power.

Water was now sporadic, and the lifts were out. So we had to plan our movements very carefully, to avoid racing up and down a hundred flights of stairs. For example, we would never head upstairs in either hotel without first using the lobby phones (which still worked) to check that the person we wanted to see actually was in their room.

In the meantime, Sabah and Mohammed had had a brain-wave—they worked out that they could hide the 40-litre fuel can for the generator inside the big cardboard box in which I had hauled the meals ready-to-eat from New York to Baghdad. They were able to get it past the front desk and up the stairs. I felt terribly guilty at the sight of an exhausted Sabah after he had finally lugged the fuel tank into the room—30 minutes after he'd set out from the lobby in a pitch black stairwell.

Just to go and visit the fugitive Burns when there was no power meant climbing or descending almost 60 flights of stairs. He was back in harness as best as could be managed by someone who couldn't return to his room and whose gear had been seized. He was filing day-by-day to the *NYT* (though not a word about his predicament) and still reluctant to descend from the top of the Palestine. He planned ahead—booking time on other people's laptops and sat-phones, as he needed it—but he didn't come visiting to our hotel.

The Sheraton's emergency power faltered tonight, just as I'd settled in to do some work. I could have jumped up immediately and kick-started the generator on my balcony, but I thought the darkness might be useful. I felt rocked to my soul by the little fellow I'd seen in the hospital today, Ali Ismail, and by the circumstances of the children in the other wards.

There are times on these assignments when no amount of emotional steel can protect you from the impact of the dead and, worse, the half-dead. It happens to most of us. On a bad day certain people around you suddenly become introspective; when you find yourself crying, you have to remind yourself that this is a normal human response. These are the times when what you see drives you on—to take more notes, to ask more questions, to give more thought . . . all in the hope that what you write will convey to distant readers a faithful sense of what you have seen and felt. Such moments can be excruciatingly painful; but they can also be very focusing and, for me, they often precede one of the best ways of coming to terms with horror, grief and indifference—writing about it.

As I sat there in the dark, my mind travelled on from Ali and the hospital to an attempt to make sense of one of the more perverse bits of the Baghdad equation—the minister and his madness. At times we were lost in a fog of propaganda but today the Americans did seem to have captured Saddam International Airport and, as best we could tell, the invasion forces were encircling the city. American commanders claimed they had met little resistance on the run up the Tigris and Euphrates valleys, which left us wondering what had become of the much-feared Republican Guards and Saddam's promise of a 'ring of steel'.

But this was where the madness of al-Sahhaf kicked in. He arrived hours late for today's briefing—rimless glasses flashing in the TV lights, Baath Party uniform neatly pressed and his black beret set at a jaunty angle. Pint-sized, but evidencing boundless energy, he danced around the lectern in a way that was reminiscent of the Monty Python knight who wanted to keep on fighting, even as each of his limbs was chopped off. But more disconcerting was the rising sense of pleasure he seemed to get from it all; the bleaker the situation, the brighter the minister. Perhaps that's just the way his face was—what we had assumed to be a Walter Matthau grin may have been simply the natural arrangement of his features—but, as he lectured us on Roman history one day or delved into the movie *Wag the Dog* in search of a metaphor on the war's progress the next, we were left wondering how seriously we should take him. More importantly, how seriously did he take us?

Control of the foreign press was still an issue for the regime. That was what the Burns brawl had been about. That was why, in the days before the start of the war, security agents under Qusay Hussein, the dictator's younger son, seized control of the Information Ministry. That was why last night I had watched in disbelief as Kadhim, the security sleeper in the Press Centre, made no pretence of who was running the show when he publicly and noisily pulled rank on Uday al-Tai, leaving the DG to look on, slack-jawed, as Kadhim harangued an editor from the Arabic satellite news service, al-Jazeera, on how Baghdad wanted al-Jazeera's staff deployed. And that was why the foreign press was ordered to work from the Information Ministry, a confirmed US target—because key elements in the regime saw us as nothing more than human shields for its own propaganda machine. The detention of Matt and Moises, and the threats against Burns, meant we could never rule out the regime wanting to upgrade our status—from that of reluctant human shields to hostages.

Al-Sahhaf's quest for hyperbolic comparisons, with which to describe the military triumphs that awaited Iraq, took us to Indochina this night and to the historic defeat of the French at Dien Bien Phu in 1954. Without actually admitting that the Americans held the airport, the minister made an obscure promise of an Iraqi counter-attack on the airport that would be, he said, 'another Dien Bien Phu'. He declared, with all the certainty of a winner: 'They are completely surrounded. It will be difficult for any of them to come out alive.' But the gem from today's briefing was al-Sahhaf's response to the speed with which the Americans had arrived at the gates of Baghdad: 'Let me say one more thing—they have not surprised us.'

As a graduate in English literature, al-Sahhaf arrived at some wonderful constructions in his second language. Talking up another Iraqi success, he declared: '"Heavy" doesn't even start to articulate the level of casualties we are inflicting.' He was a former ambassador and, for much of the 1990s, he was Iraq's Foreign Minister. Relatively unknown outside Iraq, al-Sahhaf had become a figure of fascination and amusement almost overnight because of his front man role in this war. But there was a pistol permanently on his hip and it was not the minister's ability as a stand-up comic that had won him a seat at Saddam's table, where he had been in attendance for so long that it would be hard to absolve him from complicity in the excesses of the regime.

At 63, he was of a rare Baghdad breed—a survivor from outside the Saddam fold. He was a Shia, not a Sunni; from al-Hillah, not from the Hussein family's stronghold of Tikrit. Non-conformity was even evident in his personal habits, such as in his refusal to wear the Saddam moustache. In a cut-throat regime al-Sahhaf had managed to be a constant—he had been close to Saddam since the 1968 coup that paved the way for his dictatorship. By all accounts, al-Sahhaf was fearless and gutless at the same time—to their faces, he had told Colin Powell that he was 'stupid' and Uday Hussein, the murderous older son of Saddam, that he was 'unfit to govern'; but he was said to kick his staff, literally, and, when the regime demanded loyalty, it is claimed that he showed it by betraying his brother-in-law, who was executed as an opponent of the regime in its early days.

Mostly al-Sahhaf rambled without interruption at his daily briefings. But there were exceptions. Today, after we had traipsed in from the rising heat of springtime in Baghdad, he told us: 'The Americans are not near Baghdad! Not [within] 100 miles! Don't believe them . . . they are trapped in Umm Qasr. They are trapped near Basra. They are trapped near Nasiriyah. They are trapped near Najaf. They are trapped everywhere.' After which Lindsey Hilsum of Britain's ITV, asked rather dryly: 'Minister, are they trapped at the airport too?'

It was the lanky Richard Downs, of the Irish national broadcaster RTE, who drew our attention to the fact that, as al-Sahhaf's star rose, Saddam's was being eclipsed. In the chattering lobby of the Palestine Hotel early this afternoon he told us of his survey of Iraqi TV. He estimated that normally 80 per cent of airtime was of Saddam and that the remaining 20 per cent was of the people celebrating him. But now, Downs said, the split was about 50/50. The people were seeing more of themselves. But that was about to change.

Since this afternoon Iraqi television has repeatedly run a twelve-minute clip of Saddam—smiling; cheerful, even—as he strolled the streets of Baghdad. They have also been running a speech by Saddam. Most Iraqis would not have seen either— their homes were blacked out and Iraqi TV's signal was poor after repeated US bombing—but the presidential walkabout appeared to have been shot today and in the speech Saddam seemed almost to dismiss the US encirclement of his capital as an irritant. Talking about enemy landings 'here and there', he told Iraqis: 'They involve a small number of troops that you can confront and destroy with the arms that you have.'

It was on the open plains between al-Sahhaf's unreality and Saddam's indifference that the media minders and their ministry bosses worked at manipulating and controlling our activities— but we were never quite sure when they were no longer in control. When Matt and Moises were abducted, Information seemed to know nothing about it. And Burns said that, when he had confronted Uday al-Tai about the intelligence agents' midnight raid on his room, it seemed to have been the first that the Information Ministry chief knew of it.

But al-Tai's staff were engaged in their own destabilisation exercise today. A list of 50 reporters' names had been put on the noticeboard with an order that they leave the country so that some of the reporters waiting for Iraqi visas in Amman could be allowed in to take their places. My name was not on the list. Neither was Jon Lee Anderson's and, remarkably, Burns' name was not there either. But today there was a sense that power was shifting, that the regime was on the way out and that anyone who didn't want to leave probably could take the risk of ignoring this edict.

The minder system was falling apart too. Many of them were not coming to work and, because we were pinned down at the hotels and only allowed out on ministry buses, the pressure of needing to know where your minder was at any time was starting to ease. There were always a few of them on the buses and, if a group of us got permission to go out by car, we'd negotiate among ourselves for whoever we thought was the best minder available—in our terms, not the ministry's—to accompany us.

The collapse of the public transport system meant that I was seeing less and less of Sammi Majid, the minder who had been my constant companion since early in this assignment. Perhaps this was just as well because there had developed an added complication—Sammi seemed to have taken a set against Jon Lee Anderson, apparently because he was an American. When we worked as a group, Sammi had been finding all sorts of obstacles to the simplest requests and consequently our work had started to bog down. I attempted to broker a peace so that we could all work together, but the stoush between the two of them had festered and in the end I was relieved that the issue was resolved for me by Sammi's inability to get to work.

A few days before, we had thought we had finished for the night when Vice-President Taha Yassin Ramadan, no. 3 in the regime, finished the briefing in which he threatened mass suicide bombings. But we were then called back through the dark-panelled passageway to the ballroom and who should be on the stage, drawing deeply on a cigarette, but Uday al-Tai. It seemed that he was being counter-intuitive—al-Sahhaf and the other ministers might want to play down any suggestion that war was closing in on Baghdad, but al-Tai thought other-wise and he wanted to go over what he called the 'ground rules'.

We were not allowed to use private cars or taxis. Could we all please switch to the yellow passes—and in the process pay our fees. More importantly, our movements were being severely curtailed: 'During bombing you must be in the hotel—you may be at the lobby entrance or on the roof. Cameras can shoot from the roof but, if we catch you shooting from your room window or the balcony, your cameras will be confiscated. You will not be expelled immediately but, after two or three times, we will have no option than to expel you. The guides are responsible for you at all times. You call them "minders", which is a term we do not use. These people are there to facilitate your work and to be in the middle when you are in trouble. The police and military do not know that you are journalists—imagine if they thought you were a US pilot? Especially the women among you. The guides will solve all your problems and, if I was in your position, I'd prefer to have a guide. You will look for him, not him for you, and the more you cooperate with us, the more opportunities you will have. If you are not behaving, why should I give you a scoop? Put yourself in my position—I would be proud to give you scoops if you are behaving . . . we all are friends and hopefully this friendship will last. So please be professional and respect reality.'

If al-Tai's speech was revealing about the conduct of one of the world's last Stalinist media machines, the response of some of our colleagues did not reflect too brilliantly on us. The first questioner wanted to know if he could have his Press Centre fees paid to an Iraqi embassy abroad—as if this lot was going to pass up the opportunity to pocket hard currency. 'Borrow it from your colleagues, my dear,' al-Tai told the male reporter, using the odd but accepted Arab-to-English translation of the much more poetic Arabic term of endearment, '*habibi*'. He told another male reporter: 'It's the case, my dear.'

Another journalist risked re-opening the whole enervating question of sat-phones, thankfully now dormant but working

169

to the satisfaction of all, by asking if al-Tai could just run the details of the rules past us one more time. And he nearly choked in mirth on his tobacco smoke as a woman revealed that she had two guides. 'That's because you are such a good-looking woman,' he told her. He allowed her to preen for only a matter of seconds before the boot went in: 'And if you were really pretty, we'd give you four guides.'

Al-Tai insisted that all of this was for our own protection. But what was most intriguing about his performance was that about half of the press came away laughing at his jokes, thinking they'd been given a friendly reminder. But some of us could think only of Matt, Moises and the others. And now we could throw in Burns, who tonight was hiding out upstairs. To our ears al-Tai's words were a thinly veiled threat.

Burns knew a bit about journalists who crossed this regime. He had researched the case of Farzad Bazoft, and later that night, over one of his interminable cups of tea, he recounted a British diplomat's tale of what can happen when a journalist comes to grief in Baghdad.

Bazoft, an Iranian-born British freelancer on assignment for the London *Observer* in 1989, was investigating a huge and mysterious explosion at a military complex near al-Hillah, the small city to which we had been bussed a couple of days earlier. Bazoft had dressed as an Indian doctor to visit al-Hillah, but he was arrested, charged with spying and, after a one-day trial, he was sentenced to death.

Burns: 'The diplomat looking after Bazoft was confident that, because relations between Britain and Iraq were good at the time, the sentence would be commuted. But he got a call telling him to go to Abu Ghraib prison, because Bazoft was to be executed at 9.30am that day. He was shown to Bazoft's cell and, expecting good news, Bazoft rose to greet him. The diplomat told Bazoft to sit down—he had bad news. Bazoft took it badly; he collapsed. The diplomat produced a pen and paper and at first he tried to get Bazoft to write a letter to his mother. But Bazoft had lost it, so he tried to get Bazoft to tell him what he would like to say to her.

'The letter was nowhere near complete when the guards rushed in and dragged Bazoft away. The diplomat drove 40km back to the city and, as he approached his embassy, he noticed that a small truck that was following him also slowed in front of the embassy. Even before he could get out of the car, a bundle was dumped from the back of the truck—Bazoft's body.'

DAY SEVENTEEN

Saturday, April 5

The US Captures the Airport

Filed Saturday, April 5 at 5.38pm   **Sheraton Hotel**

American tanks started moving towards the frightened heart
of Baghdad early today as the regime of Saddam Hussein tried
to rally itself in the face of the US capture of Saddam International Airport. But by mid-afternoon, Baghdad time, it
became clear that both sides in this war were over-stating their
accomplishments for the day.

The Americans claimed that they were on the ground in
central Baghdad, but they were not. Early in the day city
residents reported that Iraqi forces were diverting local traffic
from the Jadiriya Bridge, which is on the highway from the city
to the airport, at the same time as reporters with the US forces
were revealing that tanks of US Third Infantry Division had set
off again from the airport to probe the strength of downtown
defences.

But there was no truth in the claim by Captain Frank Thorp of the US Central Command in Qatar that, 'We now have troops in the city of Baghdad ... they're in the middle of the city of Baghdad.' During a 20km circuit of the inner city I found no evidence of a US presence in the central city area. More than 130 foreign media organisations are still represented here, but none reported sighting US tanks or other military vehicles in or near what could be described as 'central Baghdad'.

However, US forces are presumed to have launched the attack that destroyed two tanks and several other Iraqi vehicles, which one of my colleagues saw still smouldering at al-Dura, an industrial suburb about 8km to 10km from downtown. And several people claimed to have heard helicopters late last night, suggesting that a US special operations unit might have played a role in a firefight that took place inside the presidential compound on the banks of the Tigris River.

The Iraqis claimed that they had recaptured the airport— they have not. They appeared to be inventing the news when Information Minister Mohammed Saeed al-Sahhaf rushed in and out of a press conference in the space of less than ten minutes to claim that Iraqi forces had re-taken Saddam International Airport. 'Later, later,' he said in response to media requests for access to the airport. And for the rest of the day the hapless Mr Kadhim, a surly Iraqi intelligence agent who masquerades as an official of the Information Ministry, told us repeatedly that we'd be going to the airport 'within the hour'.

At one stage, as we listened to Mr Sahhaf, we could hear a mysterious rapid-fire gun battle going on behind him in the grounds of the presidential compound. Unperturbed, he issued a hectoring threat that overnight a 'beautiful' suicide operation would take place against US troops holding the international airport, but this in fact came to nothing.

As the first winds of summer buffeted the heavy black smoke that blankets the Tigris Valley, regime officials were forced to acknowledge that US-led invasion forces were within the city limits and the flight of Baghdadis to the relative safety of rural Iraq became a flood. Roads, especially to the north, were jammed with buses and with taxis crammed with passengers who had stacked food and personal items around themselves and on overloaded roof racks.

Saddam made a dramatic appearance—his first in public for more than two years—when he was filmed in the streets of the capital. Wearing khakis and a black beret, Saddam—if it was him—seemed relaxed and cheerful despite the suffering and damage around him, in what was a calculated debunking of US claims that he was on the run or that he had been injured—and possibly killed—in the opening strikes of the war on March 20. He pointedly mentioned the downing of an American Apache helicopter during the fighting as proof that he had survived the first days of the war.

In a televised speech a few hours earlier, Saddam acknowledged the depth of the US penetration into Iraq without referring to the loss of the airport, saying: 'The enemy has evaded the defences of our armed forces around Baghdad and other cities and has progressed, as we expected, to some landings here and there.' But, he added: 'In most cases, these landings have been made on the highways and involve a small number of troops that you can confront and destroy with the arms that you have.'

City scenes, as Saddam alighted from a luxury black sedan in the neighbourhoods of Mansur and al-Aadhamiyah, also confirmed that the footage was contemporary. There were shuttered shops and taped windows and people cooking food in the street against a sky filled with black smoke from the burning trenches of oil around the city.

Going to air from mobile broadcast units because of the bombing of its city headquarters, Iraqi TV showed Saddam being greeted by a small but enthusiastic crowd. His smiling, child-hugging appearance followed the earlier reading of a statement on his behalf, in which he promised to defend Baghdad and urged his troops and people to greater efforts: 'Hit them with force, resist them, oh people of Baghdad, whenever they advance upon your city, and remain true to your principles, your faith and your honour.'

Saddam's defiance came as wounded and bleeding Iraqi soldiers flooded city hospitals in the wake of the 48-hour fight for control of the airport, 12km from downtown Baghdad, and continued artillery battles south and west of the city. The American attacks on the city's defences also spread to the eastern outskirts, with heavy bombing and artillery barrages through the night. Power has been restored to pockets of the city after a total blackout on Thursday night, which interrupted water supplies, but distressed residents continue to flee rather than stay for what the Iraqis promise will be bloody street-by-street fighting when the Americans arrive by force.

The treatment of Iraqi military casualties in Baghdad's civilian hospitals is an indication that the regime's military hospitals are full. At al-Yarmuk Hospital, in the west of the city, a steady stream of ambulances and private cars delivered fighters from the southern outskirts of the city.

Busloads of reinforcements were seen heading south and residents of four districts near the airport told reporters that they had been ordered to leave so that their homes could be used as billets for members of the Republican Guard and the guerrilla forces of the Fedayeen Saddam. Terrified, they streamed into Baghdad. 'It was a night of hell,' a woman still trembling with fear was quoted as saying. 'We thought they had entered Baghdad. There were planes all night dropping bombs and there was shelling all night.' The US said that more than 300 Iraqi fighters died in the airport battle, but no casualty figures were available here—military or civilian.

The heavy rumble of artillery caused city buildings to vibrate, but there was hollowness in the rhetoric of the only regime official who briefed reporters early yesterday, Information Minister Sahhaf. Then he had insisted that the Americans were not within 100km of Baghdad. But by yesterday evening he had changed his tune, claiming that the Americans, whom he has taken to describing as the 'desert animals', had fought their way into an Iraqi trap that was to be sprung overnight.

Harking back to Dien Bien Phu, the months-long Vietnamese siege that marked the 1954 demise of the French in Indochina, he said: 'Maybe tonight we are going to show them another Dien Bien Phu —it will be difficult for any of them to come out alive.'

A foul odour hung in the wards of al-Yarmuk Hospital as doctors and nurses fought to save the lives of wounded soldiers with minimal equipment and no pain-killing drugs. One patient screamed in agony as a doctor used forceps in a failed effort to remove shrapnel from deep wounds in his legs.

As blood-soaked staff and family members tended the patients, Omar Bahadeen, a 23-year-old member of the special operations division of the Republican Guard, insisted that he would quickly overcome a bullet wound that had torn his lungs. With a tube draining blood from his lungs to a plastic jug on the floor under his bed, he said: 'We are not afraid. I'm injured but, as soon as I recover, I will go back and fight till I become a martyr.' This soldier told how he had watched American troops parachute into the airport, trapping his and other units in a hard-fought battle.

In the bed next to him lay a fellow fighter on the verge of martyrdom. Family members pleaded with him, using a local colloquialism to rally his spirits—'My eyes, my eyes.' An interpreter explained that this meant that the injured man was loved as intensely as the speaker of the words loved his own eyes. 'You are a lion,' they told him.

It seems these men had been lucky to survive thus far. The street talk in Baghdad is that the Iraqi soldiers who engaged the Americans in the airport battle were so scared that they were ordered to attack by senior officers who held guns on them. And when it was all over the dead were carried away, piled high on pick-up trucks.

At about 9pm yesterday there was a fifteen-minute eruption of gunfire in the presidential compound on the west bank of the Tigris. There was no way of knowing if this was Iraqi soldiers getting jittery or if they had encountered US special operations forces, who are said to have penetrated into the downtown area of Baghdad. But a few minutes after the gunfire died down there was a single, powerful explosion as a bomb was dropped on the compound.

▲

We had one toe in the vacuum. The city centre, the heart of Saddam's regime, was empty. The Americans were fanning out from the airport, but they didn't have the city; the regime had not collapsed, but it seemed to be going. A swirl of anticipation, a whiff of fear and an overwhelming sense of uncertainty stretched our nerve-ends so tightly you could have played them as a drum. There were trucks loaded with soldiers in the streets and the few cars in the city were being driven so badly they were ploughing into each other—at the traffic lights near the hotel, a small crowd was arguing loudly around a banged-up Passat sedan and a solid four-wheel drive.

The air of desertion was in the suburbs too. Traffic was heading out of town, piled high with anxious families and domestic stuff. But most of the side-streets were abandoned to the wind and the worry of war. Families who couldn't flee were keeping children indoors. At Baladiyat, in the south-west of the city, two American cluster bombs fell yesterday. On the total scale of things, the physical damage was mild; but the psychological trauma was huge. This part of the city is home to about 50 000 Palestinian refugees—it seems that, no matter where they go in the world, they can never escape violence.

There were only a few bomblets in the streets—the hideous little canisters of death that spew from the cluster bombs. But a man, who gave his name as Samir, said that eight people had been wounded and several cars and houses had been gouged by the exploding bombs about mid-afternoon the previous day. Even I, an adult, was tempted to pick up the salt-cellar-sized bomblets, so it was easy to imagine how tempting they were for children.

That's why all the children in Samir's street were being held indoors. He walked me through a dimly lit apartment—the power was still off—and children and adults were sprawled asleep on the floors. Only an old woman sat up, as though her watching and her praying would be of use: '*Allahu akbar . . . Allahu akbar . . . Allahu akbar,*' over and over.

Burns had begun the careful stage-management of his descent from the upper levels of the Palestine Hotel. When I dropped by—trudging up and down 54 flights of stairs by the time I got back to my room—he suggested that he might go for a walk in the lobby and asked me to join him. He said it would look less obvious if he wandered through chatting to someone rather than standing alone under the gaze of the minders. We headed down in the lift and soon found that his gut instinct had been right—the minders were still around, but there were fewer of the spooks and there was no attempt to arrest him as he chatted with colleagues before deciding that he would not push it too far. He went back upstairs.

The money—the $US100 000 that was being couriered in to us—was supposed to come over the border last night. But there were problems. A man who was carrying the bulk of it—$US40 000—baulked at the last minute and refused to make the crossing. The remainder was broken into small amounts, which were carried by members of a big CBS news team coming back into Iraq, but Burns was still trying to track down the individual couriers and to establish just how much they were actually carrying.

Sabah the driver was heroic, but even he could be defeated and distracted. There were nights when he came back empty-handed from his search for food and he could no longer turn to Madam Sabah because she and the rest of his extended family had fled to the country, rather than risk urban combat in Baghdad. We'd eaten well for almost two months and in that time I had only had one very mild stomach complaint. I had tried to stick to the sensible rules of the road—don't drink suspect water and eat only in restaurants you know and trust. But it never works, especially in Islamic cultures, where hospitality is a duty.

The previous month I had visited one of the last of the Marsh Arab communities in the south of Iraq. Conditions there had been appalling and every fibre in my body had said don't eat the food, don't drink the water. But when the communal glass was handed to me, I drank; and when I was invited to the community's meeting tent for a local feast, I hoed in. The rationale was simple—if I didn't eat and drink with these people and accept them on their terms, why should they bother to tell me their stories? In truth, I love exotic food and the memory of the warmth of their company at such times is often the only souvenir I can take away from such communities.

Tonight the tables were reversed. I decided to have one of the MRE pre-packed dinners. Sabah watched in amazement as

I opened the various packets of food—a chicken main course, rice, vegetables, a fruit dessert and crackers with cheese—and proceeded to heat some of them, using just-add-water chemical sachets provided for this purpose. He watched intently and with rising disgust—there was no way he would accept me on my terms tonight and he certainly wasn't going to eat any of this when it was offered to him. For my own part, I had no doubt that there would be a few more such meals in the coming days and weeks. Some restaurants were still opening, but they were harder to find.

Despite Minister Sahhaf's predictions of a spectacular Iraqi counter-attack on the US forces at the airport last night, nothing happened. But I heard of a disturbing incident at the Palestine Hotel. Early yesterday an attractive woman reporter had been embarrassed to find that her Thuraya satellite phone, outlawed by the Iraqis, had been discovered and handed to Uday al-Tai, the Director-General of Information. Everyone knew it was hers—her name was written on it. And everyone knew what the consequences were—confiscation of the phone, at the very least. But al-Tai handed it back and assured her that the incident would be forgotten. Actually, it wasn't forgotten—at 2.30am he was knocking on her door; he was alone and he was demanding to be allowed in. She could see him through the peephole, but she had the presence of mind to keep the lights off and pretend she was asleep.

Public transport was falling in a heap. Some of the buses still ran, but they were hit-and-miss; taxis were going to the highest bidders. Near the central bus station hundreds of people lined the pavements, hoping to thumb a lift out of there. On Saadoun Street, the al-Tuhaffa coffee house had been boarded up and the Petra Hotel and the al-Khyama restaurant were bricked up, in the hope of protecting them from looting. Oddly, a butcher's shop was open and he had meat hanging on the hook.

Overhead, US surveillance aircraft sounded like motorcycles in the sky and a new rumour was doing the rounds—American paratroopers had landed in the east of the city. A handful of journalists had arrived from Amman, but American soldiers had redirected them off the usual east–west route, making them veer northwards so that, when they approached Baghdad, they drove south on the road that ran between the capital and Saddam Hussein's home town, Tikrit. This was where Saddam was expected to make a last stand, and they reported that the road was bristling with arms—in one small pocket alone, they counted 60 tanks and other heavy weapons.

I went to the Latakia Restaurant with Richard Downs from RTE—a pretext to get out of the hotel in the mid-afternoon. We heard massive bursts of smallish explosions, a bit like a chain of Chinese penny-crackers going off—but with much more menace than ever was heard at Chinese New Year. At first we thought it might be a cluster bomb, but the evenness of the rate of the explosions sounded more like a rapid-fire airborne machine-gun.

The Pyramid supermarket—where a few days earlier Burns, Anderson and myself had spent another $US1400 on groceries, because the Americans seemed to be bogging down on the road to Baghdad—was closed for the first time since the start of the conflict. A notice had been put up in the lobby of the Palestine Hotel: 'We can't do laundry because we have no electricity or gas.' And the last and the bravest of the city's shopkeepers had finally succumbed to invasion fear and looting worry, and they too were bricking up and going home.

Only one or two chai carts—ordinarily an essential part of Baghdad society, selling glasses of sweet tea, dry bread rolls and hard-boiled eggs at any time of day—were open. But the reality was this: Baghdad had finally closed for war.

DAY EIGHTEEN

Sunday, April 6

The Americans are within Greater Baghdad

Filed Sunday, April 6 at 3.07pm   Sheraton Hotel

The crowds that hang around the Information Ministry's Press Centre at the Palestine Hotel are thinning. Usually the lobby is thick with leather-jacketed spooks who, with little pretence, move in beside the different knots of journalists to eavesdrop on their conversations. By mid-morning they have evaporated.

The city streets tell different stories. For the last two weeks we have assumed them to be empty. But today they are utterly and scarily deserted. Driving the length of the usually teeming, ritzy Arasat Street, a stray cat is the only sign of life.

But further out, past the bombed-out headquarters of the General Directorate of Security, we find the tail-end of the straggling refugee convoys——a beaten up red Passat sedan with fifteen people in it; a black Chevy with mattresses and boxes of bottled water strapped to the roof; a truck with five families and their food and bedding bundled on the back.

One man tells how he was moving seventeen family members to a village on the Euphrates River, about 200km to the north. Mohammed, my driver, who is making several trips to ferry his extended family to a village in the east, says that traffic is so thick it takes him two-and-a-half hours just to clear the city. Whole city blocks are emptying as families with cars, some of whom leave behind a single male to protect their property, queue frantically at petrol stations and others waste their life savings on taxis charging fifteen times the usual rate.

There is an increasing sense that this is the end for the regime. Families are voting no confidence in Saddam's undertaking to protect them by sending their teenagers of conscription age into hiding rather than to the frontline. I am told that the desertion rate in Iraq's regular army has rendered it almost totally ineffective. But the troops of the Republican Guard and the diehards of the Fedayeen Saddam are moving into abandoned civilian homes, preparing for street-to-street battles.

For the first time Iraqi tanks and cannons are on city streets. I see a convoy of tanks crossing the Jumhuriyah Bridge and four howitzers, towed by trucks loaded with shells, wheeling into Abu Nuwas Street. My heart stops because we have often discussed whether they—the regime—would come for us. However, the convoy does a last-minute U-turn and digs in on the river bank, about 200m from the Sheraton. Oddly, it disappears two hours later.

The gun crews, with their red Republican Guard insignias, cheer and wave to reporters. Also in city streets for the first time are the Kalashnikov-armed Fedayeen Saddam, whose black uniforms stand out in the militia gatherings at street corners and around key buildings, as they ready mortars, anti-aircraft guns, heavy machine-guns and rocket-propelled grenades. The Fedayeen are the guerrillas whose ferocious fighting surprised the Americans in the south, but at this stage it is difficult to assess their numbers or likely effectiveness in the capital.

There are more than 130 foreign news teams in Baghdad and we all head off in different directions, doing 20 or 30km each. But there are no sightings of the Americans.

I find my way to Mahadia, about 10km south of the city in the al-Dura district. In the middle of the road north from al-Hillah is the burnt-out wreck of an American Abrams tank. A tennis-ball sized hole is in its side, where it was pierced by an Iraqi anti-tank missile, and a deep crater is next to it, created when US jets dropped an explosive to destroy it rather than leave it for the Iraqis.

The Iraqis treat the wreck as a war trophy, but for the next 3km the road screams defeat. It is littered with the bombed-out wreckage of Iraqi military hardware—armoured personnel carriers, troop carriers, fuel tankers, pick-ups, four-wheel drives and a dozen or more charred and up-ended field guns. Some bear the insignia of the Republican Guard. Locals say that the battle lasted about three hours, after which the column of US Third Infantry Abrams tanks and Bradley fighting vehicles continued in a wide sweep towards the airport before slowing down for another intense fight, this time with the Iraqi defences in well-heeled Yarmuk.

The Americans are indeed in greater Baghdad. Their claims of success—between 1000 and 2000 Iraqis dead—are challenged without great conviction by the locals; they have bloodied Saddam's nose and will demoralise the city's defenders. Yet, what happened out there was not street-by-street fighting and where it happened was not downtown Baghdad. If you take a close look at the map, it seems as though an armoured US column set out from the airport and got itself on a freeway loop that took it all the way back to the airport, fending off the enemy forces it encountered along the way.

In Qatar this was rather spuriously presented to the world media as an 'audacious muscle-flexing' to demonstrate to city residents that the US military was at the gates of the city.

Suddenly there is an eruption of gunfire outside our hotel. It's a convoy of police cars and Baath Party diehards patrolling the city, waving Iraqi flags and firing one-handed Kalashnikov volleys. They are rallying support for Saddam and apparently celebrating the 're-taking' of the airport.

As fighting rages on the city's outskirts, an erratic whistle heralds the flight of an unidentified missile, which explodes harmlessly with a huge crack on the river beach about 100m from this hotel. Two others explode at a distance later in the evening.

The smell in the air in Baghdad is the acrid stench of burning oil, not of an imminent Iraqi victory. We don't get the promised visit to the airport and by the end of the day it seems that, apart from the destroyed Abrams tank, all the Iraqis have captured is a US service uniform—the trousers and jacket from some battle fatigues marked with the name of a Corporal Diaz. The fate of Diaz is unknown. But Iraqi soldiers parade his uniform in the city and, as if it might somehow stave off the inevitable arrival of American troops in downtown Baghdad, they perform one of the ultimate Arab insults— they use the uniform to clean their boots.

▲

The issue of Sammi had arisen again, mainly because of Jon Lee Anderson's need to get away from the 'goat-fuck', a term my American colleagues use for a story that has too many reporters working on it. The war in Iraq was a classic in the genre.

Because he worked on a weekly, Anderson could only have his say once a week, while the rest of us could address different aspects of the goat on a daily basis. Being the consummate writer and reporter he is, he tended always to have something cooking on the side, an exclusive or intriguing aspect of the evolving story that would startle us when it finally appeared in print. He had a marvellous and original stratagem, claiming that he had a back ailment which required regular visits to doctors—this allowed him to meet people in private.

But Anderson's plans fell in a hole again this morning. Sammi, whom we had already tried to replace, threw another wobbly. By chance we now found that a minder called Kiefah, who was working with *The Sunday Times,* wanted to switch teams. We talked to him and, after consulting Mr Moysen, one of the senior minders, it was agreed that Kiefah would work with us. *The Sunday Times* went ballistic, demanded the return of Kiefah and we were stuck with . . . Sammi. Anderson had previously had a bad experience with a minder named Muslem, so now, feeling hemmed in, he marched around the room ranting: 'Muslem the slug! Sammi the snake! Kiefah is stuck with *The Sunday Times*—and I don't have a minder!'

We headed downstairs for the day. The erratic running of the hotel lifts now meant that 'popping up to the room' was something we didn't do. So we actually clambered down the stairs, hauling bullet-proof vests with us—mine weighed 14kg— and making sure we had a torch in our pockets. We had to think in terms of not going back upstairs till the day's work was done. The loss of the city power supply affected the running of the two hotels hugely, but the Palestine much more so than the Sheraton.

Others at the Sheraton were now cutting the same power deal that I had secured with the hotel's engineer. When water came through the taps, it was hot; and there was a good chance that at least one of the lifts would be in service when you needed to go up into the tower. At the Palestine things were a bit grimmer—their auxiliary power system was not as sophisticated and there was no hot water. And, in the absence of power, a great sense of gloom settled on this hotel because its tiny windows allowed very little daylight to penetrate.

There was to be an outing and, surprisingly, the men from the ministry said that we could use our own cars. Anxiety was getting to Sabah—he was worried about his family, whom he had sent out of the city, and he feared street fighting in Baghdad. So he was driving like a maniac and we had to plead with him repeatedly to slow down. Sometimes the headlong pursuit of our journalistic objectives unintentionally made us seem a little less caring than we might have been about the impact of the war on ordinary Iraqis. This was their city, their home, and Sabah was entitled to be very stressed.

Our destination this morning was al-Dura, in the south-west suburbs. Wherever we went in the city now we could always hear gunfire, particularly when we headed away from the centre. Clearly the Iraqis thought that the road we were taking was a likely American invasion route. As we approached the double-decker Great Saddam Bridge, men armed with rocket-propelled grenades were dug in every 100m. Closer to the bridge they had an assortment of heavy guns ready to pick off immediately anything that crested the rise and attempted to enter the city across the river here.

We arrived at a seared strip of highway in al-Dura to inspect what the Iraqis clearly believed would be a PR triumph for them—sitting in the middle of the road was the burnt-out hulk of a US tank. It had been disabled by Iraqi fighters and destroyed on the spot by US bombers so that it would be of no use to the Iraqi forces. This was the loop of highway that had been travelled by a column of US armour the previous day; the American commanders claimed they had killed between 1000 and 2000 Iraqi fighters. But, as we examined the tank, we were given a graphic display of the technological gap between the two opposing forces in this war.

More than 100 regular Iraqi soldiers and members of the civilian defence militia gathered around the hulk, chanting pro-Saddam slogans and firing volleys from their Kalashnikovs. But then a US fighter jet drifted lazily in from the south and its pilot proceeded to play with the crowd, much as a cat does with a mouse. The jet would circle away and then noisily dart back, and every time it did the Iraqi crowd would scatter like a cluster bomb, on a road littered with the wrappings of the MRE breakfasts that Americans soldiers had eaten as they drove by yesterday. I spoke to a nearby resident, 48-year-old Sahab Obeid, who told me: 'Yes, this is a historic moment; a climax in Arab history, especially for Iraq and for Saddam Hussein.'

The streets had been abandoned by all but the military. They were digging new foxholes and speeding around in weapons-mounted pick-up trucks that had been smeared with mud, in the hope that this would camouflage them against US attack. Big machine-guns were being dug in at street corners.

The millions who had not been able to flee the city knew that they were now at the mercy of the randomness of war. They knew this from bitter experience because just up the road from the smouldering remains of the US tank was the Bilat al-Shuhada memorial, for the hundreds of children who had died when their school was hit by an Iranian missile in the Iraq–Iran War of the 1980s. Across town was the al-Amiriyah bomb shelter, where 400 Iraqi civilians died during the 1991 Gulf War, when sloppy US intelligence led the Americans to bomb it in the mistaken belief that it was a military command post.

Everyone's greatest fear was Saddam's threat to make his last stand in Baghdad. In war, no city of this size had ever been captured without a bloody awful body count. Downtown Baghdad would become a shooting gallery; its jumble of avenues and lanes would become rows of death if the Iraqis stood and fought. The US had said it wouldn't hit civilian targets, but in the Balkan wars they hadn't meant to attack the Chinese Embassy in Belgrade; likewise with the al-Amiriyah shelter here. So, if the sabre-rattling of Tariq Aziz and Sultan Hashim meant anything, all of us in Baghdad— civilians, military and media—were inching towards a new crunch point.

Meantime our own personal dramas deepened. News reached us today that the BBC's most high-profile corres-pondent, John Simpson, had been injured in Iraqi Kurdistan. When we learnt that the injury wasn't serious, our relief was quickly followed by good-natured banter. I think it might have been me who said: 'God, he'll be insufferable now!' It was impossible not to admire this man's work, the energy that drove him and his enviable knack of being in the right place at the right time on big stories. We laughed—Anderson and I—as we recalled how we had sat in different corners of the backblocks of Afghanistan, late in 2001, and listened to Simpson's booming voice on the BBC World Service as he made his now legendary claim that 'the BBC has liberated Kabul', by dint of the fact that he had just walked into town.

But the jokes stopped as soon as we got more information. Simpson had received only the slightest of wounds, but eighteen others were dead after a US friendly-fire attack on a convoy of Kurdish fighters and US special forces south-east of the city of Erbil, in the autonomous Kurdish region in the north. Among the dead was Simpson's interpreter, Kamaran Abdurazaq Muhamed. And hours later there was more bad news for journalists—the non-combat death of 39-year-old David Bloom, a co-host of NBC's *Today* breakfast program. Bloom's gritty reporting as he moved north through Iraq with the US Third Army Infantry Division won much praise and he was so prolific—in one day he filed thirteen reports—that *The Washington Post* dubbed him America's 'unofficial tour guide to

Iraq'. Bloom died from a pulmonary embolism as he boarded a military vehicle to go on a field mission.

For the first time in almost a week John Burns today ventured beyond the lobby of the Palestine Hotel. He came visiting with our money—well, some of it. And not before time—Tyler Hicks, the *NYT* photographer, was down to his last $US12. Burns was still pursuing individual couriers and working the sat-phones to Amman, reasonably confident that he and his Amman middleman would get the runaway courier with the $US40 000 back up to the mark. In the meantime, he had $US10 000 for each of us and a promise of $US15 000 to come. As he handed me my first instalment, he couldn't resist another jab at the story of my recall from London: 'You'll have a few trips on that, mate,' he laughed.

In the midst of so much propaganda from both sides, I started a sweep on when we would first sight a US tank in downtown Baghdad. As the night closed in, the war seemed to be everywhere—there was small-arms fire in the city, and we could hear out-going multiple rocket launchers and anti-aircraft fire. The American F-18s had been overhead all day. But this was a different war to what we had been experiencing for the last couple of weeks—till now the pilots had dropped their earth-shattering bombs and gone home. But tonight, from out on the edge of the city, we could hear a ground war that might engulf us at any time.

Here's how we anticipated the American arrival in the heart of Baghdad:

Paul McGeough: Noon, Monday, April 7
Jon Lee Anderson: 4pm, Thursday, April 10
Tyler Hicks: 6am, Thursday, April 10
John Burns: 2pm, Saturday, April 12
Larry Kaplow: 6am, Monday, April 14

DAY NINETEEN

The Push into the Heart of the City

Filed Monday, April 7 at 4.29pm   **Sheraton Hotel**

At precisely 8am explosions in the four elaborate gatehouses of Saddam Hussein's presidential compound, once the nerve centre of his reeling regime, signal the start of a powerful American push into the heart of Baghdad.

Minutes later, US missile attacks on the imposing sandstone Republican Palace, nestled deep in the compound's manicured and date-palmed gardens, send huge sprays of debris and smoke into the sky. Intense mortar and machine-gun fire erupts up and down the 3km-long compound, which runs along the west bank of the Tigris River, from the green-railed Jumhuriyah Bridge to the cable-slung July 14 river crossing.

Throughout the night it seemed that advance parties of US special operations were moving around in the compound, preparing for today's assault. I watched through the night as flashes of light mingled with sporadic exchanges of gunfire and heavy, intermittent explosions.

At first, the Iraqi forces put up a strong fight against a 130-vehicle column of Abrams tanks and Bradley fighting vehicles that rumbled in from the Saddam International Airport, negotiating an Iraq minefield that had been newly laid in the early hours. F-16 fighters and 'tankbuster' aircraft flew ahead of them, bombing Iraqi tanks and positions that dared to challenge their advance into the capital.

But, as I watch from the twelfth floor of the Sheraton Hotel, directly across the river, a group of vehicles that has broken away from the US column moves in from the south, prompting many of the Iraqi defenders to flee. Under incessant American fire—machine-guns, mortars and small missiles—the Iraqis run from two directions, pouring out of the centre of the compound and from a heavily armed sand spit that intrudes into the Tigris, before bolting north along an access road that services the dozens of buildings within the fortified complex.

These are supposed to be the fearless Republican Guards but under fire there is no bravery and little dignity as many of them abandon their posts, some of them struggling to strip to their underwear as they flee, hoping that half-naked they will not be identified as members of Saddam's crack force. When they are confronted with a security fence that extends into the river they are so desperate to get away that they jump in, swimming 50m out from the bank before returning along the opposite side of the fence to pick up the access road again.

Shells erupt in the islands of bulrushes in the river and bullets skim on the water as the fighting takes on the sound and fury of a discordant, explosive symphony. Prayers are sung from mosque minarets and an ammunition dump explodes spectacularly as some of the remaining Iraqi fighters ignite pre-prepared trenches of oil—filling the air with thick black smoke that never gives them the cover they are seeking.

But those who are pinned down on the spit do not have a chance. They come under heavy bombardment from the Bradley vehicles. After an hour, US infantrymen emerge from the vehicles, crouch in their shadow and pick off the remaining guards one by one.

I can hear fighting from all directions within the dense foliage of the presidential compound. When Iraqi snipers appear on top of a clock tower to the west of the compound, it is demolished by American tank fire.

But the high tech of this war is not confined to weapons. In a satellite phone call from New York, I'm told that Fox News in the US is running live footage from the steps of the Republican Palace—just across the river from me—of an American commander waving his University of Georgia flag and declaring that he is going inside to have a shower in one of Saddam's gold-plated bathrooms.

The funereal base-drum boom of very heavy artillery and tank fire is coming from around the city and I can hear the spitting sound of outgoing surface-to-air missiles as US Warthogs and unmanned drones flying low in a hazy sky provide cover for the US fighters.

But, even as this is happening, the Iraqi Information Minister, Mohammed Saeed al-Sahhaf, bounces into the Palestine Hotel to deny it all. Agitation is starting to show behind his customary joky manner; with the noise of the fighting interrupting him, he abandons his practice of formal press briefings in a dim hotel conference room and instead addresses a knot of reporters and cameras on the hotel's roof-top terrace.

Mr Sahhaf insists that the Iraqis 'slaughtered three-quarters' of the US forces at Saddam International Airport the previous evening and that American claims that they have encircled the city are 'a part of their sickness'. Before dashing away in great haste, there is another spasm of hyperbole: 'Be assured that Baghdad is secure and the city's heroic civilian population will keep it that way. I have just come from the al-Rashid Hotel—where the mercenaries say they have us surrounded—and there are only civilian Iraqis with machine-guns in the lobbies. The Americans are beginning to commit suicide at the walls of Baghdad! They tried to come in with two armoured personnel carriers this morning, but we besieged them and killed them all.'

The morning weather has been still but suddenly a wild wind blows up, ripping maps from the wall of my room and dragging the smoke plumes through a full 360 degrees in a matter of minutes, before settling the smoke like a theatre curtain between the Sheraton and Saddam's compound. There are loud explosions around the hotel—possibly from a multiple rocket launcher I saw pulling into a side-street earlier. It seems that fighting has broken out on the east bank of the river—civilian Iraqis tell me that during the night paratroopers dropped into the area and later I hear that a palace on this side of the river is also under US attack.

I'm distracted by a fracas on the riverfront below my balcony. A TV crew, which has been filming the fighting from the east bank, is being hauled away by angry Iraqi soldiers. Officials from the Information Ministry and the soldiers play tug-of-war with a screaming cameraman and they manage to drag him back to the hotel, a much better outcome than the prison where the soldiers are likely to have dumped him.

Saddam seems to be desperate. The opening battle for Baghdad is underway and he has one of his associates on State TV and radio offering cash incentives to his defence forces in a bid to hold his army together—15 million dinars (about $A15 000) for any fighter who destroys an allied tank, armoured personnel carrier or artillery piece. Also Information Minister Sahhaf is back on the airwaves, seeming to threaten any Iraqi who does not take up arms—he says that they should all be in the streets and that those who do not shoot at the Americans would be 'cursed'.

When I finally get out into the streets, the atmosphere is bizarre. There is fighting to the east and to the west, but on the main commercial strip on Saadoun Street some stubborn traders insist on opening for business. The Information Ministry puts on a bus, to show us that all is normal in Baghdad. Yet this is not the case. The relentless shoeshine boys are still out and about, but the Princess of Legs boutique is shuttered, like most other businesses.

However, a businessman, carrying a leather briefcase with gold fittings on the corners, is walking purposefully on the pavement and a man in traditional dress emerges from a chicken shop with a bag under his arm as though this is just another day in Baghdad. A cigarette hawker—selling by the packet or individually—defiantly sits at his card table on a street corner and customers are banked up at a service station.

But the sand-bagged positions that have been manned for weeks are abandoned and the soldiers who have been loitering in side-streets are gone. Presumably they have been sent to fight or they have done a runner. The guards have gone from the Trade and Foreign ministries. Despite US claims that they had circled the Information Ministry, only Iraqi guards are on duty and Iraqi bureaucrats can be seen going to and from the bombed-out building.

The ministry denies that the Americans have surrounded the al-Rashid Hotel but, rather than allow us to see for ourselves, its minders route the press bus back to the Palestine and Sheraton hotels instead of driving an extra two or three city blocks to the al-Rashid. Traffic is light, but Iraqis are still fleeing Baghdad; some of them are reduced to getting away from the city on donkey-drawn carts.

I worry about the commander and his shower. The fighting has been going on now for seven hours and there are still massive explosions and the crackle of machine-gun exchanges coming from the palace. The Iraqis are blasting the compound with surface-to-surface missiles and mortars; the Americans are hitting it with missiles and, clearly, this is not the right time for a shower.

But I'm more worried about Sabah, one of our drivers. He would not listen, and now he's out in all of this, insisting that he must fetch lunch for us.

Filed Tuesday, April 8 at 2.24pm

Looking deep into the Baghdad blackout, I can see the tiniest point of red light. But this light casts a beam that is as enormous as it is confronting. It's on the levee wall that stops the Tigris River from flooding into what was Saddam Hussein's presidential compound. Tonight this sprawling complex is the forward base for the US thrust into Iraq and the red light marks the bivouac of a US infantry unit.

But the turbid waters of the Tigris separate more than the US soldiers and me. I'm on the east side of the city, just back in my room at the Sheraton Hotel after a dash at breakneck speed to the middle-class suburb of Mansur. With missiles still falling on the city our drivers are going berserk—fast and dangerous is the only speed they know.

Along the way I could see that most of the armed Iraqi men who were previously behind sand bags, guarding government buildings, are gone. The Foreign Ministry, the Information Ministry and the Planning Ministry stand naked to US attacks.

But there is still one guard near the inter-city bus station, and he seems to be there for the long haul. He cradles a grenade launcher as he sits by his pavement post in a brown, crushed-velvet armchair.

There are signs of the morning's progress through the city of the US armoured column that took the presidential compound—the road near the bus station is cratered, the station's perimeter wall has been blasted, and an incinerated police car lies off to the side of the road.

On Saadoun Street a man dressed in black jeans, a black open-necked shirt and a black leather vest approaches and tells me: '3000 today.' I think he is talking about the war's death toll, but it turns out that he's a currency dealer, offering 3000 Iraqi dinars to the US dollar.

We speed past al-Zawra Park—where Iraqi forces are hiding cannons and truckloads of ammunition in the shadow of the gum trees—and past another public garden, in which there are convulsions as four Iraqi surface-to-surface missiles streak westwards towards the setting sun. Then we lurch around a traffic island adorned with a jowly bust of the Caliph al-Mansur.

It was Abu Jafar al-Mansur who built the ancient round city of Baghdad in 762 AD. He had traits in common with today's leader—he had an edifice complex and he was security-paranoid. But not even he could have had the high-powered, high-tech US Third Infantry in mind when he mused, as he did centuries ago, about how the Tigris River trade route would bring the world to a city that had yet to become the setting for the tales of *The Thousand and One Nights*—Sinbad, Ali Baba and Aladdin.

I've broken away from observing the battle for the presidential compound to look at a gaping hole in the ground in Mansur. But it is the second visit of the day to this neighbourhood for the silver-haired Sabah, who is more than a driver to us. Earlier, Sabah had walked out of Mansur's al-Saah Restaurant with our take-away lunch only minutes before a huge explosion made shards of its plate-glass windows, lacerating customers and freaking the neighbourhood. But that is nothing compared to the real damage a block away. Four or five houses have literally disappeared and in their place is a crater that is maybe 30 to 40m in diameter and 15 to 20m deep.

Some of the press photographers use a chilling term they picked up from the US military in Afghanistan to describe what might have happened to a dozen or more people thought to have died in this missile attack—they have become 'pink mist'. The smouldering crater is littered with the artefacts of ordinary middle-class life in Baghdad—a crunched Passat sedan, a charred stove, the wrought-iron front gate of one of the houses, the armrest of a chair upholstered in green brocade and a broken bed-head.

The top floors of surrounding buildings are sheared off. Mud thrown by the force of the blast cakes what is left of them, and the nearby date palms are decapitated. Bulldozers and rescue crews work frantically, peeling back the rubble in the hope of finding survivors. Neighbours and relatives of the home-owners weep openly in the street, some embracing each other to ease the pain and all of them wondering why such a powerful missile was dumped on them after the US has stated that its heavy bombing campaign is over.

But this was a very deliberate, opportunistic strike. Four bunker-busters—powerful, 2000lb JDAM bombs—were dropped from a B-1B aircraft on the house, in which US intelligence 'believes' Saddam, his sons and other top officials 'might' have been meeting. Anonymous US officials are quoted as saying that they received intelligence of a high-level meeting in Mansur of senior Iraqi intelligence officials and, 'possibly', Saddam and his two sons, Qusay and Uday.

This might explain the solid sand-bagged defence positions at the end of the street and a cryptic claim attributed to a bystander in the crowd around the crater that Uday Hussein might have been in the house that was targeted. But that cuts no ice with the neighbours.

The nearest house that still stands—sort of—has stood for 43 years. Now it is on the verge of collapse and the adult children of the blood-splattered engineer Fadel al-Imam, who is 75 years old, are working to convince him that he must leave. With his back to the door of his wrecked library, where there are floor-to-ceiling shelves bulging with a lifetime's collection of engineering texts and a shattered photograph of his father—a policeman in the service of the last Western occupiers of Iraq, the British—he says: 'I reserve the right not to obey any government. This will create more enemies for the Americans. Even those who were feeling good about the arrival of the Americans will want to fight now.'

We can only guess at what will happen next.

▲

If we had stayed in the Palestine Hotel, we'd have seen little of this. The balconies of Rooms 1208 and 1209 at the Sheraton, home to Anderson and myself, were dangerously exposed—instead of a solid concrete wall, behind which we might hide, there was only a louvred rail of flimsy timber. But the view we had of the full majestic sweep of the Tigris River was uninterrupted and stunning. From here, the presidential compound was so visible and so close that we didn't need binoculars to observe it. Without leaving our suite, these two balconies and another window that was next to my desk gave us a 270-degree city vista—west to the al-Rashid Hotel and beyond, south to the oil refinery and north to the suburb of al-Aadhamiyah.

A bush telegraph ran up and down the front wall of the hotel as reporters called to photographers, and photographers yelled at each other, about what might happen next. I was yelling to Tyler Hicks and to Caroline Cole of the *Los Angeles*

Times—one above me, the other below— to keep an eye on the flagpole that still stood atop the Republican Palace. I fully expected that at any minute the smoke-soiled Iraqi tricolour would be yanked down and the Stars and Stripes would take its place.

I won the sweep. We had never agreed what should be in the kitty but, until the facts on the ground made me a winner, Anderson was confidently predicting that he'd be walking away with my waterfront apartment in Sydney. I had punted on a US arrival before midday today out of a sense that the Americans would want to keep up the pressure on the Iraqis and at the same time convey to the world a sense that, after getting bogged down on the road *to* Baghdad, there would be no messing around *in* Baghdad.

It was hard to know whether to stay upstairs in the hotel and watch the battle unfold, or to head out. We hung in for a while, but by late morning a choking mixture of fog, smoke and dust interposed itself between the compound and us. The show was over.

Sabah was forever clucking over us—wiping down our desks two or more times in an hour, often infuriating me as he moved things around me while I was trying to work. But after his close shave at the al-Saah Restaurant, it was now our turn to make sure that he was okay and we had been trying to fuss over him a bit. We headed downstairs on foot, kitted out for the day— with our body armour and helmets, torches and bottles of water.

I had been using Sabah as a barometer of local feeling for weeks and this morning he gave me one of his clearest signals yet on what he thought could happen. When we got to the hotel car park, there was no Mercedes Benz. Instead, he climbed behind the wheel of a banged-up Nissan sedan, in which he clearly expected us to join him. The Mercedes was the love of his life and Sabah was taking no risks—it had been locked away for safe-keeping against looters, and he would only bring it out of hiding after the war.

We were blocked from leaving the hotel—the minders said they had yet to decide if we would be allowed out and, if so, whether we would go by car or bus. So I went to speak to Uday al-Tai, who was wandering aimlessly in the hotel forecourt. He seemed to have a bad case of the Sahhafs. In response to my 'What's happening' opener, he told me: 'There are no US troops in Baghdad. This is a clean city. This is a media war.' But we did manage to get out twice—once by bus for one of the ministry's 'everything's okay in Baghdad' tours and later by car to visit the Mansur bomb crater.

The only phones that worked appeared to be our sat-phones, but continuous power and water had been off for almost a week now. So the operation of the McGeough–Anderson suite had become somewhat basic. The water came on at odd times, which meant that we had to be quick to get a shower. It didn't always work, so there were times when we'd go for three days or more without a shower. We already had big tanks of water set aside for toilet flushing and washing dishes and a stash of bottled drinking water. But because Mr Anderson was a bit of a fusspot—even when there was tap water he insisted on using bottled water to make his coffee—we were going through it at a great rate. It's best that we don't talk about the bed sheets—they hadn't been changed in more than a week.

Yesterday the Atlas Restaurant was being bricked up against looting—today it was deserted. The sand-bagged Trade Ministry was empty of staff and guards. A man was walking across the street in full-length blue robes—carrying a bag of sugar. People still gamely walked across the city's river bridges, possibly because there was not a bus to be seen at the bus station. Outside the station, the hucksters had abandoned their stalls. In the early evening small groups of men took to sitting in doorways and at street corners, but this seemed more like neighbourhood chat time than a meeting of Saddam's local militia. One pavement cigarette vendor clearly was staying on the street for the night—he had a paraffin lamp set up on his card-table stall.

It was hard to tell who was who anymore. Men in plain clothes walked the streets with RPGs—rocket-propelled grenades. These weapons were wrapped in plastic, as though they were not going to be used any time soon. Black-clad members of the Fedayeen Saddam mingled with other military, police and security types at street corners and under bridges, but there was a sense of uncertainty about them that elicited in me a premonition that perhaps there was not going to be a serious battle for Baghdad.

Two more journalists were dead. Thinking they were doing the right thing in not getting swept up by the urge to get to Baghdad as quickly as possible, Christian Liebig, of the German weekly magazine *Focus*, and Julio Anguita Parrado, of the Spanish daily *El Mundo*, decided to stay at a US field head-quarters, south of the capital, rather that accompany the unit with which they were embedded on a push into the city. However, they died in an Iraqi missile strike that came from the rear of the base, which also killed two soldiers and injured fifteen others of the US Army's Third Infantry Division.

It was going to be another sleepless night, so I was trying to grab an afternoon catnap when the phone rang. It was Joel Simon, the acting director of the New York-based Committee to Protect Journalists, who in his role as our professional guardian angel was emailing and sat-phoning around the Baghdad press pack to get as much information as he could about where people were and what strategies they had for emergencies. It was a subject we had debated at length, but Simon's call forced me to confront again what we had always felt could be the most difficult phase of this assignment—our personal security in the power vacuum.

Getting right out of Baghdad had ceased to be an option some time ago—there was fighting to the north and west. I had been issued with a visa to Iran just before the war started but, when I went to have it stamped in my passport in Baghdad, a security guard at the Iranian embassy informed me that the last diplomat had fled to Tehran just twenty minutes before my arrival. If we were desperate, Jon Lee and I did have a pre-arranged safe house in the suburbs, which we had stocked with food and water; we were confident that Sabah would get us there safely. We were now absolutely dependent on Sabah—he liked that!—because Mohammed, who had been going back to see his family outside Baghdad every night, didn't arrive for work this day. I had my first pang of anxiety about the younger man's safety, because last night he had promised explicitly that he would be here today.

I don't know if it was based on sound reasoning or wishful thinking, but my security summation for Joel Simon was this: 'One of the first things the Americans will do when they get into town will be to throw a security cordon around the Sheraton and Palestine hotels. We're the only significant and exposed concentration of Westerners in the city and, if the regime wants to strike, we're the obvious target. I also think that when the regime collapses it'll be quick. Saddam is all that holds it together, so when the word goes out that he's done for, collapse will be instant. If there is street fighting, our significance will be diminished as the armies go after each other, in which case it'll be safer for us to hunker in the hotel than to attempt to find our way to the safe house through streets that have become the battlefield.'

John F. Burns, however, was taking a much more practical approach to planning for the vacuum. He clearly had decided that time was nearly up for the regime—and he was determined to get his confiscated gear back before the staff of the Information

Ministry melted away. As the minders had disappeared or become distracted, Burns was moving about more—coming over to the Palestine to use our computers and phone links, materialising at midnight or later and vanishing while I was asleep. Now emboldened by today's noisy arrival of the US troops in the presidential compound, he went to the Palestine lobby and accosted Uday al-Tai, whom he had already caused to blanch with warnings that the DG might end up in Guantanamo Bay, or even before a US firing squad, should anything happen to Burns.

Now The Most Dangerous Man in Baghdad was demanding the return of the equipment that had been stolen on the night the security squad barged into his room. He was holding to his theory that his *NYT* business card was as good as a Kevlar suit. Later he explained it this way to a TV interviewer: 'I was able to send messages to officials I knew in the Iraqi government, saying to them that these facts were known to *The New York Times* and were known to the US government and that, if any harm came to me, these Information Ministry officials would be answerable for it and that I judged that the penalty they faced would be severe. And here I am.'

DAY TWENTY

Occupation at a Terrible Cost

Filed Tuesday, April 8 at 11.46am   **Sheraton Hotel**

There's a man who goes up to his roof terrace every time the fighting starts. Often he's in his underwear; he watches with his hands spread nonchalantly on the parapet wall. In a vegetable patch down by the Tigris River, a family of gardeners always crane their necks to see what is happening as the F-18s, usually in pairs, wheel in from the south. And right now, a Vespa scooter is careering erratically down Abu Nuwas Street—its rider with his face turned to the sky as an Iraqi surface-to-air missile whistles off in pursuit of an American fighter jet.

The jet is so low that I can count the missiles clipped to its wings—five. The Iraqi SAM seems to be catching up but the jet does an evasive belly-roll, clears the area, takes a new bead on the downtown high-rise that the pilot and his colleagues are attempting to demolish, and fires. It's a direct hit.

Baghdad is gripped by a fatalism about life and death. People can't run, so sometimes they don't even bother to hide as the world's most ferocious firepower is turned on a sprawling city with a defenceless civilian population of five million.

The instinctive reaction of parents is to get their children out of the city—some are even making them walk to the country. But Wael Sabah was struck in Baladiyat, on the city's far eastern flank where, as hospital staff tell it, she thought her children were out of harm's way. In fact, their descent deep into hell starts the second the pilot in a low-flying F-18 pulls the trigger, unleashing a missile that rips apart their home and their lives.

Tiny twelve-year-old Noor, her long black hair a tangle of blood and dust, is dead; in the next bed in the al-Kindi Hospital trauma ward her younger brother, Abdul Qadir, is dead; and across the way their mother is dying in a sea of her own blood. If it is possible to have a nightmare within a nightmare, the al-Kindi is it. The horror of war in Baghdad is distressing, but it is not possible to walk into this hospital without questioning the very essence of humanity as we think we know it.

The al-Kindi has too much death and too much pain. It doesn't have enough medical staff, drugs and equipment; it's running out of body bags and clean water is dependent on electricity in a city of day-long blackouts. Patients facing emergency surgery can be given only 800mg of Ibuprofen, the same as an Australian doctor might prescribe for muscle pain, and there is a critical shortage of anaesthetics. They have resorted to making their own fracture-fixing frames with lengths of steel and moulding clay.

There is not enough hygiene. The hospital wards and emergency rooms are filthy and, because the laundry has been forced to close by the blackouts, doctors are making do with torn gowns instead of towels and wipes.

Patients keep arriving in a procession of racing ambulances, muddied pick-ups and battered taxis. An army of exhausted, weepy support staff help them on to gurneys, scattering the flies that feed on the blood of the last patient. Dozens of relatives stand in the shadows of the forecourt, consoling each other about the dead and waiting for news on the half-dead. Men cry openly, uncontrollably; women wail, clutching each other for support. Anger at the West occasionally becomes violent—guns have been cocked and punches thrown at foreign reporters seen to be intruding on Iraqi grief.

A woman drops to the floor in the waiting area, screaming out her twelve-year-old son's name: 'Feran! Feran! Tell me where he is!' Another of her sons attempts to console her, assuring her that he is merely wounded after an air strike on their neighbourhood, and that he's going to be fine. But Feran was declared dead on arrival at al-Kindi.

A pick-up races in—its lights on, horn blaring. On the back, an old man sobs broken-heartedly. He cradles a small boy who seems lifeless—his eyes peer blankly from pools of his own blood; the rose-coloured stain on his white shirt is getting bigger all the time and his tongue hangs from his mouth in a foamy mess. His head is split open. There is no time to learn his story.

He is wheeled into the hospital. A medical team takes one look at him and decides he needs services they can't provide so he is wheeled back out into an ambulance that screeches off through the hospital gates, to another medical centre. The pick-up gives chase, with the man on the back still in tears. And nobody has time for the two corpses next to him, which have been locked in an intimate embrace by the movement of the vehicle.

Al-Kindi's twelve surgical theatres operate around the clock. A haggard and tearful Dr Tarib al-Saadi stands outside the hospital, trying to have a break, hoping to compose himself as the wind whips at his soiled white coat. 'I have done twelve operations today—crushings, fractures and amputations. You see that these Americans are hitting civilians—their homes, their streets, their cars and even those who walk about. They hit anyone. One of the ambulance drivers says they have struck al-Yarmuk Hospital, so now we worry about a strike here.'

Lips quivering and his cheeks stained by his own tears, he goes on: 'Everyone is anxious and angry. Maybe I'm the only calm one here.' He glances at a disconsolate woman in black, slumped against a wall. He makes me look at her beautiful face, into her tragic eyes, and he says: 'She was driving in the car with her 23-year-old son. They put a bullet in his head because he failed to stop at an American checkpoint.'

The woman cuts in: 'He was innocent. We were on our way home. Why do the Americans do this? God forgive them!' Dr Saadi asks: 'How can anyone who comes to liberate a country do this—lacerate and destroy our people? Do they really think that somehow, after a few days, this woman will love them?'

The numbers have been rising steadily at al-Kindi—today it received more than 200 injuries and 35 corpses. Six other hospitals serving the city report similar figures and now they are having the overflow from Iraq's hard-pressed military hospitals foisted on them.

Nothing prepares a visitor for the scene at the hospital morgue. I've been into several in Iraq now and I think I know what to expect—the bodies are always mangled, frequently burnt beyond recognition, but usually treated with as much dignity as each having its own cold metal tray allows.

But when the double refrigeration doors are opened in one of several buildings out the back at al-Kindi, there is just a pile on the floor. Maybe 20 or 25 corpses—it is hard to figure out. Some of the faces are scorched black. Some have their clothes ripped off, their intestines hanging out. Limbs protrude from the pile, lying across other corpses, and it is impossible to tell who is who in this Dalian drama.

The traffic to and from the morgue is pitiable. Hospital orderlies wheel the dead in and families bring makeshift coffins to take the dead out. A colleague tells me that when a group of foreign cameramen moved in to film the scene, the four men charged with moving the bodies in and out of the morgue reacted badly, angrily chasing them away. 'Why are you taking photos? For Bush?' one of them yelled, waving his arms. 'Tell him to go to hell.'

Filed Tuesday, April 8 at 1.02pm   **Sheraton Hotel**

American forces today mounted two new thrusts into the heart of Baghdad, attempting to capture one of the ten bridges that span the Tigris River at the same time as they closed in on a huge Iraqi military complex in the south-east.

Three US tanks nosed out of the American-controlled presidential compound early this morning, taking up strike positions at the western end of the ten-span Jumhuriyah Bridge. A spectacular battle unfolded as the Americans struck at Iraqi-held positions. They attacked from the air and the ground, engulfing buildings and troop positions in fireballs and the deadly spray of rapid-fire munitions.

Huge explosions reverberated across the city. Shell fire from two US tanks at first, and then a third, raked a twelve-storey government office tower which the Iraqi resistance had been using as a shooting platform. The battle on the bridge may well be a foretaste of the damage that could ultimately be inflicted on the fabric of Baghdad if the Iraqis can muster a defence force and strategy.

At dawn, missile, tank and small-arms exchanges broke out at the northern end of the presidential compound, which the Americans have controlled since they pushed deep into the heart of Baghdad on Monday. This corner of the compound was subjected to repeated and intense bombing in the weeks before the US arrival in the capital.

Soon after 8am, low-flying propeller-driven Warthogs swooped in almost at stall speed, firing off high-powered rapid-fire machine-guns on Iraqi forces still holding out in the area. To the accompaniment of wild, crackling explosions, they climbed out of their attack paths, discharging fireworks-like decoys to shield them from Iraqi surface-to-air-missiles as they went. After one of half-a-dozen passes, windows popped on all twelve storeys of the adjacent Planning Ministry as showers of white fire exploded against its red-brick, southern façade.

At mid-morning the Americans opened a second front, launching multiple missile attacks on the al-Rashid military complex about 15km from the city centre. Two US helicopters were circling at low altitude as great plumes of smoke and debris leapt to the sky. This huge military complex had been the first target in the war when President George W. Bush ordered a 'decapitation' strike. Today's renewed assault on the complex is thought to be intended to clear the way for a US column moving in from the south-east. Heavy exchanges of machine-gun fire could be heard from the complex, which was lost in a cloud of smoke and dust.

Shortly after 9am today a huge fireball engulfed the neo-classical headquarters of Saddam's Baath Party, a building that has been bombed and reconstructed three times since the Gulf War, and throughout the morning F-18 fighters bombed Iraqi positions on the west bank of the Tigris.

▲

One of the very few Sheraton housekeeping staff who had stayed on duty throughout the war was James, a Sudanese migrant built like a whippet. Today, when he came to wrestle with the mess in our rooms, he said he had something to show us and he took Anderson and myself to an adjacent room that had good views to the south-east. For us it was a new front—the Americans were making mayhem at what we quickly established was the al-Rashid military complex, about 6km away.

We were aware of a huge US column pushing up from that quarter and obviously the complex would make an excellent staging post. But, for now, Apache helicopter gun ships were circling above and Iraqi units still on the ground were taking a belting. Back in the city, three tanks had broken from the north-east corner of the presidential compound and they were jockeying for position on the western end of the Jumhuriyah Bridge, teasing and testing Iraqi units at the eastern end of the crossing. Some of the Iraqis were buried in the greenery close to the river bank; others seemed to be on different floors of a nearby high-rise, the offices of the Board of Youth and Sport.

We were all being bombarded with interview requests—Burns and Anderson had become regular talking heads for US TV and radio; I was holding my end up in Australia and Ireland. This morning I did a pre-recorded interview for ABC Radio's *PM* program and was writing for the next day's *SMH* when Jenny Brockie of SBS TV rang—would I do a live cross from the APTN uplink disk on the roof terrace at the Palestine Hotel at 1.30pm Baghdad time? She knew the rules: 'Yes, if I can make it,' I told her. Suddenly a producer from *PM* was back on the line—'Could we reschedule the interview because of the attack on the Palestine Hotel?' I was flummoxed—the what?

The sat-phone handset was cordless so, with the producer still on the line, I went into the twelfth-floor lobby, where the windows gave a clear view across the street to the Palestine. It looked fine, no problems, I told her; and we quickly agreed that there was no need to rework the interview.

I finished writing and tramped down twelve flights of stairs by the light of a torch, to emerge into the sunlight and utter chaos of the forecourt of the Palestine Hotel. In the time since I had spoken to *PM,* half the people who had been in the Palestine had evacuated—many in body armour and helmets; most of them distressed. Now they were milling around, trying to make sense of what was happening.

Uday al-Tai, the media enforcer, was there and minutes earlier he had been seen tearfully embracing one of his colleagues. When I asked what was happening, he exploded: 'They are targeting the journalists—al-Jazeera! Abu Dhabi! Now this!'

'This', I quickly learnt, was a missile strike. It had slammed into the upper north-east corner of the hotel, wounding five reporters—two of them seriously. Seconds later there was a commotion and al-Tai was scuffling with an Argentinean journalist—they had to be dragged apart. In interviews with colleagues, the Argentinean, Gustavo Sierra, was amplifying his belief that it was an Iraqi strike on the Palestine: 'We were on the sixteenth floor! It was a rocket from the north—I don't believe it was from a US plane. They know we are here—why would they hit us? That's a stupid idea!' he shouted.

Not quite. Within hours the Pentagon would admit that it was a US missile—fired at the Palestine by one of the tanks on the Jumhuriyah Bridge. The al-Jazeera attack had happened shortly before 7am. Tareq Ayyoub, a 34-year-old reporter for al-Jazeera, was standing on the roof of a riverfront villa that was the network's Baghdad bureau when a US missile struck the building, killing him instantly. In Amman, one of our colleagues reported the horror that Ayyoub's wife had endured this morning—she had watched her husband report live on the 5am news; she heard that the bureau had been bombed on the 6am news; she saw the announcement of her husband's death on the 8am news.

Ayyoub had just done me a great favour, which Burns told me about when he came to our room tonight to shove another wad of cash into our hands—Ayyoub had been the courier who had brought one of our parcels of money across the desert from Amman. Last night Burns saw him—he had come by Burns' room to drop off the cash. And Anderson saw him today—his body was on top of the pile of corpses in the over-flowing morgue at al-Kindi Hospital. It was useless to him now, but he was still wearing his al-Jazeera bullet-proof vest.

Shortly after the blast at al-Jazeera, a US tank shell struck a nearby villa that was occupied by al-Jazeera's Arab-language competitor, Abu Dhabi TV. There were no serious injuries, but for many hours afterwards the network was pleading for a break in the fighting so that it could evacuate 30 people who were pinned down in the building. Then, a minute before noon, a tank shell crashed into the Palestine Hotel—seriously wounding Reuters cameraman Taras Protsyuk, 35, who was on a fifteenth-floor balcony, and Spanish Telecinco cameraman José Couso, 37, who was one floor below him. Three of Protsyuk's Reuters colleagues were wounded as well—though less seriously.

Burns was in a room four floors below and about 35m up the corridor from the Ukrainian Protsyuk when the shell hit the hotel. He said the whole building shuddered as if an earthquake had struck. Ann Garrels of National Public Radio was four floors below the strike point, but she thought that the shaking of the hotel was just another bomb or missile strike somewhere out in the city. The blast caused mayhem in the hotel. Reporters ran from the building as others used blood-soaked sheets and mattresses to get the injured down to ground level and then to hospital. There was much distress and a lot of yelling and screaming.

Jon Lee Anderson was in the parking area not long after-wards, when a car pulled in. His friend, the French photographer Jerome Delay, alighted in tears—he had rushed Protsyuk to al-Kindi Hospital, but the cameraman had died soon after they got there. I was told that the Spaniard, Couso's, surgery was delayed while a sat-phone was brought to the hospital for his wife to call from London to give the doctors formal approval to amputate his leg. The operation took three hours, but he died soon after. That night someone showed Patrick Graham, a reporter for the *National Post* in Canada, a picture of the wounded Couso being bundled into a car to be dashed to hospital. What struck Graham most was the role reversal: 'Couso was looking at the camera as if he knew exactly what was happening—he had probably done it himself so many times.'

Ross Benson, a charming if dog-eared Fleet Street dandy, was clever at sending up himself and our profession. When we had Turkish coffee in the Palestine Hotel coffee shop one afternoon, I had asked if he'd written for the day, to which he replied: 'No— I have yet to find my cliché!' But today he was filled with anger. 'It was unnecessary, incompetent and tragic, and the anger here is profound. Dealing with this regime of butchers is hard enough without the added stress of having to worry about what your own side is doing,' he wrote in London's *Daily Mail*.

Robert Fisk of *The Independent* described it as murder. The *National Post*'s Patrick Graham felt it was unimaginable that the US would deliberately shoot at the media hotel. British TV correspondent David Chater was convinced it was deliberate: 'I never heard a single [Iraqi] shot . . . It was aimed directly at this hotel, directly at journalists. It seemed to be a very accurate shot.' Swiss TV reporter Ulrich Tilgner was pretty blunt too: 'In three weeks I have not heard a single shot fired from the hotel and I have not seen a single armed person enter.'

We were stunned. Our anxiety had always been about the Iraqis—would they take us hostage? Would they bait the Americans by drawing their fire to the hotels in the hope of creating a mess for Washington? There was no security at either of the media hotels, so we were sitting ducks if individual Iraqis or elements of the regime wanted to embark on revenge killings against vulnerable Western targets. But the tone of the Pentagon response today was that it didn't feel any particular responsibility for our welfare and that, in its view, the hotels in which we stayed were legitimate targets if the Americans thought someone was shooting at them from there. General Buford Blount, commander of the US Third Infantry Division, which was now based at the Baghdad airport, told reporters: 'The tank was receiving fire from the hotel, RPG [rocket-propelled grenades] and small-arms, and it engaged with one tank round. The firing stopped.'

But that was not the case and Herve de Ploeg, a cameraman with France 3 TV, was able to prove it. He had been filming the tanks on the bridge from the hotel for some time—for a while there is no action in his footage, but then the turret on one of the tanks turns and the barrel is aimed directly at the hotel. In the few minutes before the tank shoots at the hotel, no gunfire that might have emanated from the hotel can be heard. De Ploeg's video then shows a bright golden-orange flame coming from the tank and, about two seconds later, the image jumps erratically as the impact of the shell hitting the hotel jolts the Frenchman's camera.

Al-Sahhaf arrived at the Palestine Hotel soon after the attack. He was ferried there in a dusty Nissan dual-cab pick-up—not the usual spit-and-polished ministerial Mercedes Benz, even though this turned out to be his last appearance before the foreign press. Deviating only slightly from his usual credo, he was prepared to admit that the Americans had occupied one of the presidential palaces. But he rallied quickly: 'We'll burn them in their tanks. We'll destroy them and they will be forced to surrender.' It occurred to me that, during his drive to the hotel this morning, al-Sahhaf must have made a conscious decision to keep talking nonsense and at some point in that journey he must have acknowledged to himself that we could see his madness, because he knew the US tanks were on the bridge and that we could hear them and, as of this morning's attack, feel them.

By late afternoon the tanks had failed to dislodge the Iraqi fighters in the Board of Youth and Sport building. But pretty soon F-18 fighter jets arced in through the setting sun, rolling like puppies as they shot missiles into the building. As they lined up, the Iraqis fired SAMs at them from only 400m south of the Sheraton. Once these missiles had locked on, the jets would roll, spraying brilliant magnesium flares that bamboozled the SAMs and sent them limping off to explode uselessly down the river.

The jets would then line up for another run. As they crossed the river I could see their missiles part company from the planes—one of them racing ahead to hammer into a corner of the Youth and Sport building; another making a huge gouge in the south face of the building as the jets belly-rolled again and tore on up the Tigris valley and away from Baghdad. Clearly the Americans were attempting to demolish the building; with each missile strike a flock of long-necked water fowl would flap and shriek in protest from the bulrushes on the river.

It was mesmerising. People hung from just about every balcony on the front of the Sheraton. One young Iraqi was particularly ecstatic and, at a spectacular moment when the building was enveloped in a fireball, he turned to us from his perch two balconies away, punching the air, giving a vigorous thumbs-up and yelling: 'Yes! Yes!'

Burns was on our balcony and called out to him: 'So, you are happy?' But clearly we were still in Saddam's Iraq and unguarded displays of such feelings were dangerous—life-threatening in fact. The young man then pulled himself together, affected an air of indifference and snapped back: 'No. Fucking Americans!'

I spent considerable time at the al-Kindi Hospital as dozens of dead and wounded Iraqis were being brought in. The war in Iraq was becoming more and more of a wild American shoot-out.

As I interviewed a patient, I heard a familiar voice and suddenly John F. Burns materialised beside me. The fact that he had sprung himself from hotel arrest was proof indeed of the collapse of the Information bureaucracy, which had been a cornerstone of the old regime.

It had been a bad day for Iraqi civilians. As evening took hold, a strange silence settled on Baghdad. It was impossible to tell if the armies were spent or merely drawing breath. It had been a bad day for journalists too. I get very uncomfortable when journalists become the story, but in this war reporters were dying—proportionately—at a rate that was about ten times greater than the US and British military deaths.

At a vigil on a lawn between the hotels tonight, people were upset when a man rose to remind them that the city's hospitals were overflowing with Iraqis who were dead and dying. Should journalists commemorate their dead? Maybe they should do it in private. Burns tackled the issue in print—delicately: 'The journalists at the Palestine organised a twenty-minute candlelit vigil after dark, and debated among themselves whether there was justification in grieving for three dead journalists in a city where dozens of Iraqi civilians—people who mostly had no choice about being in Baghdad, unlike the journalists, all of whom were volunteers for the wartime assignment—had been killed on the same day.'

After the vigil, reporters talked in small groups before drifting back to their rooms up in the towers of the two hotels. Later, close to midnight, Uday al-Tai embarked on what would be his last round of calls on the foreign networks. But he was offering neither sympathy nor understanding. Al-Tai wanted money. He demanded that each network make immediate cash payment of their outstanding Press Centre fees. He issued no receipts and he collected an estimated $US200 000. Al-Tai then disappeared into the Baghdad night.

DAY TWENTY-ONE

The End of Saddam's Regime

Filed Wednesday, April 9 at 1pm   **Sheraton Hotel**

Jubilation and wholesale looting in Baghdad today signalled the end of the regime of Saddam Hussein as thousands of US troops met little or no resistance on their way into the heart of the city.

There were wild scenes as residents—some in tears, others singing and dancing—crowded onto city freeways, showering the Americans who rode into town atop their tanks with flowers and the classic Iraqi greeting for foreigners: 'Welcome! Welcome in Baghdad.'

'Today Baghdad is like Berlin in 1945,' an egg seller told me. There was no sign of any arm of government. The Information Ministry, which has attempted to keep the foreign press on a tight rein, was abandoned and none of the agencies that might maintain law and order was on the streets. But while the people clearly felt that they had shaken off the Saddam yoke, US officers said there was still some resistance—small and disorganised, but fierce.

There was no word on the fate of Saddam or his sons, Uday or Qusay, all of whom were targeted by US planes that dropped four 2000lb bombs on a residential area in Baghdad yesterday. But, presuming Saddam's era had ended, a man yelled at foreign reporters: 'People, if you only knew what this man did to Iraq. He killed our youth, he killed millions.'

The looting was on such a scale that it caused traffic jams in the eastern suburbs as huge crowds ripped all that they could from government buildings—air-conditioning units, ceiling fans, hat stands and anything else they could carry. They brought trucks and packed their cars so high that much of the loot fell off as they drove away. With great high spirits they hijacked police cars and motorcycles, full-length curtains and sports trophies. They used wheeled office chairs to push their loot away into the suburbs while some guarded their booty on street corners, waiting for family vehicles to return to collect it. One of them said: 'This is our peace dividend.'

When they had done with the high-rise Transport Ministry and the headquarters of the Iraqi Olympic Committee, a part of Uday Hussein's personal fiefdom, they torched the buildings. And they stole dozens of Uday's thoroughbred horses from a nearby stables complex. On Palestine Street, a favourite regime venue for rallies and shows of military and Baath Party support, Iraqis looted a Trade Ministry warehouse, coming out with air conditioners, ceiling fans, refrigerators and TV sets.

Posters of Saddam were shredded, statues pushed over and many people cheered 'Bush! Bush!' and 'America! America!' as others tore up 250-dinar notes that bear the face of Saddam. Not far away a bare-chested young man danced in the middle of an intersection, madly swirling his shirt over his head.

And they relished saying the things that a few days ago would have had them tortured or imprisoned. They spat at portraits of the dictator and they denounced him with great bitterness. Murtha Odari, a 27-year-old army deserter, said: 'He is a criminal—he killed so many of our people. He made us fight against Iran; he invaded Kuwait and now he makes us fight the world. Now we are so happy.' Asked why he had joined in the Saddam cheer squads over the years, he said: 'We were scared. We did not have a choice.'

Standing outside the blazing Olympic headquarters, 46-year-old Abu Mantazar condemned the looting. While he celebrated the arrival of the Americans, he had a warning for them. 'Before it was so bad for us—so this makes us happy. We look forward to having a new government and an end to this mess,' he said. 'Look, the US is welcome here—but not for long. Just for a while—to help the next Iraqi government get going. And after that they have no right to stay here; and while they are here they must see us as human beings and not as barrels of oil.'

Streets in the centre of the city were virtually deserted. Small numbers of men in civilian clothing carried Kalashnikovs and local people said that a group of militias still stationed at the eastern end of the Sinak Bridge were diehard Syrian volunteers.

US infantry units began pushing in from the east and the marines from the west last night, planning to link up on Tahrir Square in the centre. They claimed to have secured all routes into the capital as the last resistance they faced was put down in the early hours of today. As his men set up checkpoints at an intersection about 3km from the city, Marine Lieutenant Geoff Orazem told me: 'I love being in Baghdad.' But one of his men was a bit confused. He asked: 'Hey man, what city is this?'

Iraqi tanks and armoured personnel carriers were abandoned across the suburbs with articles of military clothing scattered around them—apparently those of fighters who had changed into civilian clothing for their getaway.

In the inner city, a white-haired man took a poster of Saddam and beat it with his shoe—a traditional insult. Others gathered to spit on the portrait or to kick the image of the face of Saddam. 'Come see, this is freedom. This is the criminal, this is the infidel,' the man said. 'This is the destiny of every traitor. He killed millions of us.'

But an old man who has spent the last few weeks quietly telling me how much he longed for this day, said simply: 'Now we dance.'

▲

We were doing high-fives on a traffic island in the east of the city, halfway between Saddam City and downtown Baghdad. We knew from the eerie silence in the early morning that something was different. This was the silence of the vacuum. How long would it last? Which way should we go? Where were the marines, the Republican Guards and the Fedayeen Saddam? All the exit routes we had planned were closed. We jumped into the first car heading out from the hotel—it was a Korean photographer's—and we headed east to this island where we found the marines.

All the suffocating anxiety of the last month evaporated in an instant. We knew we were safe, not because we had gone from the Iraqis to the Americans, but just because it was over. The atmosphere was festive as cheering looters went past with their booty. We—Burns, Anderson and myself—had an awkward, blokey embrace; we laughed and choked on emotion at the same time. We had come out the other side. We'd get Burns' four-leaf cluster for the sheer madness of having wanted to be here in the first place; but, more importantly, for somehow having survived it on our own terms—both personal and professional.

Words will never describe the relief. We chased around after the looters before I hitched a ride back to the city to file a story. The others went off in different directions, with Burns at one stage getting ahead of the US advance. When he came across a well-armed, menacing group of young men, he opted for the language of the morning. 'Bush good?' he asked. But they snarled back: 'Bush down shoes! America down shoes!' As they spat on the ground, the message was clear—Bush and the US were good enough only for the soles of their shoes, a terrible insult in this part of the world. Burns beat a hasty retreat.

We knew that the Americans were creating concentric security circles as they approached the centre and I knew they'd arrived at the centre when a massive explosion threw the pictures off the wall in my room at the Sheraton. I rushed to the balcony to see a cloud of smoke drifting away from one of maybe 50 US tanks and other fighting vehicles that were encircling the two press hotels. But they weren't just protecting us—they were moving in, taking the space vacated by the Information Ministry. Their first task in both hotels was a door-by-door security sweep—all with guns at the ready and accompanied by much yelling in American accents.

Washington's glee was obvious. But a Pentagon spin-doctor might have been disappointed with the turn-out in the streets of Baghdad when the marines came to town. At first glance the numbers looked good; but if you put the looters to one side, things became a little dicey. And if you took the foreign press and the marines out of the crowd in Firdos Square as the marines stage-managed the demolition of a towering bronze of Saddam Hussein, then the numbers were disappointing for an army that came here as liberators. For such a momentous occasion in Iraqi history, perhaps only 500 Iraqis watched. Most Iraqis were so consumed with questions and worries about the future that they didn't even stop to savour the moment, let alone the day. And, in the face of so many imponderables, many simply shrugged their shoulders.

I went back out into the street, spending an hour or two watching Saddam get snapped off at the knees. Later Anderson and I attempted to get to the Russian Embassy, to check out a British report that Saddam had taken refuge at the embassy, but we simply couldn't get there. As we headed back down Saadoun Street towards the hotel, we saw a car coming towards us with sparks flying in its wake. At the end of a length of cable the car was towing the bronze head of Saddam, which had been hacked from the statue that the marines had brought down. We chased it for a while with the mad idea of buying the head of Saddam for $US500, but we gave it away after we were forced to stop at a US military checkpoint, and we returned to the hotel to do some work.

We had not given it much thought up to now, but suddenly the realisation dawned upon us that a new army was marching on Baghdad—the hundreds of reporters who had been embedded with the US military, and the hundreds more who had attempted to follow the Americans from the north and the south, and yet hundreds more who had been camped in Amman, waiting for the first opportunity to get into Iraq.

Anderson and I were in the wonderful position of still having our spare rooms—830 and 905 at the Palestine. Burns snaffled 905 from us to tide over two of his colleagues who were sleeping in a Humvee and I loaned 830 to Geoff Thompson from the ABC. Meanwhile Sabah was downstairs putting money on the manager's desk to nail a couple of rooms for the Nine Network's Paul Barry and his cameraman who had phoned, sat-phone to sat-phone, from 30km out to ask for help. Sabah got them the rooms, and later I sent them off to see Firas for help with a local fixer.

DAY TWENTY-TWO

Thursday, April 10

A Tyrant's Statue Falls

Filed Thursday, April 10 at 12.42pm   **Sheraton Hotel**

After the looting came the soul-searching. Jubilant Iraqis had not even beheaded the statue of Saddam Hussein in Firdos Square before they started asking questions. Every Iraqi who spoke to me had a warning or a question for Washington that revealed a deep distrust of America's intentions.

It was the restive Shia of Saddam City—a nice Saddam touch to give his name to the area into which he herded so many victims of his oppression—who first sensed that power had shifted overnight on Tuesday. Always champing for a go at Saddam, this cinder-block slum erupted into euphoric and, at times, violent looting. Shops and stores were quickly stripped bare and torched; then the mob piled into vehicles and went in search of richer pickings.

They found them. But they also found Lieutenant Geoff Orazem of the First Marines, a shiny-faced Californian, whose column of tanks and fighting vehicles took much of the heat out of the looters—for a while. By the time I got to the intersection where he was establishing a security cordon, about 4km from the city centre, a remarkable procession was heading back to Saddam City—a boy carrying trophies from the Sports Ministry; men trying to herd a dozen of Uday Hussein's thoroughbred horses to their home; six men in single file, each with two ceiling fans from the Transport Ministry over their shoulders; and a man whose arms were filled with soccer balls as he kicked three more along the road in front of him. They went through the buildings like a plague of locusts. As fire engulfed the Transport Ministry and the nearby Iraqi Olympic Committee headquarters, where Uday ran his own private torture and prison operation, people danced in the streets.

Every street and highway is crowded with looters taking their haul away—on trucks, in an ambulance, in cars and taxis, on foot, or on wheeled office chairs which they have roped together as makeshift trolleys. They pause in their pilfering to shower the Americans with flowers and they chant praise for George W. Bush—just as they used to do for Saddam. They tear down the ubiquitous posters of their deposed leader and they shred his money bills.

The raw energy and spirit is something I have not seen in more than a decade of assignments in Iraq. It adds a high-spirited madness to the looting which, beyond Saddam City, is mostly confined to what the Pentagon would describe as 'regime targets'—ministries and other arms of the government.

There are exceptions. When I asked who owned a palatial riverfront home in the city, its looters looked at me cheerfully and said: 'Not us.' A man walked past with a pile of full-length drapes from some senior bureaucrat's office.

Lieutenant Orazem's men were still trying to read the Iraqis. Some of his soldiers were hunched and others prone, but all had their weapons cocked and pointed into the crowds. Yesterday they shot—and wounded—a man who didn't obey their orders.

Iraqis watched with an amazement they dared not express before yesterday's tumultuous collapse of the regime as the dictator's aura of power faded to something akin to that of a petty thief on the run. It was as though they had awakened from a long troubling sleep.

Faced with the threat of prison, torture and death, Iraqis had come to accept what the regime said. They had learnt that it was best to ignore Saddam's excesses and to accept his rhetoric as an article of faith. It was dangerous for people to acknowledge objective truth, so they had embraced regime truth.

On Tuesday I walked Saadoun Street. Normally it is a teeming, colourful commercial strip but now it was deserted, with the exception of a man who wandered along with a small teapot in one hand and a box of sugar and a tea-strainer in the other. When I had asked him what he thought about the imminent arrival of the marines, he had answered in pure Sahhafese: 'They are not in Baghdad; they will be defeated.' Despite the fact that he could see with his own eyes the ugly rosette where a US tank shell had hammered into the Palestine Hotel, killing two journalists, he repeated: 'There are no Americans in Baghdad.' As we'd walked on, even Kiefah, my rotund government minder, was bemused: 'He has read the speeches so well!'

So when the regime had said that Abu Ghraib was merely a prison, not a centre of brutal torture where many of them had a friend or a relative, they had readily suspended their critical faculties and gone along with it. When the regime had said that Iran had gassed the people of Halabja in 1988, they'd nodded in agreement.

Just as our drivers were having difficulty coping with such dramatic change—the Information Ministry press office at the

Palestine Hotel had been abandoned but we had to explain in great detail to Sabah that he no longer required the spooks' permission to take us places—so too were people like 27-year-old Raad. A gaunt-faced, hungry-looking student, he still thought it too dangerous to give me his full name as he became the first of many to reveal his family's personal pain at the hands of Saddam. Cryptically, he said: 'My brother was taken by Saddam's security people—it caused us great pain and we had to pay many bribes to save him.'

We decided to cross to the west side of the city, to visit some of Saddam's outrageous palaces. But as we went through Tahrir Square, where Saddam hanged the Jewish spies in 1968, the approach to the Jumhuriyah Bridge over the Tigris was so littered with rubble from American bombing that it was impassable.

Parts of the centre of the city were still deserted. As we went north to cross the Sinak Bridge, a group of fighters from the Fedayeen Saddam—Syrian volunteers, according to the locals—shooed us away as they lay in wait for the Americans to cross the bridge. The body of a dead fighter lay on the access ramp to the bridge.

It was time to head for the wilting gardens and dry fountains of Firdos Square, where it became difficult to tell who was helping whom in efforts to topple the 6m-tall Saddam statue—the US military or the locals. The rope that was first produced was American. So were the chains and, when push came to shove, so was the fighting vehicle that was then trying to pull Saddam flat on his face.

In the crowd I found Moyiad Jumaa, a mature-aged student in traditional grey robes. Like most people in Baghdad he was intoxicated by the day's developments. However, the message he said he wanted to send to the global anti-war movement seemed better directed to the White House. He said:

'We know that the US has a bad policy on Iraq—we know this better than most. But these people must understand that for 30 years we have not been allowed to talk or even to breathe freely. If the devil himself came to free us, we'd say "yes". We don't know what the US will do, so why jump to conclusions; wait and see—and if it is bad we have a long history of revolution. If they end up treating us as Saddam did, we will revolt again.'

As we were talking, a crowd of young men had hoisted themselves up onto Saddam's huge pedestal while others took turns, attempting to smash the statue with a heavy sledge-hammer. The road around the square was filled with US military machines, some of them grinding their tracks on the bitumen. A young student wanted to practise his English but he was remarkably ambivalent when I asked if he felt good or bad about the day's events. 'Between . . .' was all he said.

There were cries of '*Allahu akbar*'—God is great—and one of the ring-leaders, a huge-shouldered man who earlier had swung the sledgehammer, made a brief speech: 'Saddam will fall down; this is the destiny of dictators. Saddam would have been over us for 100 years if the US had not come to free us; he is a cancer in the Arab world.'

A greying gentleman by the name of Salim Jaffar declared himself happy with the arrival of the US marines and infantry. He said: 'I now feel very free; I know that I'll be able to sleep now. Saddam Hussein assassinated my brother in 1977—he was hanged in prison for insulting the president. It was August 5, 1977 and since then my family has been punished by the security services. Saddam's Iraq was a dictatorship of torture, war and terror. So today is the first day I can speak.'

Jaffar, who is on the Baghdad staff of the World Food Program, then used his new-found freedom of speech to address the White House. Looking around at the beaming faces in the crowd, he said: 'Everyone is happy for the time being.

But what will happen about our new government and its policies? This is the start of a long and difficult period. It will be a disaster if the new government is based on religious percentages of the population—the Shia want to control everything and they know only about religion.'

This particular statue of Saddam wore a three-button suit, with a hankie stuffed in the breast pocket. He had an arm outstretched and his serious gaze was fixed down the length of Saadoun Street. People were now throwing stones and their shoes at the statue, but suddenly there was movement—one of the US Bradley fighting vehicles was crunching through the gardens and over the marble forecourt towards the imposing figure.

And now there was a new, much more exciting distraction. As the locals mounted the fighting machine to be part of the demolition, they discovered the marines' supply of MREs— meals ready-to-eat. Suddenly there was a burst of very serious looting—they went mad, throwing packages to friends in the crowd as dozens more clambered up to rip their liberators off with much more enthusiasm than anyone was directing towards up-ending the statue.

It was about then that this American helping hand for the Iraqis became a public relations disaster. An American flag was produced and, as one of the marines helped to put the noose around Saddam's statuesque neck, he wrapped the head in the Stars and Stripes. The US flag didn't get as big a cheer as it might have had and a colleague informed me of the stunned reaction of an ophthalmologist in the crowd who said: 'I thought this was liberation—not occupation.'

Suddenly it became an international incident. In the global village, this whole drawn-out exercise was being telecast live by CNN, which immediately expanded the coverage to report that those watching at the Pentagon were appalled by what they were seeing. I don't know if the Pentagon called the fighting vehicle direct, but suddenly a ten-year-old Iraqi flag was produced—we know this because it didn't bear the Saddam-written inscription *'Allahu akbar'*, which the statue's inspiration added to the flag after the 1991 Gulf War. The US flag disappeared into a soldier's pocket.

Later a cigar-chomping marine declared: 'That felt really good.' But he insisted that the Iraqi instigators of the escapade had requested the use of the rope, then the chains and, finally, the engine power.

Abrahim Dalami, a 38-year-old driver wearing a close-fitting Lycra outfit, was visibly shocked: 'We want this to happen; but we don't want the American flag. We want freedom—not occupation.' His family too had suffered at the hands of the regime—his two brothers had been jailed and, when he refused to reveal the whereabouts of one of the brothers, he was hauled in and made to stand in water through which an electric current was run.

His story is interrupted by the final toppling of Saddam. As the fighting vehicle applied tension to the chains around Saddam's neck, the statue snapped off at the knees and hung for a while before smashing to the ground. Mohammed Abass, who described himself as a wealthy businessman, emerged from the crowd with his worries: 'An end to the war is good. But what happens now? Is the US a genuine friend of Iraq or does it just want our oil? Anyone coming to Iraq is better than Saddam—he finished off our money and he killed four million Iraqis. But what does the US want?'

Across the street a bearded former Iraqi Airways pilot, Khalid Ali, is asking the same question: 'What is to happen to us now? Will the Americans stay? Will we get good government or just more of what we had?' Ali—whose bitterness for Saddam is due to the loss for 22 years of his father, who was captured by the Iranians during the Iraq–Iran war and held for all those years in a Tehran prison—sounded a little daunted about the future: 'We have a long way to go and none of it is going to be easy.'

I rounded out the day over dinner with Kiefah, our former Information Ministry minder, whose courage in the face of the regime's policy of telling us as little as possible so impressed us that we have retained him as a translator. Kiefah is another who didn't even stop to savour the day.

Over a meal of braised lamb and chicken shawarma, he revealed his own personal contest with Saddam Hussein—and he's claiming victory. 'Some years ago,' he said, 'I was in Britain briefly and someone suggested that I stay there and become a refugee from Iraq. But after the 1991 war Saddam accused people who were leaving the country of failing their patriotic duty because they were seeking a softer life while he and Tariq Aziz were defending the country in the face of the UN sanctions against Iraq.

'I couldn't have lived with Saddam claiming that he was patriotic and at the same time having my patriotism questioned. So I came back from Britain to a bitter life. Because of his high principles about patriotism, I have no job, no family and no house. And I didn't leave the country—and now it is Saddam who is trying to leave.

'That is why I'm happy today. Saddam has proved my theory—he is not the historic leader he claims to be; he is a nothing and now he is like a rat. He could not defend Baghdad because he is a coward who was only ever interested in the power. I didn't leave my country and now Saddam is trying to leave his. That means he lost—and I won.'

▲

I had never seen so many hat stands. It seemed that every looter had either a ceiling fan or a hat stand. The Mansur Hotel was being stripped, the Information Ministry was smouldering and a massive bomb had flattened a supermarket on the opposite corner. So many weapons had been looted that the black-market price for a Kalashnikov was down to $US3. When Sabah slowed at an intersection, we were overtaken by two hospital beds loaded with medical equipment.

The al-Rashid was being carted away by the trolley and truckload, which upset Sabah greatly—his life had revolved around this place for more than twenty years. Despite the pleasure he took from the overthrow of Saddam, he still couldn't fully appreciate how radically things were going to change. He had yet to come to terms with the loosening of the regime's grip on the minutiae of his life—it hadn't occurred to him that the old certainties, like the tightly controlled transport pool at the al-Rashid, might now be a thing of the past. Or what impact these tumultuous events might have on his dream acquisition of a GMC.

The looting was very disturbing. The protective wall of bricks thrown up by shops and hotels backfired for some. In Mansur, just across from the al-Saah Restaurant, where Sabah might have died in the US bomb attack that was meant for Saddam and his sons, the bricked-up doors and windows of a shop were taken by looters as an invitation to attack—they must have figured that, if there was a wall, there had to be something valuable behind it.

We went back to the al-Kindi Hospital and were almost reduced to tears by what we saw—the locust-like speed of the looters had paralysed a hospital that had been a mainstay of the city's emergency health system during the war. An American soldier, who had taken up guard duty at the hospital today, showed us the note that a runner from the al-Kindi had carried to his checkpoint. It read: 'In the hospital there are terrorists. Please help.' But by then it was too late.

The patients, including little Ali, whose arms were ripped off in the US missile strike on his home, had to be evacuated to another hospital, this time in Saddam City, where the local mullahs were now imposing their own strict law-and-order regime. At the gates of the al-Kindi we met Haider Daoud, a wearied volunteer guard, who told us: 'Yesterday I asked the US for protection for this hospital, but they told me they weren't here to protect hospitals. I'm so disappointed that a big army like the USA can't protect a little hospital like this.'

This looting was not an accident. There was rising criticism of the US, as each ministry building was stripped and torched, that they did not have a crisis management plan for Baghdad. But when an American security cordon went up around the Oil Ministry, it dawned on me that the anarchy was actually a part of the plan.

In the meantime, it was as though the terror of Iraq's past was oozing up through the cracks in the pavement. It was everywhere. Everyone I spoke to, as the Saddam statue came down yesterday, had lost a relative or a friend to state brutality. And today, at the Directorate of General Security, the home and interrogation centre of the national security police, there was an oppressive, deadening air about the series of bunkers that till now had been off-limits, behind high walls on the eastern outskirts of the city.

The looters were just about done by the time we got there. We found a couple of surly men who seemed to know about the place, but didn't want to admit to having worked there. Yet they wanted us to know that all the prisoners had been released three days earlier. How many? 'No one ever knew,' one of them said. 'They were kept in tunnels underground.' We could not find the tunnels but, as we left, small groups of Iraqis began arriving, saying that they were looking for relatives who had disappeared within the security system.

I had taken to careering around the city with Kiefah, over whom we'd previously had the argument with *The Sunday Times*. The demise of the minder system meant that Kiefah was now able to make his own call on whom he'd work for. If Sabah were not available, I'd hire a freelance driver from the mob with their hands up for work at the front of the hotel. My biggest worry was the disappearance of Mohammed. No one knew for sure where he had taken his family in the country and Firas the fixer, who had set me up with Mohammed as a driver, had heard nothing. My anxiety only heightened when David Blair, of *The Daily Telegraph* in London, told me that his driver had been killed in the last days of the war.

The best of the former minders were the first to reappear, offering themselves as translators and fixers. I was especially pleased to see Saalar Mustafa working for Larry Kaplow. Saalar was an individual who, within all the limitations of the Information Ministry, always managed to conduct himself with dignity and to command our respect.

Not so Mr Moysen—the hapless director of the Press Centre, who had always laboured in the shadow of the dreadful Mr Kadhim. Moysen was last seen yesterday morning, running down Abu Nuwas Street. He had been loitering near a four-wheel drive, which had been confiscated from a group of Italian journalists who had entered Iraq without visas during the war. The journalists were still under hotel arrest in the Palestine and one of them watched as Moysen began loading his personal gear into their four-wheel drive. Burns told me later that one Italian raced out of the hotel and slashed the vehicle's tyres with a pocket knife while his colleagues gave chase to the fleeing Press Centre director. Moysen quickly ran out of puff, and when they caught up to him, he pulled out his Information Ministry ID tag and shredded it in front of them before setting off again along the embankment of the Tigris.

The last we heard of the Information boss Uday al-Tai came from some of our Spanish colleagues. They had braved the creaking beams in the bombed-out Information Ministry building to find their way to al-Tai's office. They found a big box of Viagra in the top drawer of his desk and a pile of 'me with the leader' photographs from official gatherings—charming pics of al-Tai and Saddam together. Elsewhere in the building they found bundles of files—including one labelled 'John Fisher Burns'. It was all in Arabic, but they promised to get the file to Burns.

Curious and welcoming crowds were gathering around the US vehicles—Humvees, Abrams tanks and Bradley fighting vehicles in the streets. There was genuine warmth as the Iraqis saw soldiers eating local bread and kebabs and frequenting shops, which of course were springing open as the pressure eased. But some locals could not contain their anger at the failure of the US to halt the looting. Dr Gailan Ramiz, a 62-year-old professor of political science at Baghdad University, fought his way through the cordon around the Palestine Hotel and a few of us spoke to him in the lobby. 'There has been no war in history that was more talked about and more written about than this one—so where was the plan? We thought the US were the experts in logistics and planning,' he lamented.

I spoke to Dr Ramiz about the silence of Iraqis in the face of Saddam's excesses, but he cut me off: 'We were never silent in our souls—maybe that is why I look so old. Because there is no greater spell than the imprisonment of the human soul, either by dictatorship or by foreign occupation. If I had spoken of democracy they would have chopped off my head. But it is good news that we can start to build something now—we can rebuild our society and have a dialogue on how to get the US out of Iraq, or we can sit and grind our teeth because we ended up as we did and because foreign tanks have us up against a wall. Future generations might be able to explain this, but for now we have to look to the future with the scars of dictatorship. And we have to believe in the values of democracy and freedom. I'm optimistic.'

We were not seeing a lot of Jon Lee Anderson this week. He had gone off down a burrow and we would not know what he would be bringing back till we saw the next edition of *The New Yorker*. But today he saved a hospital.

The story he was working on required him to go to the Wasati Hospital in the Alawiya district. He had discovered that among the patients was Paul Pasquale, one of the Reuters staff injured by the US tank strike on the Palestine Hotel, and that the hospital was fighting a losing battle to keep persistent looters at bay. Anderson marched back to the Palestine Hotel, found a marine commander and soon was leading a five-Humvee column back to the hospital, where he briefly had to direct operations. Anderson wrote in his subsequent piece for *The New Yorker*: 'The marines got into combat stances facing the hospital. I pointed out that it was the hospital that needed to be protected, and they turned around and took up positions at the entrance gate.'

DAY TWENTY-THREE

A Time for Revenge

Filed Friday, April 11 at 12.49pm   Sheraton Hotel

Khalil Abu Sheikh is running for his life. In his 60s, he wears the cheap grey suit of a Baath Party informer and in the Baghdad heat he sweats as he strives to close the distance between himself and a US military checkpoint at the end of the Sinak Bridge.

The unshaven Abu Sheikh is a miserable creature. In the dog-eat-dog world of the Iraqi regime he made a living rounding up young army deserters. He did it at gunpoint and he'd turn his captives in to the authorities for a pittance bounty—about $A18 a head.

Last year he hunted 26-year-old Mazhar Ali Mahmoud. On the night of October 17 he chased him through the alleys of Bab al-Sheik, in the centre of Baghdad, bringing him down with two bullets in the back. He then gave Ali Mahmoud such a whipping with a wire rope that the welts on his back and chest are still livid. 'Now I want to kill him,' a panting Ali Mahmoud said.

The collapse of Saddam Hussein's regime has turned the tables—now Ali Mahmoud and a gang of his friends are hunting Abu Sheikh. The informer is desperate to get across the Tigris River, which means clearing a jumpy US military checkpoint. It is like a scene from *Apocalypse Now*.

The barrier in front of three US Abrams tanks is made up of four burnt-out cars, in which are strewn the scorched and bloated bodies of at least five Fedayeen Saddam fighters. Their buckled and burnt weapons are by their sides. They have been in the hot sun for three days now—two of them can be identified as human only by the odour; the others are like grotesque shop-window dummies.

The soldiers are alarmed as Abu Sheikh slashes his hand across his throat, shrieking that his pursuers are trying to kill him. He drops to his knees, pleading. They order him back—into the arms of his would-be assassins. But Abu Sheikh sits on the road, refusing to go back. In the pandemonium shots are fired.

Abu Sheikh, the informer, survived. In the end, the marines made him lie face down; they tied his hands behind his back and went through his pockets. Then they took him away.

As Baghdad slides further into anarchy, tens of thousands of regime loyalists face the same fate as Abu Sheikh. US forces are preoccupied with military objectives and all Iraqi police and security staff, like the rest of the regime, have melted into the population which they used to keep in a tight vice of state and party control.

The rampant looting that first targeted the regime spread to embassies, hospitals, businesses and private homes today. Even the al-Kindi Hospital, which performed so heroically as it dealt with appalling casualties during the American bombing of Baghdad, was looted of beds, electrical fittings and other equipment. In this power vacuum the marines say they are cracking down but today there was no sign of it as troops invariably watched, but did not act against, the looters.

The German, Chinese and Turkish embassies were done over and the French Cultural Centre on the riverfront was stripped bare. Around the corner, guards at the French Embassy nervously toyed with their Kalashnikovs after stretching layers of coiled barbed wire around the Ottoman compound.

A Red Cross worker is dead and two from Médicins Sans Frontières are missing. Arguing that US forces should confront the lawlessness, Amanda Williamson, a Red Cross spokeswoman, said: 'It's not possible to distribute medical and surgical supplies or drinking water to the hospitals. The situation is chaotic and very insecure. At this stage they could at least do everything possible to protect vital civilian infrastructure, like hospitals and the water supply.'

But in the Baghdad vacuum it's every man for himself. The military operation is insulated from the looters who, in turn, are oblivious to the fate of the likes of the informer Abu Sheikh. Having toppled the regime of Saddam Hussein, the challenge now facing the US and its war allies is as daunting as it is enormous. The pent-up anger, energy and frustrated ambition of millions will demand urgent proof that life after Saddam Hussein will be worth the pain of war.

The looting is just a crude start. And the brutal murder at a Najaf mosque yesterday of pro-US Shia leader Abdul Majid al-Khoei is a warning of the fraught and possibly irreconcilable differences between Iraq's long-suffering majority Shia community, the marginalised Kurds of the north—who are also a significant portion of the population—and the Sunni minority, which ran the regime for Saddam.

Twelve years of sanctions have crippled the economy and a bureaucracy that needs to work immediately to give Iraqis their post-Saddam peace dividend—urgent humanitarian assistance, good schools and hospitals, and an environment in which a potentially rich oil-based economy can function and grow.

Washington has proposed an interim government representing all the Iraqi factions under the supervision of retired general, Jay Garner, who already runs the Pentagon's Office of Reconstruction and Humanitarian Assistance. He is expected in Baghdad soon. He will have to eliminate the Saddam die-hards at the top of each ministry and encourage lower-level managers to work alongside American 'advisers' at a time when payback will be rife—it's very easy to eliminate a competitor by branding him a Saddam loyalist—and when Iraqis are looking for proof that they have been liberated, not occupied.

General Garner's first mistake could be the airlifting into Iraq of about 100 exiled Iraqis to help him. Invariably, after such wars, there is nothing that offends the millions who have sat through the oppression and then the pain of the war more than to arrive back at work and be greeted by a new boss who has sat out the hardship in the comfort of exile.

The US is trying to head off revenge acts against Iraq's 50 000 Baath Party members by broadcasting appeals—run on Freedom TV, which operates from US aircraft flying over Iraq—for those who have not been involved in 'criminal acts' to be allowed to return to their posts after the war.

The US is banking on the task of rebuilding being easier than in Afghanistan. Deputy Secretary of State Richard Armitage said: 'Unlike Afghanistan, Iraq is not a failed state. It was a torturous, oppressive state, but it had education. Where Afghanistan was about 20 per cent literate, here we're over 60 per cent literate. They have a very well-developed middle class. You have capable technocrats below the sort of leadership levels in, I think, every ministry.'

Iraqis also are deeply anxious about the fate of their huge oil resources, which critics claim the US wants to control so as to supply the US market. This is judged to be mainly as a way of controlling global oil supply at a time when Saudi Arabia, the only other producer with the capacity to hold prices at levels acceptable to Western economies, is seen to be less stable.

Any attempt to manipulate control of Iraq's oil or, as some in the Bush administration have suggested, to impose a levy to pay for the cost of the Iraq war, will be a damaging political tool in the hands of Iraqis who oppose an American presence here and in the Arab Street, which can be easily whipped up into anti-US anger.

In the void that now exists, the handling of these critical issues will be the measure by which Washington makes the leap, if it ever can, from being a fearsome and distrusted superpower to being an ally that is tolerated or even admired.

In the meantime it's mayhem in Baghdad. A rifle shot in the air, or a tank shot outside a building being stripped, would send the looters back to the suburbs. But for now Mohammed Abboud is busily strapping down booty stacked high on the back of his pick-up outside a warehouse at a palatial home in the process of being built in suburban al-Dura for one of the most feared thugs of Saddam's regime—Ali Hassan al-Majid, better known as Chemical Ali.

Al-Majid, a cousin of Saddam, was killed in an American bombing run over Basra early this week, the successful conclusion of one of the targeted US manhunts during the war. He earned his nickname from his enthusiastic use of chemical weapons against the people of Halabja and other Kurdish communities in the north of Iraq in 1988. He also crushed the Shia uprisings against Saddam after the 1991 Persian Gulf War.

So there was a certain irony in the manner of his death and the humiliating looting of his household goods, given that in

1988 he had made a tape-recording in which he said of the Kurds: 'I will kill them all with chemical weapons! Who is going to say anything? The international community? Fuck them! The international community and those who listen to them.'

Yesterday Chemical Ali's collection of Saddam portraits was smashed; his furniture and bedding, his racing car wheels and his jet ski, his kitsch African and Renaissance wood carvings were being sifted through by the very people he had oppressed.

'It's anarchy,' Abboud said as more trucks and vans drove through Chemical Ali's palm plantations and his irrigated orchards to get to the burgeoning warehouse, which was about half the size of a football field. 'Will the Americans stop us looting? We don't have these things in our houses—refrigerators and TVs. Is it thievery when the people are hungry? Look at these riches and how we have lived for 30 years. Our oil bought this.'

The four-storey house being built next to the warehouse was of marble, onyx and sandstone. Huge sculpted friezes of life in ancient Baghdad adorned the façade and a sweeping staircase went to bedrooms half the size of a tennis court. In the warehouse men, women and children rummaged excitedly, but selectively, through personal items and the fittings for the house—ceramic tiles, light fittings and restaurant-sized kitchen fittings.

Vases, chessboards and statues were going out the door. The portraits of Saddam were smashed; medals bearing his image and a promise of 'unity, freedom and socialism' were scattered on the floor. There was little interest in a pile of spent tank shells—mementos of a particular battle?

His video collection was trampled rather than taken. It included: *The Big Easy*, *Lethal Weapon II*, *Skin Deep*, *Iran: The Inside Story*, *Weekend Warriors* and *Lifestyles of the Rich and Famous*. His family snaps were shredded on the spot, including one in which he looked very pleased with himself, dancing as a crowd of tribal elders looked on sombrely.

As I was leaving, one of the looters thrust a Saddam wall clock at me. He said: 'This is a gift for you.' Me: 'Thank you very much.' Looter: 'Don't mention it—it's not mine.'

▲

We were still hanging out for the rest of our money. We were not overly concerned, just anxious to be able to account for it to the bean counters at home, who would never understand the risks and dangers people took to get it to us. Burns had given us the initial $10 000 when it arrived and, after the drop-off by Tareq Ayyoub, the al-Jazeera reporter who died, he had been able to make another distribution of $US7500 to each member of our syndicate. So we were each short $US7500.

The key middleman in the deal was an enterprising Jordanian by the name of Amjad Tadros. He was a big-time fixer for CBS, but he also did deals such as ours on the side. At this time, the single biggest issue in CBS's Baghdad camp was that 'Dan' was on the way. 'Dan' was Dan Rather, one of the biggest and most prestigious names in American TV news, and we fell to wondering if the movement of our funds had been slowed to help cover such a big-ticket item as a visit by Dan. The CBS drivers liked to brag about having to drive Dan to the Jordanian border, where he would be picked up by a helicopter so he would not have to endure the three or four hours drive on to Amman.

But Amjad assured us the money was coming. In the meantime he had opened a new business—he had two Thuraya sat-phones brought in from Amman and he had retained a couple of local helpers to stand in the street near the Palestine Hotel under a sign that offered international calls at $US10 for two minutes. Iraqis were queuing up at such a rate that he had to retain the services of Mr Jamal—the Information

Ministry cashier who had no fingernails—to manage the money that was pouring in.

Journalists were pouring in too. We estimated that maybe 400 arrived yesterday and another 200 to 300 today. As Jon Lee and I drove past the al-Rashid Hotel today we passed the latest convoy arriving from Amman—about 50 vehicles in it. They were crowding out the hotels and breaking down the rhythm of life as we knew it. But I suppose the end of the war had already done that. Burns looked at them all this morning and muttered darkly: 'Maybe we've had our trips, mate?'

We had thought that the end of the war would mean an end to the satellites being jammed but last night we were off the air for almost five critical hours—it was an absolute debacle, very tense, as our offices and homes, and the TV and radio stations expecting to interview us, didn't have a clue what was happening. Anderson was desperate to file his big piece on the collapse of Baghdad but, after trying to get a satellite line for three anxious hours, he fell into bed exhausted and defeated. I had been working on a big weekend piece and had hit the mattress earlier. I was back up at 5am, stabbing at the redial button and watching—hoping and praying that the digital measure of the signal strength on my sat-phone would rise to the requisite 520-plus. It seemed like forever that it hung in the low 400s.

In the meantime, as we knew would be happening, the editors at *The New Yorker* were frantic—they had been holding the magazine open late for this one piece from Anderson. My office couldn't get me and neither could Fox News' Greta Van Susteren program, which had arranged an interview with me. When my wife, who was fielding urgent calls from Fox, couldn't raise either of our sat-phones for hours on end, pangs of anxiety kicked in at home. But finally I hit the jackpot—a satellite signal of 520 and rising. I dragged the fully-clothed Anderson off his bed; without completely waking up, he managed to transfer his report to a floppy disk, which we stuck into my computer and sent by email to his editor Sharon DeLano. It got there late, but in time to catch the magazine; Greta Van Susteren missed out on her interview. But we were back on the air and I filed for the *Herald* just on time.

The soldiers of the new regime, boys from Omaha and Texas, were getting around Baghdad smoking cigars and with flowers in the webbing on their helmets. It was going to be a while before the detailed, inside story of the collapse of the previous regime emerged. But the threads of its demise were already known. There was little or no support from the civilian population. Apart from al-Sahhaf, whom we had last seen on Tuesday morning, none of the ministers of the regime had been sighted for days—there were rumours that they had bussed themselves and their families to Damascus and elsewhere. The Baath Party leadership and the officer corps spread the word quietly among their underlings on Tuesday night—go home, we have neither the weapons nor the energy for this contest. And within a matter of hours one of the most talked-up and most feared military machines in the world simply evaporated. All that was left were the weapons and uniforms abandoned by men so desperate not to be identified as part of the regime they had propped up for years that they were prepared to walk the streets of Baghdad half-naked.

The insular environment in which they were forced to live and the lies that they were deliberately told meant they could not comprehend the technological superiority of the US. They were unlikely ever to be inspired to military greatness under nepotism run amok. So by dawn on Wednesday the military had made themselves scarce, the bureaucrats had decided to stay at home and the heavies were on the run. That included Saddam, but little was known of his whereabouts—even by the high-powered CIA team that was said to be on the ground scouring Baghdad.

Dr Wamid Nadhme, the political scientist who had worked out that Burns' minder was a spy, had lived under Saddam's regime for long enough to understand its foibles and never to allow others to put words in his mouth. As we drank tea, he was very critical of the exiled Iraqis who were returning from abroad with a claim on power. So, when I asked if these people might be the dregs of Iraqi society, he stopped me: 'I don't think they are the dregs and we do need people to be appointed to these positions initially. But some of these people are hated and despised, and one way or another they are linked to the worst aspects of the old regime—that's why Colin Powell opposed them.'

With the old regime gone, Burns wasn't sure who to turn to about his stolen equipment. But today a man who claimed to have links to the Mukhabarat approached him. He invited Burns to accompany him to his home and there he handed over most of *The New York Times'* equipment—the sat-phones and the laptops. The cameras and the cash did not come back.

DAY TWENTY-FOUR

Saturday, April 12

The Looting Spree

Filed Saturday, April 12 at 10.58am   **Sheraton Hotel**

The gaudy Sajida Palace was one of Saddam Hussein's favourites. When the Americans bombed this overly decorated mansion, which the dictator had named after his wife, he faithfully rebuilt it and restored its huge manicured gardens, orchards and linked lakes. That was in 1998.

But with repeated American bombing in the last few weeks it was trashed again. And today, with Baghdad still in the grip of post-war anarchy, looters trashed the memory of Saddam and his family as they hauled away every stick of furniture and any fitting they could unscrew or break off.

In a darkened stairwell, I passed a man with a chandelier from one of the grand bedrooms clutched to his chest. A whole family was stripping the decorative brass-plating from the towering front doors. Others were lugging out tacky Louis XIV and Queen Anne reproduction lounge and bedroom suites.

In the best tradition of fallen dictators, from Africa to Eastern Europe, it seems that Saddam's taste in home decorating was pure dictator kitsch. But such is the fear of the man that—despite the toppling of the regime—none of the looters was prepared to be named, even in a newspaper in a country as distant from Baghdad as Australia is.

They paused briefly in their pillage to play-act life in the wreckage of the Saddam household. They pretended to be at a banquet at a huge table that would seat more than 100 for dinner; they lolled briefly on a bed in one of the cavernous bedrooms—one of them suggesting that this was where 'little Saddams' were made; and they made use of what was left of the marble bathrooms.

Across town, at the palatial home of Saddam's much-feared older son, Uday, looters took away wine, whisky, guns and paintings of half-naked women. They also stripped a luxury yacht moored in a private marina in the grounds of this riverfront house and they made off with Uday's prized white Arabian horses. But there was little else to amuse in Baghdad today.

The torching and looting of government and other buildings escalated, and it now seems that the failure of US-led forces to quickly curb lawlessness in the Iraqi capital will add billions of dollars to the cost of national reconstruction for a population that has suffered war and privation for more than twenty years. More than half a dozen key government ministry buildings were ablaze; the Rafidain Bank headquarters was pouring smoke into the Baghdad sky; the Mansur/Melia Hotel was stripped and on fire; and the fabled al-Rashid Hotel, home to foreign journalists in Iraq for years, was looted of its entire contents.

Plumes of looters' smoke had taken over from the trench oil-fires in blackening the city skyline and it seemed that the decision by the US not to stop the banditry was overnight creating a huge criminal class in a country where the absolute power of the state had kept crime in check for decades.

The US says it is attempting to regroup the Iraqi police force, but this will be a slow process because it is insisting on a screening procedure that is likely to take longer than it will take for the looters to burn the remaining office towers—towers that should be the home of the local and national bureaucracy in the new Iraq.

'Each individual officer will be assessed for where he sits politically,' said Major David Cooper, 40, a reserve marine public affairs officer. 'We're going to find out who they are and see if we can work with them. We are not going to put war criminals in positions of authority. If we can, we stop and chase the looters away . . . But we don't have the resources to chase them from every store.'

After local pleading, the marines posted guards at a few hospitals and other vital installations. But, according to Major-General David H. Petraeus, commander of the 101st Airborne Division: 'We're not going to stand between a crowd and a bunch of mattresses.'

Baghdad remains in the grip of an electricity and clean water crisis. Millions of families, already terrified of being looted, are being forced to spend evenings and nights in blacked-out suburbs. They are having to rely on untreated water in a country in which more than 500 000 tonnes of untreated sewage is dumped in the river system daily.

Lieutenant-General William S. Wallace, the senior army officer in Iraq as commander of V Corps, said that army engineers were attempting to locate civil authorities who knew the work-ings of the electricity grid, which failed a few nights before the fall of Baghdad with each side in the war blaming the other for its demise. But he warned: 'Getting water and power and sewage back on in this city is going to be a monumental task.'

Many people in the city are blaming the poor Shia community for the looting. But as I drove through several of the city's well-heeled suburbs today, I saw families with BMWs and other expensive cars returning to their homes with piles of stolen goods. In suburbs like Mansur and Karada, neighbourhood vigilante groups have thrown up roadblocks and they have posted armed groups in each street to deter would-be looters.

In Karada, 42-year-old Makram Abdul Said said: 'There is no safety. Homes in this area have been looted and this isn't what was supposed to happen. I think the Americans are allowing it to happen; it's to allow the Kuwaitis to have their revenge for what happened in 1991. Why do we still not have power? Why do they not control this barbarian looting? This is miserable—everyone has a weapon and nobody can be trusted.'

Josept Risculla, a member of one of the new volunteer urban defence squads, said: 'If we don't do this, we'll be next.' Demanding that the US troops defend state and private property, he went on: 'When George Bush says on TV, "I want to give freedom to the Iraqi people," what freedom is he talking about? The freedom to steal from houses and hospitals?'

Gunfire could be heard regularly across the city and rotting bodies still littered the streets. Today I watched a family stripping a crashed Nissan minibus, even as the bloated corpses of two Fedayeen Saddam fighters, who had been in the vehicle, lay on the median strip only two or three metres away.

The marines were blowing up Iraqi ammunition dumps across the city, but they were slow off the mark to stop hundreds of looters making off with scores of Kalashnikovs, hand grenades, pistols and rocket-propelled grenades and launchers from the Planning Ministry, on the Tigris west bank.

A combination of looting and a lack of medical staff forced the closure of the al-Kindi Hospital on the east side. But in the west the al-Yarmuk Hospital was dealing with gunfire and knifing wounds inflicted in looting clashes and with children and babies who had been seriously injured in cluster bomb explosions and were still dying. Visitors to the al-Yarmuk reported that its floors were thick with stale blood and that its wards smelled of gangrene. Orderlies in blue carried Kalashnikovs to ward off marauders as patients in soiled sheets cried in pain because they lacked pain-killers and hospital equipment, which had been looted.

The cause of the injuries among the new admissions was difficult to ascertain. Some of them were the victims of jittery US soldiers who, in the wake of continued suicide bombings, shoot up suspect civilian cars; some have been injured by the detonation of unexploded US and Iraqi munitions lying around the city; and some are the tail end of the Iraqi resistance to the US presence.

The most brazen looting took place at a treasure-loaded museum on the west side that celebrates the life and leadership of Saddam. Pistol-packing looters, who seemed to know exactly what they were looking for, used steel bars to smash open plate-glass display cases before making off with many of the priceless gifts presented to Saddam by foreign leaders over the years. They included a diamond-studded watch presented by the Sultan of Brunei, a gold-plated Kalashnikov from a former head of the Soviet KGB and swords from French President Chirac. A jewel-encrusted throne and a bundle of rare elephant tusks also disappeared.

At the museum's entrance an old woman in head-to-toe black sat on guard over her booty—replica models of a sailing ship that stood about two metres tall and a mother-of-pearl inlaid model of the Dome of the Rock, one of the holiest of Muslim shrines, that was about one metre tall. One looter rode off on his motorcycle with a couch, two armchairs, two standard lamps and several decorated boxes piled precariously in the sidecar.

Back at the Sajida Palace few of the looters paused in the congested car park to take in the significance of a Koranic inscription sculpted into an alcove on one of the outside walls. My translator said it was difficult to give its precise meaning in English, but this was the gist of it: 'Everything belongs to Allah . . . all that is and all that was and all that will be . . . and he gives and takes according to his will.'

▲

Anderson and I were going to the Sajida Palace—it too was being looted. We had to be careful because our unannounced arrival at such venues often unnerved the looters, many of whom were armed. So we took to loudly announcing ourselves as we entered each new building: '*Sahafi! Sahafi!*' This was the Arab word for 'reporter' and usually it was sufficient to put the thieves and bandits at ease.

But at the Sajida Palace we had to lower our voices. In the midst of the bombed rubble, just outside the great brass-trimmed metal doors, stood one of Saddam's very kitsch brocade-and-gilt armchairs; sitting in the chair, sound asleep at 10 o'clock in the morning, was John Burns. He'd had his own share of anxiety and tension on top of all that we'd had and, suddenly, it had caught up with him.

It was catching up with us all—Anderson and I found that we were literally falling asleep in the middle of interviews. I stepped back to take a photograph of Burns with my digital camera, but, as eloquent proof that professional photographers are still a necessity, I later discovered that I'd forgotten to put a data card in the camera. Suddenly there was a ruckus that woke Burns up—a band of looters came through the main door with Sajida Hussein's egg-shell-blue four-poster bed.

We found out today about the fate of the safe house that Sabah had arranged in Mansur if we had needed to get out of the hotel in a hurry. It was the unoccupied home of a diplo-mat. Soon after the war started, Heider, the caretaker of the house, was bailed up by a bunch of intelligence officers looking for somewhere to hide. They tied him up and fed him only bread and water, while they ate and drank their way through our supplies and then stole the petrol Jon Lee had stashed at the house.

In the worrisome absence of Mohammed, I'd been taking on other drivers on a day-by-day basis. Today my driver was Mohammed Jawad Ali, a former sea captain who spoke seven languages but who was reduced to touting for work as a translator for the foreign press. He seemed to know everything. As we passed the al-Buniya Mosque, I asked after the wealthy family that had built it and for whom it was named. He said: 'The rich can go where they like—one of the brothers is up on the Syrian border; the other is in Amman.' When we got back to the hotel the thought of lugging my body armour up twelve flights of stairs was too much, so I left it in the boot of Mohammed Jawad Ali's car. Yes, he said, he'd work as a driver for me tomorrow.

Colleagues were catching up. Byron Pitts, a great friend and a correspondent with CBS, who had been embedded with the US military, arrived in Baghdad today and will be gone tomorrow. I had met him first in very difficult circumstances in Afghan-istan—I had just survived the Taliban ambush, in which three of my colleagues died. We caught up regularly in New York, though not as often as we'd have liked given our rota of assignments. But we had been emailing each other during the war about catching up in Baghdad. It was great to see him.

Heathcliff O'Malley, a highly entertaining photographer with *The Daily Telegraph*, moved into the spare bed in Jon Lee's room. His name had become a perennial joke in the last war because of the Afghanis' efforts to pronounce it, in which they usually replaced the 'ff' with a 'tt'. O'Malley had been in

Baghdad before the war, but was ordered out by his editor. Thomas Dworzak, a German photographer who worked regularly with Anderson, was on his way down from Iraqi Kurdistan. I was anxious at having lost contact with Sam Kiley, who had infuriated the Iraqis last year by using a motion-sensitive camera to capture security agents going through his possessions at the al-Rashid Hotel. As a result of this, they had subsequently refused to give him a visa (and had delayed mine for months because we were mates), so he covered the war from Iraqi Kurdistan.

Kate Geraghty, a photographer colleague of mine, was about to arrive from Kuwait. My Fairfax colleague Mark Baker also was coming in to Baghdad and, although my original plan had been to stay for at least three weeks after the fall of the city, I was starting to feel that, after ten weeks of working eighteen to twenty hours a day every day, exhaustion was getting the better of me. I decided to book a GMC for the desert run to Amman and the first available flight out of Amman to New York.

You could tell it was time to leave. The hotel had got the muzak back in the lifts and all four of them were working. Restaurants were reopening and, as I went up to the twelfth floor this afternoon, I eavesdropped on speculation that, within ten days or a fortnight, Virgin Airlines could be flying into what I'll always think of as Saddam International Airport.

DAY TWENTY-FIVE

Sunday, April 13

A Cultural Catastrophe

Filed Sunday, April 13 at 11.26am   **Sheraton Hotel**

They knew what they were looking for. It needed to sparkle in the light of the burning oil-soaked rags that the looters use to light the darkness as they continue to maraud in Baghdad. But, as they searched for ancient jewels from civilisations dating back millennia, they utterly destroyed one of the world's finest collections of antiquities, the Iraq National Museum.

It is a cultural catastrophe. Today the museum's exhibition halls and security vaults were a barren mess—display cases smashed, offices ransacked and floors littered with handwritten index cards recording the timeless detail of more than 170 000 rare items that were pilfered.

Worse, in their search for gold and gems, the looters gained access to the museum's underground vaults, where they smashed the contents of the thousands of tin trunks in which curatorial staff had painstakingly packed priceless ceramics that told the story of life from one civilisation to the next down through 7000 fabled years of Babylonian, Assyrian and Mesopotamian history—from the birthplace of Christianity, Judaism and Islam.

In tears of anger and frustration, Mohsen Hassan, 56, an archaeologist and deputy curator, began to itemise the pieces he was certain were stolen: a priceless solid-gold harp and the sculpted head of a woman from Uruk—both from the Sumerian era, which began about 3360 BC; golden necklaces, silver and precious stones from royal tombs dating back 4000 years; exquisite bas-reliefs and a rare collection of ivory sculptures trimmed with gold. Too distraught to talk about the collection, he showed journalists a copy of the catalogue for *The Grand Exhibition of Silk Road Civilisations*, which toured the world in the late 1980s and for which the museum set aside its traditional reluctance to allow any of its treasure abroad.

All of the items that made it safely around the world and back to Baghdad have been looted. They include irreplaceable centuries-old stone carvings—of birds and beasts, and kings and queens; ivory goddesses and Sumerian cuneiform tablets covered in picture writing similar to Egyptian hieroglyphics; Mesopotamian tapestry fragments; 5000-year-old carved marble plaques; early texts showing an understanding of geometry at least 1500 years before Pythagoras; and friezes of ancient warriors and ceramics dating back to civilisation's first cities. 'All gone, all gone,' Mr Hassan told me, breaking down. 'All gone in two days.'

The looting of the museum, in the Karkh district of the inner city, underscores the story of the anarchy that has beset Baghdad since the arrival here on Wednesday of US-led forces. Every public building has been raided by the mobs and most of them torched, sometimes accidentally because of the use of oil-soaked rags for light. Hospitals have been reduced to empty shells. Iraqis who care are infuriated by the loss and by the transmission to the world of the most appalling images of their society in greedy chaos. The looters are a product of the regime that has shaped them—poorly educated, hungry for revenge after decades of oppression and unable to appreciate the damage they are doing to the country that is theirs.

The Americans have come here pursuing a military objective. Now, when it is too late, they say they will confront the looters. But we have seen little sign of this. They say they will impose a curfew, as if that matters when most of the looting is done in broad daylight in a city that has become a patchwork of vigilante-patrolled no-go areas and a killing field for those bent on revenge against the individuals who made up the regime of Saddam Hussein.

Those who are hungry for power are asserting themselves with menace. The long-oppressed Shia majority, centred in the south, is taking control of a key area of Baghdad—the endless slums of Saddam City. Aggressive and angry young Shia, in the bearded garb of the mosques of Karbala and Najaf, have taken over the streets and the hospitals, imposing their own brand of law and order and issuing warnings such as this from Ahmed Mohammed, 27: 'We thank George Bush. But if he stays here, he is just another Saddam. The Americans are becoming like Saddam. The two of them are exactly the same.'

And Baghdadis are acutely aware that the marines threw a cordon around only one public building when they pulled into town—the high-rise headquarters of the Oil Ministry.

The US Defence Secretary, Donald Rumsfeld, brushes it all off: 'Yes, it's untidy; but freedom is untidy,' was his flip response to the mayhem. He needs to think again, because how the Iraqis read the conduct of the US forces in these early days will inform their acceptance of the US presence for years to come.

'The Americans have disappointed us all. This country won't be operational for at least a year or two,' said Abbas Reta, 51, an engineer and father of five, who was among hundreds of Iraqi professionals who volunteered yesterday to help restore services. 'I've seen nothing new since Saddam's fall. All that we have seen is looting. The Americans are responsible. One round from their guns and all the looting would have stopped.'

Nezar Ahmed, an electrical engineer, spoke for many when he said: 'We've been wanting to kill Saddam Hussein for twenty years but we couldn't. So we are grateful to the Americans, but they are letting thieves take everything from the Iraqi people. It is their responsibility to maintain security but they let the thieves do whatever they want.'

As the tracks of another passing tank screeched on the Baghdad bitumen, and its crew turned a blind eye to the looting, Fuad Abdullah Ahmed, 49, blurted: 'The army of America is like Genghis Khan. America is not good and Saddam is not good. My people refused Saddam, and they will refuse the Americans.' Meanwhile, in the crowd that gathered to protest near the Palestine Hotel there was an ominous warning for Mr Rumsfeld from the mouth of Raad Bahman Qasim, 30: 'If this continues in Baghdad, we'll kill any American or British soldier.'

The ransacking of the museum took two days—interrupted only for 30 minutes when pleading staff persuaded members of a marine tank unit to go to the museum and scare the looters with a few warning shots over their heads. Abdul Rahman, the museum's 57-year-old live-in guard, was a gibbering wreck as he told of the arrival at the museum of a shouting crowd armed with axes and iron bars to smash the doors and display cases.

He explained: 'They said there was no government; that everything belonged to them. There were women and children. They stuffed the pieces into bags and I couldn't talk because there were too many of them. So I stayed in my room. They were yelling that there was no government and no state and that they would do whatever they liked.'

Just like Saddam Hussein, the guard admitted that in ten years on the job he had never bothered to look at the museum's displays. And now that there was no Saddam and no museum collection? 'I'm a guard. I don't bother myself with stuff like that.'

Clearly the looters had been given a hand—the Fort Knox-like doors to the vaults must have been opened for them, because they were unmarked. None of the museum staff is going to admit this, and anyhow the chances are—in this atmosphere of violence and fear—that whoever held the keys would have been slaughtered on the spot if they had not done what they were told.

Another of the museum archaeologists, Ra'ed Abdul Ridha Mohammed, 35, was one of the staff who raced to fetch the marines. He told me: 'I asked them to bring the tank into the museum grounds and protect what was left. They refused. And when they went away the crowd was back immediately, threatening to kill me and then to tell the Americans that I was a spy for Saddam Hussein. There was no way to protect myself or the collection, so I fled.

'But if a country has no record of its history it is nothing. If our civilisation is looted, then we don't have a country. So I blame the US—George Bush promised us liberty, but this is not liberty. If we had stayed under Saddam Hussein we'd still have the collection.'

Then he escorted me through the vaults—where the aisles between the ceiling-high shelves were deep with smashed ceramics and the buckled trunks from which they had been dumped. The heads of the ancient Assyrian kings from Mosul lay chipped and broken; the ears had been broken off a stone lion from 3000 BC to 2500 BC; carvings from the early Christian era in Hatra were in pieces; and relics from Nineveh had been thrown against the wall.

I came up out of the vaults, blinking in the sunlight, and into the Baghdad battlefield, and my thoughts turned to Washington and its military strategy. The US-led forces invaded

Iraq at a time of America's choosing; but they arrived in Baghdad with insufficient boots on the ground to impose law and order, in a city where pent-up anger and frustration were always going to erupt. They lacked the manpower to protect the fabric of this society and the ancient ones that pre-date it.

A tank shell or a grenade had punctured the ceremonial gate to the museum grounds, and shopfronts and homes around it were badly damaged. Windows were smashed and masonry broken and blackened. Looters were still trundling out of the city, on roads littered with the debris of war as rubbish fires burnt on the pavements.

As I drove back towards the Sheraton Hotel, I passed a bomb-flattened department store and the smouldering Foreign Affairs Ministry. On the Sinak Bridge, over the Tigris, there was the unmistakable stench of death from wrecked cars that had been pushed to the side. As I crested the bridge, the bombed remains of the al-Rashid International Telephone Exchange came into view—a high-rise tower filled with the wondrous technology of our civilisation and seeming to to teeter on warped and spindly concrete columns, which are all that survive of its mid-section. This is after repeated bombing by the US, apparently because of concern that Saddam Hussein might make a phone call.

After witnessing three weeks of attacks on Baghdad and almost a week of looting—especially of the Iraq National Museum—questions about where the criminality lies become blurred.

▲

There were plenty of frayed tempers at work this morning. Burns, a few others and myself were trying to find the Iraq National Museum because we had been told about the criminal looting of its priceless collections. The hand-drawn map we had been given was not particularly good so, after we'd been around the block three times, Burns and I began yelling at each other. And we were both yelling at a new freelance driver I had booked for the day because this morning I could find neither of the Mohammeds. Our tiredness had turned us into zombies; the tension release created by the end of the war meant that we simply didn't have the reserves to cope with another wrong turn.

It was disconcerting to realise, as we drove around the city, that last week's square holes—the Iraqi defensive bunkers dug on median strips and in Baghdad's parks and gardens—had by this week become round holes, reshaped by the US bombs and missiles that had made craters of them.

The temperature was constantly in the mid-30s Celsius—Burns stepped out in those shorts of his every day now. Road traffic was getting heavier and women were back on the streets, doing household shopping and other chores. Under the watchful eye of US tank crews, an attempt was being made to re-enlist the services of Baghdad's professional classes to get a shattered city functioning again. At the front of the Palestine Hotel, the different professions and trades were ordered to line up: policemen, power workers, engineers and so on.

But all of this was happening in a total absence of security—at either a personal or city level. Outside the Iraq National Museum, after witnessing the impact of the barbarian looting of its treasures, I was approached by a man wanting to sell me looted medicines. He was pushy and a crowd gathered, sullen and angry. But, before anything serious could happen, our freelance driver pulled a pistol, waved it once and the crowd scattered. Ordinarily I'd be appalled, but now I was disturbed by the comfort I took from the fact that, unbeknownst to me, my driver had a gun.

While we waited at the museum, an angry Iraqi doctor sought us out. He would not give his name. He could speak English—he said he had studied medicine in Britain—but he refused to do so. Instead he spoke Arabic through an interpreter: 'Because of what I have seen, I hate the English language. The first thing we need here is security. They have destroyed eighteen provinces and injured a population of 25 million people, just to get one man. If they are talking about freedom, then let us have it with pride, not with bowed heads.'

Fires still burnt in a string of high-rise government buildings. Even the National Library had been torched and, when Burns and I went through it this evening, we could still feel the heat rising through the soles of our boots. What had been on the shelves, including the best collection of this country's ancient manuscripts and histories, was now reduced to a layer of fine white ash on the floor. Maybe 100 or 200 books from a collection of tens of thousands had been spared—because they were off in a side room, apparently awaiting restoration. And scattered on the floor of that room were some of the prerequisites to promotion in Saddam's public service—the staff's collection of pictures of themselves with Saddam and other senior officials of the regime at library functions. These were all that the looters had left behind.

My photographer colleague Kate Geraghty arrived today; she was sleeping on the sofa because the two hotels were full. I found Burns and let him know I was going to have to take back Room 905 from the *NYT* to put Kate in. But we couldn't juggle the rooms until tomorrow. Meantime, some more of our money had arrived and Burns dropped Anderson and myself another $US5000 each.

DAY TWENTY-SIX

Monday, April 14

The Shia Divide

Filed Monday, April 14 at 11.32am **Sheraton Hotel**

There was always going to be a lot of sabre-rattling, but now there is blood on the steps of the mosque. The loosening of Saddam Hussein's iron grip on Iraqi life and politics is unleashing political and religious torrents that threaten to run out of control. Intrigue abounds in Baghdad, where the street talk is laced with fantastic tales of foreign interference.

Two of the staff at the looted Iraq National Museum insisted they had seen a man of Western appearance wearing flowing white traditional dress as he was ferried around the city in a white Mercedes Benz. He alighted from time to time, they said, speaking in foreign-accented 'high' Arabic as he encouraged bystanders to join the looting frenzy that has wrecked nearly all the institutions of the Iraqi government.

A professor of political science claimed that 'Wahhabi agents'—code for alleged interference by neighbouring Saudi

Arabia—were also working the streets, stirring opposition to any political gains for Iraq's long-oppressed Shia majority.

And manipulating it all is Washington, flying in its hand-picked team of exiled Iraqis and wanting to steer the new Iraq away from any influence from Shia Iran or Wahhabi Saudi Arabia, in the hope that the country will become the Middle East satellite the US wants as its other alliances in the region come under pressure.

In Najaf—an international power centre for Shia Islam because of the burial there of Imam Ali, son-in-law of Muhammad the Prophet—a prominent and pro-US Shia activist was murdered on the steps of the city's stunning, gold-leafed mosque. And there are reports from that city that the home of the man who today is revered around the world as the spiritual father of all Shia has been surrounded by gun-toting activists, who are demanding that he leave the country within 48 hours.

As the Iraq war approached, I was repeatedly confronted with a series of imponderables that could be clarified only as facts were revealed on the ground. Some have been answered.

Would Iraqi forces put up a fight? Yes, some would, I thought. How many would die? Thousands. Would a good, hard jab in the chest cause Saddam and his regime to simply collapse and fade away? Probably. Would the US find weapons of mass destruction? Probably not, I wrote.

Now Iraqis are on the verge of answering the most fraught question of all: How will they respond to the demise of Saddam? Can the US push and prod them along a fragile diplomatic path to form what might become an acceptable representative government? It had attempted this in Afghanistan with limited success so far. Or, like Yugoslavia after the death of the dictator Josip Tito, will the country descend into a nightmare of full-blown civil war?

Tomorrow US officials are expected to convene the first of a series of so-called town meetings, at Nasiriyah in the south, at which it will seek to guide selected Iraqis, from here and abroad, in the formation of an interim administration that will serve under a retired US general until a new government is elected. The process is expected to conclude in several weeks with a conference in Baghdad, similar to the December 2001 summit in Bonn which anointed Washington's candidate—Hamid Karzai—as the interim president of post-war Afghanistan.

But freed of the tyranny of the Saddam regime, fissures have split the Shia community as old family rivalries erupt in a violent leadership struggle. Only days after the US flew into Najaf, Sheik Abdul Majid al-Khoei, accompanied by two former Iraqi military officers, was murdered. Al-Khoei, 50, the head of the London-based philanthropic Khoei Foundation and a son of the late Grand Ayatollah Abu al-Qasim al-Khoei, was an active supporter of US intervention in Iraq.

Also murdered was Haidar al-Rifaai, the hereditary cus-todian of the mosque, who was long accused of being a patsy for the Saddam regime. But another thread in the Shia schisms is resistance by those who had to stay in Iraq, and who suffered at the hand of Saddam, to any role in the new Iraq for returning exiles who have been living free of persecution in the West.

The man whose house is said to be surrounded is the current Grand Ayatollah, Imam Ali Sistani, who is aligned with the non-political Shia stream and who issued a fatwa during the war, urging Shia not to take sides. Reports from Najaf state that al-Khoei, who at times had a US military escort, went around town attempting to rally support for the US and to take control of the central mosque, the site of the tomb of the revered Imam Ali.

Last Thursday an angry crowd gathered at the mosque, and al-Khoei and Haidar al-Rifaai were cornered in a basement office. Al-Khoei managed to fire two shots from a pistol, killing a man in the crowd and further enraging it. The two men tried to escape, but the crowd rushed them. Witnesses said that al-Khoei died from multiple bullet and stab wounds while the custodian was hacked to death.

At the centre of the Shia struggle is the Iran-based Supreme Council for Islamic Revolution in Iraq, or SCIRI, set up by Ayatollah Mohammed Baqir al-Hakim, the son of another Shia Grand Ayatollah who first challenged Iraqi secular regimes as far back as the 1950s. Al-Hakim followed in his father's steps as an Islamic scholar but, when his father died in the 1970s, the leadership of Iraq's Shia was taken up by Mohammed Baqir al-Sadr, who encouraged Shia to join al-Dawa—meaning 'Islamic Voice'—an outlawed militant organisation that actively opposed Saddam.

Saddam retaliated with a brutal crackdown on the Shia leadership and, after an attempt on the life of Saddam's deputy Tariq Aziz in the 1980s, Mohammed Baqir al-Sadr and his sister were arrested in 1999. She is said to have been raped in front of him and he is supposed to have died after nails were driven through his head.

This was the point at which al-Hakim fled to Iran and to the protection of the late Ayatollah Khomeini who, before his leadership of Iran, had been exiled in Najaf. In Iran, al-Hakim set up an exiles' militia, which regularly crossed into Iraq and which, in the wake of the 1991 Gulf War, briefly took the southern city of Basra.

The overlapping relationship between SCIRI and al-Dawa is not clear. But fundamentalist, anti-Western supporters of al-Dawa are reported to have been very active since the demise of Saddam. They have taken control of Saddam City, a slum area of Baghdad, which is home to an estimated two million Shia. Yesterday they renamed it Medina Sadr, or Sadr City.

Shia in Kuwait have accused al-Dawa of the al-Khoei murder, but 22-year-old Muqtada al-Sadr, a son of the executed former Grand Ayatollah, has denied the charge.

Al-Hakim, now 63, has paid a cruel price for his political and militant opposition. In an interview with *The New Yorker's* Jon Lee Anderson in Iran earlier this year, he said: '...this period was characterised by killings, imprisonments, and I was tortured. I was burnt with cigarettes, electro-shocked. My head was put into a metal vice; I was beaten very harshly and imprisoned in a cell where I couldn't distinguish between night and day. All of this happened when I was in my youth.

'When I was an older man, five of my brothers and nine of my nephews were killed. Fifty of my relatives were killed or disappeared. I've had seven assassination attempts against me, but I depend on the Almighty to cleanse my soul, and I am not tired, I will continue.'

Al-Hakim is said to be wary of attending any of the US-convened town meetings.

▲

Mohammed the driver is safe. Anderson was the first to see him in the crowd outside the hotel. So tight is the US security cordon around us now that only those who have a press pass, or those for whom we vouch, are allowed in. Mohammed had been trying to get through for much of this morning when Jon Lee chanced upon him and told him to wait there until I could be fetched. I raced down and we embraced.

He was fine. The village in which his family had sat out the war lay beyond a military checkpoint, through which no traffic had been allowed to pass for almost a week. This meant he couldn't get into the city but, because the Americans had wrecked the phone system, there was no way for him to send a message. The main thing was that he and his family were well, and he wanted to get back to work.

The Nabil Restaurant had re-opened, hoping to challenge the Latakia's grip on the crisis market. Before the war started, the Nabil had made a bid for our patronage by inviting the entire press pack to the 'Mother Of All Battles' party. But few went. The Nabil's big advantage was that it served alcohol, but neither Anderson nor I had had a drink since the start of the war. We had scotch, vodka, beer and even a few bottles of wine in a bar in our suite. But there had been too much adrenalin in our systems and too much danger around us even to think of having a drink.

There was still no city power and, when I awoke this morning, the hotel's emergency generator, which had got the Sheraton's elevators working again, was on the blink too. That meant a noisy start to photographer Kate Geraghty's day. She was still camped on the couch, which was only metres from the generator we had installed on the balcony. I needed power and light to work, so I kick-started the generator at 5am—with apologies. Mark Baker had arrived just as Geoff Thompson of the ABC decided to leave—so we put Baker in Room 830 and today we wrested Room 905 back from the *NYT* for Kate. I've arranged for Kate and Mark to take control of the generator and I've given Mark the electric kettle. I've signed over $US5000 to each of them, to ensure that a cash crisis does not force them to leave Iraq earlier than they intend.

There was an accident today involving a vehicle in a media convoy trying to make it into Baghdad from Amman before dark. They had only 40km to go when a blow-out caused veteran Argentinean correspondent Mario Podestá, 52, to lose control. He died instantly and camerawoman Veronica Cabrera was taken to Baghdad in a critical condition.

DAY TWENTY-SEVEN

Tuesday, April 15

A Prison Visit

Filed Tuesday, April 15 at 11.36am   **Sheraton Hotel**

Even as the war started, Saddam Hussein's death machine did not miss a beat. Four days after the bombing started, the heavy steel gates at Abu Ghraib closed with a sickening, metallic clunk behind Nazar al-Jaf.

Now his friend Rashid Fluh, a sacked Iraqi security colonel who has a military-issue pistol shoved into the waist of his trousers, says he's looking for al-Jaf's body. A former inmate himself, he has returned to one of the most feared symbols of power and menace in Saddam's Iraq—with no room in his heart for hope that al-Jaf might have escaped the noose or the bullet.

The very prospect of coming to this place of detention, death and interrogation loosens tongues that till last week invariably remained tied in the presence of foreign reporters. Kiefah, my interpreter, is the first to broach the subject as we drive west from Baghdad, on a broad highway littered with bombed-out civilian vehicles and charred Iraqi tanks and armoured personnel carriers, many of them peeled open like an old-fashioned sardine tin. Coming towards us, headed into town, is a 1000-vehicle US military convoy.

Kiefah: 'At school, my cousin's child said that when Saddam came on the TV, his father would spit at him. There was an investigation and he was jailed for six months.' Mohammed, the driver, who has his elbow out the window: 'A man in my neighbourhood used the soles of his shoes to smack a poster of Saddam—a dreadful insult for Iraqis. He was executed.'

Today it appears that three kinds of people want to visit Abu Ghraib. There are former inmates like Rashid Fluh, who hopes to dignify the presumed death of his friend and to confront his own demons after spending seven years within its walls. Inevitably there are looters—one lot has come with a front-end loader, trying to steal the prison's huge power generator. And finally, it seems, there are former staff—who are drawn back for what reason? They will not be named and they will not admit to having worked the cell blocks, but they have a detailed knowledge of the prison's layout and its leaden routine. Perhaps they too are confronting demons.

Figures were never released but, by some estimates, as many as 75 000 prisoners were held here at any given time. In October last year, Saddam declared an amnesty and most criminals were freed, but not the political prisoners. In one of the offices, a file reveals that late last month 10 000 inmates remained in this forbidding complex, about 30km out of Baghdad.

The cell blocks are cramped, dark and oppressive. The only act of kindness that can be discerned is that some prisoners were allowed to cover the lower section of the steel bars to their cells with plastic—apparently to stop the draught. There is no sun. As many as fifteen or twenty prisoners were held in each of these musty cells that measure only 4 by 4m.

Fluh was jailed for what he says was a decision to join a group of security officers bent on opposing Saddam. His friend al-Jaf, also a colonel, was a part of the group which was easily infiltrated because employees in all arms of the regime were required to watch and report on each other. 'I heard that al-Jaf was executed,' he says but then he needs to leave because of the distress that the visit causes among the friends who have come to Abu Ghraib with him.

People wander the prison, alone or in couples. At the gallows house a small crowd congregates. It's a new building, apparently the only recent addition to Abu Ghraib. It is built of cinder blocks; inside, it is painted a dusty grey-white.

It's dark, but I can see the raised concrete platform at the back with a ramp leading up to it—easier for handling struggling prisoners. In the middle are two holes, about 1m square. Ropes dangle over each of them and there's a box with twin steel levers that open the hatch through which the condemned prisoner dropped to his death.

In the space under the platform there is a sickening memorial to one of the last victims—a black sandal. As I contemplate it, one of the men who knows his way around offers practical advice on death: 'Sometimes they didn't die properly, so someone would stand on their neck till it broke.'

The nooses have been severed from the ropes. One noose is still here; it is made of three-strand, waxed hemp rope with a damp white cloth wrapped around the section that would fit beneath the victim's chin. It's disturbing to think that this moisture might be the sweat of the last victims.

Wednesday was hanging day at Abu Ghraib. On Thursdays families and relatives would come to collect the coffins, usually taking them strapped to the roof of a taxi. One who made such a journey was 46-year-old vegetable-seller Karim Mulji Hashim—twice: 'My two brothers called Saddam names. One of them was an army captain who was sick in the head after the Iran war. He did not know what he was saying—but they hanged him. My other brother was jobless and they chopped his head off—like a chicken.'

Dira al-Deen, a 31-year-old public service clerk, has come from Saddam City. He clutches his father's identity card, saying: 'I'm looking for my father because they did not ask us to come for the body. He was a policeman but they said he was working for the opposition. We have been to the cemetery near here but they do not put names on the graves—just file numbers.'

Al-Deen says that most who never emerged from Abu Ghraib were from the Shia slums of Saddam City, from which he and some friends have seized about 40 000 files from the abandoned offices of the internal security service. They want assistance to set up a help group for families that want to search for victims of the regime: 'I was ten years old when my father was arrested. They took me and my three-year-old sister to prison too—one of the officers tried very hard to sodomise me, in front of my sister, to make me tell them things about my father.'

The locals say that, as US forces advanced on Abu Ghraib last week, the remaining prisoners were trucked out to an unknown destination. But not all of them made it.

As I am about to leave, 37-year-old Khalid Ahmed directs me towards an area where looters are using big aluminium milk urns to loot petrol from the prison's sand-bagged fuel dump. There is an appalling smell of death where he says that he has just finished burying five men, who might well have been the last victims of the last enforcers to flee Abu Ghraib.

He says: 'I found two of them here. And,' as he points to a place about 50m away, 'another three over there. All were dressed as civilians. Their hands were tied and they had execution masks on—a black bag pulled over their heads with a draw-string tied tightly under their chins. They were bloated from being in the sun and the dogs had started to eat their bodies.'

The looters are still at work, leaving a trail of destruction that, as with all the other government buildings that have been trashed, is obliterating some of the best evidence against Saddam Hussein—the paper trail. One of the most enduring British bequests to Iraq was an ingrained public servant's need for paperwork and bureaucracy. The worst excesses of the regime were documented on a daily basis. Now much of it is in cinders after fires lit by the looters, or it is blowing on the desert wind.

The inmates of Abu Ghraib were not left in any doubt about who decided their fate—there are huge murals of Saddam all over the sprawling complex. In the lobby of the prison's security staff office, he beams absurdly from the wall, dressed in what looks like the uniform of a Prussian officer. But here his eyes have been gouged, his face is smeared with mud and dribbles of drying spit hang from his medals.

Outside in the bright sun, the colonel, Rashid Fluh, pulls out his pistol and takes careful aim at another depiction of Saddam. He fires, making a hole next to the fallen dictator's right eye. And Karim Mulji Hashim, the young man whose two brothers were executed here, is in a fit of tearful rage. He hurls his rubber sandals at the image of Saddam. Again and again and again.

▲

The last $US2500 came today. Who would have thought that we could have moved such an amount of cold, hard cash—a total of $US100 000—halfway around the world, over deserts and through a war zone, without losing a cent as it shuffled through more than a dozen pairs of hands, many of them people whom we had never met.

We had to carry big sums of cash on these assignments—no credit cards here, no cheque accounts, no holes-in-the-wall—which meant wandering around for weeks with the price of a new car, and sometimes more than that, hidden in the folds of our clothing. Most reporters had a neck pouch or a waist pouch for their greenbacks . . . and a supermarket carry bag for their supply of near-worthless Iraqi dinars.

The city remained in the grip of a crisis. Though a few restaurants had re-opened, none had put their pavement tables out. Most nights there was shooting right across the city—much of it thought to be squabbling among looters, but some of it fierce gun battles between the Americans and lingering pockets of Saddam's resistance. My colleague Baker was in Baghdad and writing now, so I was slowing down, trying to focus on two major pieces for the Easter weekend in Australia. Anderson observed that life for us was starting to return to its normal speed. I sat in the sun this morning with Kiefah; when he heard a bird singing, he said: 'That's unusual.' To which I replied: 'No, Kiefah, that's normal.'

Mohammed and Kiefah took me to the Abu Ghraib prison, west of Baghdad. Something inside me contracted as we entered those gates. I knew I should be thinking of the thousands of Iraqis who had never left this place—one of the first sights I saw was a poorly concealed mass grave for those who probably were the last to be executed here—but a part of my brain wouldn't let go of Matt and Moises, and the other two who were detained here with them. I located the wing in which foreign prisoners had been held—I knew it well because I had read Matt's published description of it. But, try as I might to find some record of their detention, the looters had beaten me to the punch. As in every other government building, their greatest act of vandalism had been to destroy much of the mountains of paperwork left by this regime. As we left the prison a tattered paperback from the prison library fluttered in a gutter—Ngaio Marsh's *Scales of Justice*.

Today ended up being a day of near-violence for the *NYT*. Burns awoke in the pre-dawn to find the muzzle of an American M-16 about 10cm from his nose. 'We're acting on information, sir; just a security check,' he was told. It seemed that teams of marines were giving the upper storeys of the Palestine Hotel a good shakedown. And Tyler Hicks had to run for his life when he got caught in the cross-fire between looters when he was taking pictures at a downtown bank.

After the looting spree, there were now ten tanks and armoured personnel carriers around the Iraq National Museum. Veronica Cabrera, the Argentinean camerawoman who was rushed to Baghdad after a car crash on the road from Amman yesterday, died in hospital overnight. She was the first female journalist to die while covering the war in Iraq. A week after the collapse of the regime I saw a dead donkey on the Jumhuriyah Bridge. I told Anderson and we each knew what the other was thinking—we'd never got round to tracking down the owner of the donkey that brayed when the bombs fell. We said nothing.

It was time to pack. I'd be leaving the generator for Baker and Geraghty (and they would deliver it for safe-keeping to Mohammed before they left Iraq). I packed one slightly used chemical warfare suit (practice drills only) and an unused combat helmet. The atropine anti-nerve agent injections were still in their plastic wrappers in my first-aid kit and I bequeathed my left-over MREs to my colleagues. Then I received an email from my mother, demanding an explanation as to why she had never heard or read the words 'bomb shelter' in any of my reports.

DAY TWENTY-EIGHT

Where is Saddam?

Filed Thursday, April 17 at 4.45am   Sheraton Hotel

Baghdad has become rumour city. Everyone has a view on whether Saddam Hussein is dead or alive, in the country or off and over the border, getting closer by the day to the billions of dollars he is said to have stashed away for a life on the lam. But, in the absence of a corpse, the chances are that he is alive. The detailed accounts of sightings in Baghdad during the war and on the day that the city fell are proof enough for some that he is on the run, but still is in the capital.

Back in the late-50s, Wamid Nadhme, now a professor of political science at Baghdad University, was an exchange student in Cairo. He took the sort of phone call that few young Iraqis abroad would have had the courage to ignore—Saddam was on the run and needed a safe house. The future dictator slept on Nadhme's floor for three nights, before going underground. At the time Nadhme admired his future leader but, even before the US-led war against Iraq, he was emerging as a rare Baghdad-based critic of the regime.

Now, as half the world predicts that Saddam will retreat to Tikrit, his home town, for a courageous last stand, Nadhme paints a less flattering picture: 'If they try to capture him, he'll run and he'll die. He's a bully; he's not brave. He left half his bodyguards in one of the safe houses he was using in this war, knowing it was about to be attacked. Most of them were his cousins—they died in the air strike.'

We were at Nadhme's home on the banks of the Tigris, sitting in his darkened sitting room, surrounded by faded family portraits from the 50s and 60s, when he rounded off the discussion on Saddam with a dramatic flourish: 'Saddam is still alive—I spoke to a person who was with him on the Tuesday night.'

This is important. On the day before—Monday, April 7—US B-1B bombers dropped four powerful bunker-buster bombs on a house in a small street in Mansur, a well-heeled suburb but home to many Baath Party loyalists, a favoured Baghdad locale for the Hussein family and a preferred presidential bolthole during the 1991 Gulf War.

The bombs were fused to detonate less than half a second after each other so that each would drill down, digging deeper before the next exploded. It left a crater about 40m wide and more than 20m deep; a dozen civilians died and four homes were obliterated.

But it didn't take much to work out that the Americans got the wrong house—or that they knew it. Two houses away from the target is the house in which Saddam and/or some of his closest associates, including his younger son Qusay, were hiding out. The evidence is arresting. The house had been rented but not lived in; strange late-model cars came and went; five new telephone lines had been installed recently and hurriedly—the wires came from a telephone pole straight through one of the front windows and they were so new that they were coiled as though they had just been unwound from a roll—and the fancy furnishings included a solid executive desk that would satisfy the ego of the President of Iraq.

In the old days none of this could be discussed. But now people fell over themselves to talk to foreign reporters. At the edge of the crater, a voice said, 'He got away ten minutes before the bombing,' and heads nodded in general agreement. The neighbours spoke of soldiers setting up antennae in the area and of 'many luxury cars' making a fast get-away. Majid al-Lazawi, 51, a senior protocol officer in the Tourism Ministry who claimed to have met the president several times, insisted that he had seen Saddam on neighbourhood streets several times in the preceding days.

And five phone lines? Maria Marcos, who worked in the nearby home of the first secretary at the German Embassy, said: 'My boss has only one line'; another neighbour added: 'I have three. But five?' Marcos had also observed security cars in the area. She said: 'When I saw them, I thought isn't it good of the regime to put on extra security for the diplomats who live in this area because of the war.'

And how do we know that the US knew it was the wrong house? It has been making a big deal of the fact that it has samples of Saddam's DNA and would be able to match it with samples from any bomb site. But the neighbours insist that the American forces now in control of Baghdad have not been near the site.

Mansur is on the east side. But over on the west side, tucked into a sharp U-bend on the Tigris River, is al-Aadhamiyah, where the roots of the Baath Party are deepest and the US forces faced the last and most determined resistance in Baghdad. And it was on the edge of the square there, outside the Abu

Hanifa Mosque, that Saddam put in another appearance, just before the noon prayers on Wednesday of last week—the marines had already entered his city and the looters were just beginning the week-long rampage that began on the east side.

This was another of Saddam's acts of betrayal. He told the crowd that gathered that they must fight and that he would be with them—'in the same trenches'. Not quite. Hours later the aerial bombardment started, destroying the mosque's clock tower, doing much superficial damage to the grand Ottoman-style mosque itself and severely damaging the dusty cemetery nearby.

And when the US soldiers arrived on foot they clearly believed that Saddam or members of his entourage were hiding in this place of worship, despite all denials by the locals, because the military used what appeared to have been a rocket-propelled grenade to force the door on the holiest part of the mosque—the sanctuary in which lies the tomb of the holy man of olden days, Abu Hanifa.

The people of al-Aadhamiyah are proud of their loyalty to Saddam. Still. They speak in wondrous praise of him. A tyrant? No. If he had done wrong, then surely his errors were in-significant compared to those of others. But what about the tens of thousands of Iraqi political prisoners who had been executed at the infamous Abu Ghraib prison? They claim not to know much about this; every society has its criminals and they have to be dealt with, a group of them told me as we sat in the sun in the bombed-out cemetery.

After much prodding they conceded that indeed the fugitive president had visited the area, but they were not going to admit to what might have been seen as human frailty in the man—Nadhme, the political scientist, had startled us by revealing that Saddam had cried openly as he had looked across the city from al-Aadhamiyah.

So it was not till we ended up sitting cross-legged on richly coloured carpets deep inside the mosque that we got a detailed, eye-witness account of Saddam's brief visit. The mosque custodian, Maythem Shihab, is 55 years old and a former Olympic wrestler. He wore grey-brown robes and had a white cloth wrapped tightly around his head. His strong grey beard was clipped short and in these troubled times he still smiled—but not when he revealed that he got to Montreal for the 1976 Games, but was blocked from competing by political protests.

He said: 'It was a terrible offence to have these armed infidels in the mosque—they didn't even take off their shoes and they started a fire in the women's section.'

And Saddam?

'When I saw him I was filled with pride to be Iraqi. He drove over the bridge to check things, stopping just short of the square. When he got out of the car I shook his hand. He was here for maybe twenty minutes. Qusay, his son, was with him and Abdelhamid Mahmoud, his bodyguard. He wore his field marshal's uniform.'

The custodian told how, as Saddam alighted from his car, people rushed in, picked him up and stood him up on the car's bonnet. Then, running his fingers down his cheeks to indicate crying, Shihab continued: 'Yes, he was emotional. But we thought he was crying out of happiness, because it was so long since he had been among the people of al-Aadhamiyah.'

Reminded that the ancient Arab warrior Saladin, on whom Saddam models himself, always led his soldiers from the front, the custodian defended Saddam: 'He is a statesman with the authority of office. In Saladin's day it was swords and blades, but today war is lasers and computers.'

Despite all this, some of the rumours insist that Saddam has been spirited out of the country—either by the CIA in exchange for the regime's capitulation or by the Russian ambassador, who drove to Damascus before flying to Moscow early in the war, a journey during which his road convoy came under attack.

Estimates of Saddam's wealth range from $US2 billion to more than $US10 billion, much of which is said to have come from illegal oil sales, kickbacks and extortion schemes. Since the start of the war US Treasury officials have claimed that at least $US1.2 billion held by Iraqi front companies around the world remains unfrozen. But it is not clear how many of the regime's key figures have fled the country to make use of this money. The US believes that many of Saddam's family and officials are hiding in Damascus.

But US forces in Mosul in northern Iraq this week said they were negotiating the surrender of two of Saddam's closest associates—Ezzat Ibrahim, Vice-Chairman of the Revolutionary Command Council and northern regional commander, and Lieutenant-General Sultan Hashim Ahmad, Saddam's Minister of Defence—both of whom are on the US list of the 55 most-wanted Iraqis.

Information Minister Mohammed Saeed al-Sahhaf, dubbed Comical Ali by the British tabloids because of his delusional predictions of victory for Iraq, even as it faced imminent defeat, is rumoured to have committed suicide hours before the fall of Baghdad. And Saddam's half-brother, Watban Ibrahim Hassan al-Tikriti, was captured by units of the British SAS as he attempted to flee to Syria.

US officials claim that Saddam's first wife, Sajida Kheirallah Telfah, the mother of his wanted sons, Uday and Qusay, is in Syria. His second wife, Samira Shahbandar, mother to Saddam's third son, Ali Saddam Hussein, and two daughters, also is said to be in Damascus.

The President's top scientific adviser, Lieutenant-General Amer Hammoudi al-Saadi, turned himself in to US forces in

Baghdad last Saturday, insisting still—and supported by the US failure, so far, to discover to the contrary—that Iraq did not have weapons of mass destruction. He told the German TV station that facilitated his surrender: 'I was telling the truth, always telling the truth, never told anything but the truth, and time will bear me out, you will see. There will be no difference after this war.'

Surprisingly, there is little recrimination in Baghdad at the failure of the country's military forces to defend the city. It seems that most Iraqis knew what US intelligence and military planners did not know—the Republican Guard was a paper tiger, perhaps a construct of the Western media more than anything else.

Nadhme, the political scientist, is perplexed. He said: 'There is something dubious, something unclear, and something unexplainable about what happened that night.'

That was Tuesday of last week. But the pieces are coming together—the leadership took fright, and as the men in the ranks looked over their shoulders and saw the fate of their colleagues in the south of the country and on the outskirts of Baghdad, they decided to cut and run.

They abandoned their uniforms, their weapons and their war machines. Some of the smarter among them observed that their officers were going home for dinner, insisting they would return before the Americans advanced further on Baghdad. But they did not return.

The haste with which the Republican Guard and the Fedayeen Saddam abandoned the streets and bunkers of Baghdad made it one of the easiest military conquests of the war. Senior Baath officials have insisted that they were ordered to withdraw systematically, but no one has nominated who gave the order or explained why they did not pass it down the line as tidily as they might have.

A senior official said there was simply a realisation that Kalashnikovs and rocket-propelled grenades were no match for US firepower and it seems the message that the game was up might have gone out through the city's policemen. Naseer Hassan, a manager at the international airport, told reporters that at dusk on the Tuesday, a policeman alighted from a patrol car, near his position on Palestine Street, to tell him: 'Be careful tonight. We're going to leave the streets. The Americans are very close. If we stay here we have two choices—either they kill us or they take us prisoner.'

Mohammed Jowad Ali, the captain of an Iraqi super tanker until Baghdad's oil trade ground to a halt late last year, told me how more than 25 members of the Republican Guard came knocking on the door of his home, discarding their uniforms as they arrived and demanding a loan of 'pyjamas and slippers'.

He said: 'One of them was a brigadier, who left his pistol and ID papers with me. He came back two days later to collect them. We gave them every pair of slippers we had in the house.'

EPILOGUE

I spoke again to Sabah, my silver-haired old man, today.

Up and down, he's been my barometer of the mood in Baghdad. He was eager for the overthrow of the regime, but tearful when his daughter miscarried during the early US bombing and shattered when his nephew was killed by American fire as he drove an Iraqi military supply truck. His national pride kicked in during the early Iraqi military successes in the south, but he was jubilant as the marines rolled into Baghdad.

So what did he make of the very first move by the man the Pentagon wants as Iraq's new leader—the long-term exile Ahmed Chalabi—who immediately took over Baghdad's Hunting Club? Chalabi and his US military escort installed themselves in what was once the exclusive domain of the Baath Party leadership and of Uday Hussein, Saddam Hussein's brutal first son.

'Same, same,' the old man told me. 'There is no difference.'

These are tumultuous, frightening days for Iraqis. A despised regime crumbled in the face of overwhelming force but, for all its power and might, the US is still grappling to secure control of the people, the nation and its politics in the early days of what many Iraqis still feel is an occupation, not a liberation.

Life for Iraq's 25 million people has become a desperate struggle to find food and their feet after the Americans ripped away the old regime and then stood back as the only form of life and government most of them knew was destroyed in a looting rampage that many are convinced was part of the invasion plan. All functions of government are paralysed.

Americans might be offended by a comparison with September 11. But if that traumatised the US, how do we measure the impact of such a rapid, high-powered military invasion on the life of ordinary Iraqis? A tyrant is gone, but in the same flash so too is the only form of social and economic order that most Iraqis have known. As they come to terms with the emotional outpouring of all that was wrong under Saddam—the imprisonment, the torture, the executions—they must also confront the vulgarity of war and the further diminution of lives that were already grim enough, but which for Iraqis were 'normal'.

The people of Baghdad were subjected to the nightmare of constant bombing. Most of this was on the outskirts of the city but, spectacularly and frighteningly, some it was on selected regime targets in the downtown area. There was sufficient civilian death and destruction by enough errant bombs to have had them trembling in fear as they sat through long nights without electricity. And, as Iraqi forces countered with suicide attacks, any movement around the country was potentially lethal because US forces adopted a shoot-to-kill regime against a population that did not understand orders, such as 'stop' or 'freeze', when jittery Americans yelled at them in English. Iraq's highways and Baghdad's streets were littered with the dead.

On the heels of a four-week war that military historians will probably judge a triumph, Washington's confident dream of imposing its brand of democracy in the Middle East has become a lottery of anarchy and explosive politics that could go any way. And for now, instead of helping the people they claimed to be liberating, US forces look more like a self-interested army of occupation.

There are daily protest marches—a democratic novelty for Baghdadis. These rallies about law and order, jobs, the economy and the shape of the next government point to a relationship between liberator and liberated—or occupier and occupied—that continues to be based on fear, anxiety and distrust.

Just as the US forces arrived in Baghdad without a plan to prevent robbery and violence, they came without a plan for the estimated 50 per cent of the population who depended for their pitiable salaries on the government and a rigid centralised economy that no longer exists. The only plan seemed to be to protect the oil wells in the south and the Oil Ministry in Baghdad. These were quickly cordoned off with tanks and armoured personnel carriers.

When the US talks about representative government in the new Iraq, it is speaking code for what it doesn't want— a conservative or fundamentalist Shia regime that the 60 per cent majority Shia could conceivably install in a pure democratic vote. So this is a dangerous environment, in which the US and its ill-disguised agents embark on creating a democracy to America's liking.

Instead of grateful thanks, the US is confronted with slogans demanding that it quickly retreat from Iraq. It faces fighting and friction as Shia factions jockey for power. Left to their own devices, strongly nationalist Iraqis might well arrive at an unaligned, democratic society that Washington could live with. But the risk to the US, in its artless efforts to manipulate the Iraqi outcome it wants, is that the Shia in particular could look for guidance to the east—to Iran and the ayatollahs.

Iraqis did not like Saddam. But they appreciate strong leadership and in the post-war vacuum they see a need for a firm hand. One local told me: 'We need thousands of Ghandis in the governates, but we need one Saddam at the top of each and another in Baghdad to make this country work.'

My last job, before leaving Baghdad for a while, was to visit the Mother Of All Battles Mosque, a bizarre monument by Saddam to what he always insisted was his 'victory' in the 1991 Gulf War. Its lustrous white minarets—the outer four shaped inelegantly as Scud missiles, the inner four like the barrel of a Kalashnikov—were caked dismal brown by the dust storms that assail Baghdad at this time of year. Traditionally mosques are a place of refuge, open around the clock. But now the gates were chained; surly men with guns paced up and down, and an aggressive young mullah dismissed me.

I wanted to see the Saddam Koran—a megalomaniac indulgence displayed in a pavilion on the mosque lake, in which 600 gilt-edged frames each hold a page of the holy book, written by one of the best calligraphers in the land, who used the blood of Saddam Hussein as 'ink'.

Across the road some men sat in a knot in the shade of a spreading tree. They gave me a glass of cool water and assured me that dealing with this grotesque indulgence should be an early task for the new government. However, one of them said: 'It is forbidden to write the Koran in blood, but it cannot be destroyed—it is the holy book from God.'

What might have been a simple task suddenly was filled with all the contradiction and challenge of building the post-war, post-Saddam Iraq. Iraqis revere the book, but they loathe the man celebrated in this very limited edition. His oppressive shadow is gone, but they hate how the daylight came and they remember order where for now there is chaos.

And, in a corner of their hearts and minds, many of them feel they are being robbed.

▲

Madam Sabah was back from the country. But Sabah was still up to farewell me at 6.30am, insisting on carrying my bags and doing one more clean-up of my desk. Best of all, he produced one last Turkish coffee—not quite as good as Madam Sabah's—and we shared a last joke about him getting that GMC before we had a long warm embrace.

Burns thought he'd stay on in Baghdad for a few weeks more. The previous evening, I had traipsed over to the Palestine and up the stairs (as the power was still off) for the last time to see him; he was writing a piece for next day's publication. Anderson pitched to come out with me—we even talked of the slap-up dinner we'd have in Amman—but he needed a few more days on the ground to round out his final piece on war and the Baghdad regime. The three of us then living in the suite—Anderson, myself and 'Heathclitt' the photographer—shared a final dinner sent in by Madam Sabah.

After the most intense month that any of us had experienced as reporters, it felt very strange to be setting out for Jordan. I had booked Issam, my favourite driver, for the long haul to Amman. But he was impatient, so we headed off from the Sheraton Hotel about fifteen minutes ahead of a media convoy of about ten or twelve GMCs.

It was overcast, about 6.45am, and the streets of Baghdad were deserted. There is enough room in these vehicles to stretch out and sleep and normally Issam had a small television attached to the dashboard. Within minutes we were on the open highway and Issam was doing one of his more impressive juggling acts—making coffee from a kettle mounted next to the console while travelling at 160km/hr. I asked if the road would be trouble-free but all he said was: 'Inshallah!' God willing.

Bandits had harassed reporters heading into Baghdad on the previous day. But most of the vehicles we passed were bombed-out wrecks and only once did we freeze, when we saw two men suddenly moving towards the road from behind a rocky outcrop. They were harmless shepherds. As we overtook two trucks without number plates, Issam muttered: 'Him Ali Baba. Him Ali Baba too.' My body wanted to drift off to sleep; but I felt that I had to sit upright, at least until we reached the border, looking out for bandits.

I had done this twelve-hour drive so many times over the years, but I imagined this would be the last time. On my next Iraq assignment I'd be flying into Baghdad—probably on a direct flight from JFK. As we roared across the desert, my mind went over lots of things—how quickly the war was over once it started; how long it had seemed at the time; and all the dead and injured. From the start of the bombing, it had been 30 extraordinary days that gave us a window on the terrible price that the Iraqi people have paid during over 30 years of brutality, and now this war.

Suddenly, almost 300km west of Baghdad, Issam pulled up in a hurry, turned the vehicle around and started heading back towards Baghdad on the wrong side of the road, gesticulating and shouting: 'My brother, my brother.' He was chasing another GMC coming from the direction of Amman. It was indeed Issam's brother who was ferrying reinforcements for the *Los Angeles Times* into the Iraqi capital. They conferred briefly and had the same message for each other—the road was clear.

As we pulled up at the border crossing two hours later, I realised for the first time that I was doing so without a knot in my stomach. GIs manned the Iraqi side. I jumped out, set up the sat-phone and rang my home in New York and my office in Sydney, to let them know I was out of Iraq.

Within minutes we were on the road to Amman again, with Issam uttering another prayer: '*Alhamdulillah*' or 'Glory to God'. When we got there, I checked into the Hyatt. It was Saturday evening and the next Royal Jordanian flight to New York would not be till Tuesday morning. I fell into a clean bed and crashed. After twelve hours I woke up briefly, then crashed again. It was strange to be in a deserted but functioning hotel—the lights worked; there was hot water and room service.

On Monday morning I went on an errand, searching for a particular style of local ceramics that my wife liked. After striking out at three different shops, I decided to go back to where she had first seen the plates she wanted—in the lobby of the Intercontinental Hotel when she joined me here for a holiday during one of my Middle East assignments late in 2002. I was heading along a corridor of boutiques when I heard my name called. I turned around and I couldn't quite believe it—Matt McAllester and Moises Saman were heading towards me.

We embraced and then adjourned to the nearest coffee shop to order Turkish coffee. They had been home on R&R but now, after some hard lobbying of the editors at *Newsday*, they were returning to Baghdad and Iraq. They looked as they always did—Matt with his spiky hair and his scholar's glasses; Moises with his dark skin and Palestinian good looks. We filled in some of the blanks—them telling me about their time in Abu Ghraib, me telling them about Larry Kaplow's tireless campaign on their behalf in Baghdad. Dinner would have been nice, but Matt was already working on a big series that he had to file before departing for Baghdad the next morning.

I found Pam's ceramics and wandered off to look at some jewellery I knew she liked. The next morning I was on a flight back to New York.

ACKNOWLEDGMENTS

Form usually dictates that a spouse be acknowledged modestly at the end. But this book could not have happened without Pam Williams' generous good spirit and editing skills. I walked in the door after being away for ten weeks, had dinner and then disappeared into my study for three weeks, during which I worked round the clock—pushing chapters out under the door for the dead-eye reckoning of her red pen. I owe her a great deal.

Richard Walsh, of Allen & Unwin, clearly is a glutton for punishment. This project was his idea. It grew way beyond our respective expectations, but he managed to keep us both on track through another stressful books-by-email exercise. I particularly liked this gem which he fired off at 5.55am as we came down to the wire: 'I'm up—and growling already . . .' His unbelievable attention to structure and to every detail, as he shaped and directed *In Baghdad*, was awe-inspiring. I think he regards my spelling as a personal challenge. My thanks for A&U's forbearance on a tight schedule also go to Patrick Gallagher and to senior editor Colette Vella; thanks, too, to Maher Mughrabi for checking Arabic terms.

The Sydney Morning Herald was great on this story. Publisher Alan Revell and editor Robert Whitehead were towers of strength on the difficult decision of staying in Baghdad— I thank them for that and permission to reproduce my reports as filed from Baghdad. Saturday editor Lis Sterel was a conduit for sanity and foreign editor Peter Kerr and his staff did me proud with the treatment of the story.

This kind of journalism is hard and often very harrowing. But it's also a lot of fun, and all the more so when you team up with colleagues of the calibre of Jon Lee Anderson and John F. Burns. Their company and their wise counsel helped make the assignment of a lifetime all the more memorable. Baghdad would not have been the same without them. And Jason South . . . I missed you, mate.

New York, May 2003